POLITICS, KINSHIP AND CULTURE IN GAELIC IRELAND, *c.* 1100–*c.* 1690

Politics, kinship and culture in Gaelic Ireland, *c.* 1100–*c.* 1690

Essays for the Irish Chiefs' and Clans' Prize in History

Edited by

Joseph Mannion and Katharine Simms

Word*well*

First published 2018
Wordwell Ltd
Unit 9,
78 Furze Road,
Sandyford Industrial Estate,
Dublin 18
www.wordwellbooks.com

ISBN: 978-1-9997909-2-9 (paperback).
ISBN: 978-1-9997909-5-0 (hardback).

British Library Cataloguing-in-Publication Data.
A catalogue record for this book is available from the British Library.

Typeset in Ireland by Wordwell Ltd.
Copy-editor: Emer Condit.
Book design: Nick Maxwell.
Printed by SprintPrint, Dublin.

Contents

Preface

The O'Brien and Gearóid Ó Ceallaigh

The Standing Council of Irish Chiefs and Chieftains (*Buanchomhairle Thaoisigh Éireann*) is delighted to publish this, the second anthology of essays on Gaelic Ireland, four years after the first, in continued association with Clans of Ireland (*Finte na hÉireann*). We hope that this academic treat for the reader will continue well into the future.

The Standing Council was formed in 1991, and the original members (sixteen chiefs) were presented to the president at Áras an Uachtaráin after its inaugural Annual General Meeting in Dublin. Initially, the Council was active for many years and held its AGM in both Dublin and other parts of the country.

The objects of the Council are:

(a) to consider matters affecting the Irish chiefs and chieftains and the clans they represent;
(b) to submit its views and interests to government, to departments of state, to local authorities, to press and public, and to associations connected with clan and family in Ireland as well as overseas;
(c) to educate the general public in matters connected with the rights, functions and historical position of Irish chiefs and chieftains;
(d) to take such steps as may seem expedient to protect the titles, armorial bearings and other appurtenances of chiefs and chieftains from exploitation or misuse in trade or otherwise;
(e) to promote and preserve the Gaelic heritage of Ireland;
(f) any other objects related to the above objects.

In 1999 an event occurred that is commonly called 'the MacCarthy Mór Hoax', which resulted in the removal of one of the members of the Standing Council. Consequently, in 2003 the Irish government decided to withdraw its 'courtesy recognition' of the chiefs, which had been instigated by the Chief Herald of Ireland, Edward MacLysaght, in 1944. This situation still exists to this day. As a result of this decision, the Standing Council was left in limbo for a number of years and attendance at AGMs dropped significantly. There was a consequent decline in the work that the Council undertook.

We are pleased to say that the one area in which the Council is still very active is the Irish Chiefs' and Clans' Prize for History (formerly the Irish Chiefs' Essay Prize for History), started in the late 1990s. This was originally undertaken in conjunction with Dr Katharine Simms of the History Department of Trinity College Dublin and *History Ireland* magazine. In 2013 we formed a close association with Clans of Ireland, and since then both the annual Irish Chiefs' and Clans' Prize and the anthology published every four years have been sponsored jointly by the Council and Clans of Ireland.

The future of the Irish chiefs is a very important part of Irish history, as they have been around in many forms for thousands of years. The Standing Council of Irish Chiefs and Chieftains represents the descendants of the old Gaelic order, with a well-documented heritage dating back to the last *de facto* chiefs of the sixteenth century. We are depleted in numbers and it is therefore imperative that the Irish chiefs continue to survive as members of the Standing Council, in order to continue to play a part in the future of Ireland and its rich history.

In 1989 Rory O'Connor, the elected chieftain of the O'Connor Kerry clan, set out to establish an organisation for the revival of Irish clans. The result was Clans of Ireland, the purpose of which was to support and co-ordinate the activities of the various clan organisations in Ireland and around the world. To do so, a Register of Clans was created that has been maintained ever since.

Today, Clans of Ireland maintains a presence on the internet, and its board of directors meets several times a year at the Chapter House in Christ Church Cathedral in Dublin, a location chosen for its historical significance for Irish clans. Clans of Ireland holds an annual conference, usually in Dublin, at which we are addressed by academic speakers. Throughout the year we support the activities of the individual clans, in addition to organising or participating in other events around the country that typically have a balance of genealogy, history and social entertainment.

In 2010, Clans of Ireland instituted the Order of Clans of Ireland, an order of merit established to honour individuals who have made an outstanding contribution to Irish culture and heritage or who have brought conspicuous honour to their clan. In 2012 President Higgins became patron of Clans of Ireland at a ceremony at Áras an Uachtaráin. This was a significant historic milestone, as it reflected the association between contemporary Ireland and our celebrated early documented history. In the same year, Clans of Ireland also received recognition from the United Nations as a civil society non-governmental organisation. In 2015 President Higgins hosted the *Ceannairí* and *Taoisigh* of Clans of Ireland at Áras an Uachtaráin. This was a highly significant event, as it was the first occasion that a modern head of state had gathered the clan chiefs under his patronage.

The maintenance and conservation of the fundamental traditions of our Gaelic and later medieval family heritage is central to the broad purpose of Clans of Ireland. We engage in the development of public profile, as the umbrella body which unites contemporary Gaelic clans and ancient families, while promoting intellectual research into genealogy, history and culture. Our involvement as joint sponsor of the Irish Chiefs' and Clans' Essay Competition is fundamental to this.

We recognise and salute the tremendous initiative of both of our joint sponsors, the Standing Council of Irish Chiefs and Chieftains and the History Department of Trinity College Dublin, who originally developed the concept of the competition. A close working relationship has been maintained with both since our involvement with the project began four years ago. In August 2017, Clans of Ireland and the Standing Council of Irish Chiefs and Chieftains confirmed the intent of both organisations to continue the joint sponsorship arrangement for the foreseeable future.

Introduction

Joseph Mannion and Katharine Simms

The following collection of studies on the history of Gaelic Ireland is the product of four years of an essay competition, sponsored jointly by the Standing Council of Irish Chiefs and Chieftains (*Buanchomhairle Thaoisigh Éireann*) and Clans of Ireland (*Finte na hÉireann*). The works represent the winning entries and superior-quality essays from 2013 to 2016, and cover the period ranging from the twelfth to the seventeenth century. The subject-matter varies considerably from one study to the next, but similarity of content allows for the arrangement of the essays into three distinct assemblages, dealing with politics, kinship and culture on the island of Ireland during the specified period.

The opening section on political and social history begins with an essay by Stephen Hewer, who reassesses the situation of the Gaelic population living under English law during the second half of the thirteenth century and the first quarter of the fourteenth. Based on his findings, and contrary to the belief of many modern scholars, Hewer demonstrates that Irishmen were not deprived of their civil rights universally and were entitled to plead their case in the English courts in their own right. In the second contribution, Simon Egan traces the relationship of the O'Donnells of Tyrconnell with the Scottish Stewart monarchy from the late fourteenth century to the battle of Flodden in 1513. He also charts the rise and fall of the MacDonald lordship of the Isles in this context, and highlights the limitations of Tudor power in Ireland during the early years of Henry VII's reign, with the consequent potential for foreign intervention where the kingship was concerned.

The varied experiences of the Tudor crown in Ireland during the sixteenth century are reflected in the next three essays by Diarmuid Wheeler, Chris Lawlor and Stephen Kestell. In the first of these, Wheeler explores the phenomenon of Gaelic collaboration with the English authorities, as exemplified by Barnaby Fitzpatrick of Upper Ossory for a quarter of a century from the mid-1550s onwards. Fitzpatrick's remarkable loyalty to the crown was in stark contrast to the intense opposition to Tudor expansion offered by Feagh Mac Hugh O'Byrne in the upland region south of Dublin, destined to be shired as County Wicklow early in the seventeenth century. The distinct but complementary studies of Lawlor and Kestell reveal the extent of O'Byrne's conflict with the English forces and its significance in the overall context of the Nine Years War. Another rebellion, this time in 1641, provides the background for the final essay of the first section, which was penned by Gordon Bond. His subject is Mary Bux, an Irish-speaking woman of English parentage who was left among the Irish rebels to act as an informant. When her life was in danger, however, the

English garrison refused to protect her and she was eventually kidnapped and murdered.

Kinship is the theme central to the next four essays, which deal with the fortunes of a selection of chiefs and clans of Scottish, Anglo-Norman and Gaelic Irish origins. The first of these is by Brian McCabe, whose study of his ancestral Mac Cabe gallowglass clan recounts the military service they rendered to the rulers of the Fermanagh, Monaghan, Leitrim and Cavan areas from the fourteenth to the sixteenth century, and their acceptance as a clan in their own right. Declan Keenan follows with a study of Sir Richard Burke of Newtown, Co. Mayo, who was chieftain of the Lower MacWilliam Burkes when the second composition of Connacht was agreed to by the leading lords of the province in 1585. By subscribing to the new financial arrangements imposed by the Tudor crown, Burke managed to secure for himself and his heirs a significant portion of the mensal possessions that had formerly attached to the MacWilliam chieftainship.

The search for the ancient chiefly line of the O'Moloney clan of County Clare is the focus of the following essay by Gerry Moloney, where the evidence uncovered in relation to Dermot O'Mallun, the last official chief of the O'Moloneys, is discussed. Forced to flee Ireland about the time of the Desmond rebellions at the age of fifteen, Dermot spent the remainder of his days on the Continent, where he studied law, was employed by Archduke Albert and married into the Flemish nobility. Eugene McMahon then traces the undoing of his ancestral McMahon clan of County Monaghan in the period between the mid-fifteenth and late seventeenth centuries. The slow but steady decline of this prominent Gaelic dynasty, through internal division and external attack, is charted with reference to the loss of their social status and hereditary clan lands in the century leading up to the defining Jacobite wars.

Gaelic culture and the Irish church are the focal points for the final selection of essays in this anthology, which opens with a speculative piece on the formation of the diocese of Tuam by Ruairí Ó hAodha. The writer suggests that the choice of Tuam as the centre for the Connacht archdiocese can be linked to a near-fatal assassination attempt on Tairrdelbach Mór Ua Conchobair, who was wounded by his own people at a place called Áth mBó in 1115. Based on the recurrence of Áth mBó in a list of place-names in the Annals of Tigernach under the year 1127, Ó hAodha posits that the circuit of Tuam there cited refers to a grant by the king of demesne lands in thanksgiving for his recovery from his injuries. This is followed by Gerard Beggan's endeavour to identify the ruins in Killyan churchyard in County Galway with a daughter house of Kilcreevanty Abbey called St Mary's Killin, as noted in a charter from 1223. The author advances wide-ranging evidence to support his proposal, based on extensive research into the history and archaeology of this north Galway locality.

The Trinity College harp is 'the most exotic musical instrument in the world', according to Brian Manners, author of the next essay. In a compelling account, Manners provides a comprehensive history of the Irish harp and outlines the difference between the medieval exemplar and its nineteenth-century revival. Irish Gaelic culture, as portrayed in medieval literature pertaining to Queen Medb of Connacht, is the theme for the next essay by Lora O'Brien. In a questions-and-answers type composition, the different aspects of the mythical queen, as they appear in the old Irish sagas, are introduced incrementally and discussed. Colette Allen follows with a study of the place-names and landmarks in the Tallaght hills of County Dublin, in which she attempts to match mythical sagas with the local landscape. In addition, she offers corrective alternatives to earlier scholars' identifications of saga locations and argues for the geographical integrity of early Irish literature. The anthology concludes with a most interesting contribution from Con Connor on footwear in medieval Ireland, in which he gives a graphic description of his attempts to reproduce what is referred to as the 'Lucas Type 1' early medieval shoe. This was a distinctive, decorative type of footwear worn by the early Irish nobility, which inspired the author to title his essay 'In the footsteps of the noble Gael'.

Perhaps owing to the unconventional nature of the historical sources for the study of medieval Gaelic Ireland—predominantly literary in nature, the products of a professional class of poets and genealogists—this field of Irish history has been often neglected at university level, although greater attention has been paid to the activities of the Gaelic chiefs and their followers in the sixteenth and seventeenth centuries, when the native sources are supplemented by English state papers, correspondence and financial records. Yet the multiplicity of local history societies, and clan organisations, testify to the continuing interest felt by the Irish at large, and those of Irish descent abroad, in the society and culture of their ancestors, and much independent research is undertaken by private individuals for their own satisfaction.

The first anthology in this series, *Gaelic Ireland (c.600–c.1700): politics, culture and landscapes*, edited by Katharine Simms (Wordwell Press, 2013), was the fruit of a competition then sponsored by the Standing Council of Irish Chiefs and Chieftains, with the objects of encouraging research into Gaelic Ireland among budding postgraduate historians and of reaping the harvest of independent researchers, while always requiring a full academic apparatus of footnotes and bibliography. The continuance of the competition, and the appearance of a second anthology under the joint sponsorship of Clans of Ireland and the Standing Council of Irish Chiefs and Chieftains, testifies to the success of the original project. The essay competition continues to this day and will hopefully go on to achieve its joint aims of spurring the interest of a rising generation of Irish researchers and of disseminating information about a somewhat under-studied but vital part of our nation's past.

Part I: Political and social history

1

An introduction to the free Gaelic people in English Ireland, *c.* 1250–1307[1]

Stephen Hewer
(2015 prize)

With the septcentenary anniversary of the Bruce Invasion of Ireland this year [2015], perhaps it is relevant to address a topic often associated with the invasion: the so-called 'Remonstrance of the Irish princes'. This is the name given to a petition sent to Pope John XXII by Domhnall Ó Néill *c.* 1317 which contained a list of grievances against the English magnates and administrators in Ireland.[2] The petition claimed, among other things, that the experiences of the various Gaelic peoples were universal under English rule, and that the settlers denied all Gaelic people access to the English courts and prevented the Gaelic chiefs from becoming accepted members of English society.

> [In the English courts in Ireland] any Gaelic person, whether cleric or lay . . . is denied from bringing any court actions by that very fact (i.e. being Gaelic).

This claim sat well with many modern readers, and absolute discrimination against the Gaelic people has become a popular myth.[3] We would be better equipped, however, to understand medieval society in English Ireland and its internal relations with the Gaelic inhabitants if this petition were treated as an editorial in a newspaper, meant to incite emotions with liberal use of hyperbole.

The reality is that while there were unfree Gaelic people in the English-conquered and English-held areas, there were also free Gaelic people living in English Ireland. Many historians have discounted the latter's existence because of a 'lack of evidence'. Some have theorised that any and all free Gaelic people were hidden under English names,[4] while others thought that they were disseised (removed from their lands) before the surviving court records were made (1252).[5] On the one hand, there is evidence for many 'Anglicised' Gaelic people in English Ireland, such as John son of John (nowadays called 'FitzDermot'), great-grandson of Domnall Mac Gilla Mo Cholmóc, king of Uí Briúin Chualann, south of Dublin.[6] On the other hand, there is a great deal of evidence, previously neglected by historians, for the existence of free Gaelic people in English Ireland with Gaelic names. This evidence may be found in the court records left by the English administration, which show us how

English law in Ireland was actually applied in practice.

The main factor to remember is that only persons who were of free status could win a case in the English royal courts in Ireland. In addition, the English did not allow unfree people to hold free lands. They were clear on this fact when in 1261 the itinerant court at Limerick took the house and goods of David Goer in Killone, Co. Limerick.[7] He had not lost a case; he had not been defeated by a plaintiff; he simply was unfree and the house was taken 'into the king's hand'. We can compare his treatment with the fate of nine men from County Kerry in 1252. Thomas son of Thomas Cradoc accused these nine men of disseising him of his lands, but the court ruled that the lands belonged to the nine defendants. Four of these men had Gaelic names: William Dun (*Donn*), Gillin Dun (*Giolla Eoin Donn*), Gilbert Ofynan (*Ó Fionnáin*) and Raghenild Omolkeran (*Raghnall Ó Maoil Chiaráin*).[8] They were left in peaceful possession and Thomas was fined for a false claim.

While in the latter case the English royal court played a passive role, in some it actively confirmed that the Gaelic people involved were free and that the courts and administration would protect them. In 1260 Robert Duf (*Dubh* or *Ó Duibh*?) recovered six acres in Cloncrayth (Claonráth?), Co. Cork, from the abbot of Tractan and Maclachelin (*Mac Lochlainn*), a brother of the house, after they had illegally and recently disseised him.[9] In 1261 Neel Ocrofthelhyn (*Niall Ó Criomhthainn*?) recovered twenty acres from Hugh de Anton and Robert David in Gortenchauely, Co. Limerick, for the same.[10] In 1290 Elena Scolog (*Ó Scolóig*?) and Agnes, her sister, recovered a house and five acres in Clonerkyllethan, Co. Limerick, from Rhys Clon. Their father, William Scolog, had been officially recognised as the rightful owner, and sometime between his death and the court case Rhys had taken their inheritance. In 1302 Richard Scolog, son of Henry Scolog, recovered eight acres in Fanleoston, Co. Cork, from John le Flemeng, which John had taken after Henry's death.[11] These cases were all assizes, the quickest form of court case, which required the plaintiffs to be above reproach, and they demonstrate that free Gaelic persons were able to win property cases in the English royal courts in Ireland.

To entice English people, especially merchants, to move to their lands, the earliest conquerors and settlers created boroughs. These boroughs—and the five royal urban centres of Dublin, Wexford, Waterford, Cork and Limerick—were granted privileges, confirmed by charter, which allowed them semi-autonomous government and freedom from tolls. Among the lists of burgesses and citizens (the name for the members of boroughs and cities respectively) we can find many Gaelic people. On the Dublin list of free citizens we find Gillefintan (*Giolla Fiontain*), Gillecrist (*Giolla Chríost*) who was with Ralph de Lamore, Bridinus (*Brídín*?) Ruffus, Padinus (*Paidin*?) Hibernicus Sutor and Thomas Maloc (*Ó Maolóig*?) de Nass.[12] At Clonmel in 1300 we find Roger Otoyk (*Ó Tuait*?), William Fagan (*Ó Fechín* or *Ó Fiacháin*?), William Boyk (*Ó Buadhaigh*?), Robert Boly (*Ó Baoighill*?), Henry Ker (*Ó Ciardha*?), John Okyk/Okilt (*Ó Caoilte*?), Adam Ohany (*Ó hÉanaigh*?), Thomas Colyn (*Ó Coileáin*?)

and John Fagan listed as free men and burgesses.[13] Seven years later, King Edward I's Irish council decided that, by custom, even an unfree Gaelic person who owned a house in an enfranchised borough became a burgess and free person in English Ireland.[14] The records from Dublin and Clonmel support the council's ruling, although the Dublin citizens and Clonmel burgesses could have been free from birth.

Free Gaelic men were accepted as attorneys by the courts and by the English lords who hired them. In 1252 Bricius Ocohelan (*Breac Ó Cochláin*?) appeared in the itinerant court at Limerick as the attorney for Leliath.[15] In 1280 Edmund son of Henry de Roche sued Anna, the widow of John de Cogan, at the Dublin Bench. Edmund's court representative was John Obut (*Ó Buidhe*?).[16] In the same Dublin Bench session, Philip Odrey (*Ó Draoi*?) represented Henry Hog in a civil case relating to the illegal use of force.[17] In 1285 Emmeline, the widow of Hugh de Aston, sent Hugh Oglawth and Adam Oglauth (*Mac an Ógladigh*?) as her attorneys to the Dublin Bench, and they were received by the Bench after the king of England, Edward I, confirmed their suitability.[18] Attorneys at that time were not the same as solicitors or barristers today, but they would have spoken the same language as the justices of the courts and known the court procedures.[19]

English lords also hired Gaelic bailiffs for their manors. Before 1290 Condoly Mackyngnery (*Condálach Mac an Airrí*?) was Emmeline de Longespée's bailiff of the manor of Corcomohide, Co. Limerick.[20] Neyvinus Odonagh (*Neamhain Ó Donnchadha*) and Molok Omolkyny (*Maológ Ó Maoil Chaoine*?) were bailiffs of Lemkillecan (or Lemgillothan), Co. Cork, for Thomas son of Philip,[21] and Donenold Ohanly (*Domhnall Ó hÁinlighe*?) was the bailiff of Balytannyth, Co. Dublin, for Eustace le Poher before 1298.[22] Bailiffs collected rents from all of the tenants, presided over the manorial court, enforced the mandatory labour services of the free and unfree tenants (mandatory manual labour was not a sign of unfreedom) and then sent all of the profits to the lord. Bailiffs were also, customarily, the representatives of lords in the English king's courts, but this practice fell out of use with the advent of professional attorneys.

In 1242–3 the *vicecomes* (viscount, nowadays called a 'sheriff') of Dublin was Simon Murdagh/Muridac (*Ó Muireadaigh*?).[23] He had custody of County Dublin and Dublin Castle until 1245, when he was ordered to deliver seisin to John son of Geoffrey, the new justiciar of Ireland.[24] Simon's achievement seems incredible because many historians have—*ex silentio*—argued that no Gaelic person held such a position of secular power in English Ireland.[25] Other records demonstrate that *vicecomites* of counties and seneschals of liberties employed Gaelic men to serve as their deputies as part of their royal or franchisal retinue respectively. In 1295 James Omattus (*Ó Mac Cais*?) was sued along with William de Valence, lord of Wexford, and Gilbert Sotton, the seneschal, for exceeding their administrative powers.[26] The next year John son of John son of Henry, seneschal of Wexford, William Nivel, Maurice de Caunteton, another seneschal of Wexford, and Daniel Omathus (*Ó Mac Cais* or *Ó*

Máighiú?) were sued by Gilbert de Sutton for the same.[27] In 1302 James Omaccus—probably the same man from Wexford—was fined for seizing the goods of a man outside his jurisdiction. James was gaoled but was released after providing sureties to pay a fine of 40*s*.[28] The record also mentions that James was the sergeant of Dublin, and that he summoned and distrained men to appear before lay and clerical panels.[29] Omaccus was clearly a deputy of the English administration, paid for his muscle and given legal power and privilege in return.

With the free Gaelic people identified, the next question is what happened to them. We may never know what happened to the majority, but we can see the disappearance of some.[30] A few Gaelic people who were recognised as free members of English society did not produce a male heir. Their lands went in marriage with their daughter(s) to an English husband. Around 1250 Domhnall Ó Longáin held Loughane in Bohillane, Co. Cork, from Richard de Carew of Castlecor, and gave Loughane and Sleveen with his daughter Raghnailt to Philip son of Tancard Cristofre before 1260.[31] Diarmaid Mac Carthaigh held the cantred of Glinshalewy in fee and hereditarily (directly from a lord, probably in exchange for military service).[32] After his son Cormac died, his three daughters claimed all of his lands. Robert Cusyn and Rathenild (*Raghnailt*) seized most of the lands, and then David de Prendergast and Dernorguyl (*Dearbhorgaill*) and Thomas de Kaninges and Edina (*Éadaoin*) sued Robert and Rathenild for two-thirds of the cantred.[33] The usual practice for multiple female heiresses was to split all property evenly between them. Each daughter was theoretically entitled to a third of the cantred. No one objected to their ethnicity or their ability to use the English courts in Ireland.

A case from Waterford in 1253 partially reinforces the old anti-Gaelic discrimination theory, but not entirely. A jury reported to John son of Geoffrey, the justiciar, that six Gaelic men holding in chief of Henry III should be legally disseised in order to place English tenants on the same lands. It believed that the rent of these Gaelic men was too low, and that English tenants would be to the benefit of the king's treasury.[34] Some, but not all, of the Gaelic men were subsequently disseised; the rest paid higher rents.

From 1280 to 1381 several Uí Cheallaigh sued to recover lands in north County Dublin and east Meath from English men and women. The Uí Cheallaigh were the lords (or kings) of Brega, which encompassed that region. In 1280 Donenald Okelli (*Domhnall Ó Ceallaigh*) brought a few cases but the results were not listed, and so we cannot tell whether the English courts recognised his rights to Lougher, Duleek, Meath.[35] In 1287 the lordship over William Okelli junior's lands was sold to a church. While William did not lose all of his lands, the same record states that 30 acres that he had previously held had been granted to the same church.[36] The Uí Cheallaigh continued to sue for lands in Brega, but by 1381 the English courts and society determined the Uí Cheallaigh in Duleek to be unfree Gaels and therefore unable to recover lands in court.[37]

A final way in which the free Gaelic people disappeared was through land grants. In 1263 Thomas O Regan (*Ó Riagain*) repaid a debt of 22½ marks to Robert de Emly, the bishop of Limerick, by granting the latter all of his lands, burgages and tenements in Clonnawyll and Clonchenn.[38] Cecily daughter of Donald Oconnean (*Domhnall Ó Coinín*?) granted Richard Costard 21 acres and a stang of arable land in Maymoch (Mayne, lib. Kilkenny) in exchange for 23 marks, a robe and 12*d.* annual rent.[39] In 1277 Agnes Odurne (*Ó Duirn*), probably the daughter of Conibyr Odyrne (*Conchobhar Ó Duirn*), granted twelve acres in Corbally to Thomas de Lega the younger, and Alexander son of Alexander Mol (*Maol*) sold his rights to 100 acres in Rathno, Co. Cork, to Philip son of Gilbert.[40] Without holding any free land, they could have been reclassified as unfree like the Uí Cheallaigh of Brega, remained in those areas but died without heirs, or moved to an enfranchised borough and purchased a house—becoming free and accepted members of English Ireland. Unless new evidence is discovered, however, we may never know.

The existence of the free and accepted Gaelic people may come as a surprise now, but they were well known to thirteenth-century Ireland. Excluding a few rhetorical claims, only recently has their existence been denied. These few cases cannot be taken as representative of the majority of experiences. Thirteenth-century society was stratified, and the magnates and prelates did oppress peasants with harsh labour services and denial of access to the royal courts. Nevertheless, the idea that *all* Gaelic people were treated in one way, or that the so-called 'Remonstrance of the Irish princes' was an accurate and objective statement, clearly needs a fresh appraisal and critical analysis of all of its claims.

Notes

1 Many thanks to Eoin MacCárthaig, Damian McManus and Seán Duffy for their advice on rendering the Gaelic names from the Anglicised form written in the Latin court records. All of the suggested renderings in this chapter are merely suggestions; any infelicities are entirely my own.

2 Walter Bower, *Scotichronicon*, ed. N. Shead, W. Stevenson, D.E.R. Watt, A. Borthwick, R.E. Latham, J.R.S. Phillips and M. Smith (Aberdeen, 1991), vi, pp 384–403.

3 B. Murphy, 'The status of the native Irish after 1331', *Irish Jurist* 2 (1967), pp 116–28; G.J. Hand, *English law in Ireland 1290–1324* (Cambridge, 1967), pp 198–210; A.J. Otway-Ruthven, *A history of medieval Ireland* (London, 1968), pp 125, 188–9, 235–6; R. Bartlett, *The making of Europe: conquest, colonisation and cultural change, 950–1350* (London, 1993), p. 214.

4 A.J. Otway-Ruthven, 'The native Irish and English law in medieval Ireland', *Irish Historical Studies* 7 (25) (1950), pp 1–16, at 6–7. Professor Otway-Ruthven *assumed* that all of the free Gaelic people had written grants of access to English courts that have not survived.

5 K. Nicholls, 'Anglo-French Ireland and after', *Peritia* 1 (1982), pp 370–402, at 374. Robin Frame reluctantly acknowledged the existence of free Gaels but claimed that they were not recognised by the English courts and could not bequeath their lands to their heirs. He provided no evidence for this absolute claim and placed the counter-evidence in a footnote, dismissing it as completely anomalous.

He even had some doubt about Nicholls's theory that there were recognised Gaels before 1252: R. Frame, 'Ireland after 1169: barriers to acculturation on an "English" edge', in K. Stringer and A. Jotischky (eds), *Norman expansion: connections, continuities and contrasts* (Farnham, 2013), pp 115–41, at 119.

6 Domnall's name is standardised to pre-1200 conventions, whereas the other Gaelic names in this chapter are rendered in the post-1200 conventions. E. O'Byrne, 'FitzDermot (Mac Gilla Mo Cholmóc), Sir Ralph', in J. McGuire and J. Quinn (eds), *Dictionary of Irish biography* (hereafter *DIB*) (Cambridge, 2009): http://dib.cambridge.org/viewReadPage.do?articleId=a3129 (19/11/14); *idem*, 'Mac Gilla Mo Cholmóc, Diarmait', in *DIB*: http://dib.cambridge.org/viewReadPage.do?articleId=a5047 (24/4/15). It is important to note that this family—who, in fact, were never called 'fitz Dermot'—quickly became almost entirely English by blood and custom. John son of Diarmaid married Clarice daughter of Gilbert son of Griffin. John son of John married Ralph de Pitchford's daughter. Therefore Ralph son of John son of John son of Diarmaid was three-fourths English: J. Mills, 'The Norman settlement in Leinster: the cantreds near Dublin', *Journal of the Royal Society of Antiquaries of Ireland* (5th ser.) 4 (2) (1894), pp 160–75, at 162–3; Frame, 'Ireland after 1169', pp 128–30. The descendants of Mac Gilla Mo Cholmóc are only remembered as being Gaelic because their patrilineal descent can be traced back to a Gaelic king, completely erasing their maternal lineage from history, and subsequently their mothers and grandmothers as well.

7 C. McNeill, 'Lord Chancellor Gerrard's notes of his report on Ireland: with extracts from original Irish records exhibited by him before the Privy Council in England, 1577–8', *Analecta Hibernica* 2 (1931), pp 92–291, at 251–2.

8 'Records Commission calendars of plea rolls', 1819–23, National Archives of Ireland (hereafter NAI), RC 7/1, p. 143.

9 NAI, RC 7/1, p. 243.

10 NAI, RC 7/1, p. 361.

11 NAI, RC 7/2, p. 425.

12 P. Connolly and G. Martin (eds), *The Dublin Guild Merchant Roll* (Dublin, 1992), pp 114–16, 118. Gillefintan and Thomas Maloc are also on the guild merchant roll ('Thomas Maloth'): ibid., pp 51, 53.

13 NAI, RC 7/6, pp 77–8, 80–2; RC 7/7, pp 24–31, 165–7, 176–81; RC 7/8, p. 158.

14 J. Mills (ed.), *Calendar of justiciary rolls . . . Ireland, 1305–7* (Dublin, 1914), p. 352.

15 NAI, RC 7/1, p. 130.

16 NAI, RC 7/2, p. 5.

17 NAI, RC 7/2, p. 6.

18 H.S. Sweetman (ed.), *Calendar of documents relating to Ireland* [hereafter *CDI*], *1285–92* (London, 1879), no. 62.

19 P. Brand, *The origins of the English legal profession* (London, 1992), pp 33–69; *idem*, 'The early history of the legal profession of the lordship of Ireland, 1250–1350', in D. Hogan and W.N. Osborough (eds), *Brehons, serjeants and attorneys: studies in the history of the Irish legal profession* (Dublin, 1990), pp 15–50.

20 NAI, RC 7/3, p. 357.

21 NAI, RC 7/5, p. 18.

22 NAI, RC 7/5, pp 282, 294, 328, 342–3.

23 M.P. Sheehy, 'Unpublished *notitiae* and *epistolae*', *Collectanea Hibernica* **6–7** (1963–4), pp 7–17, at 9. Seán Duffy proposed that Simon Muridac may have been a very Gaelicised Ostman (Simon mac Muireadaigh).

24 H.S. Sweetman (ed.), *CDI, 1171–1251* (London, 1875), no. 2792; *Calendar of patent rolls, 1232–47* (London, 1906), p. 467; Á. Foley, 'The sheriff of Dublin in the fourteenth century', in S. Duffy (ed.), *Medieval Dublin xii* (Dublin, 2012), pp 264–88, at 268, 279.

25 'There were no native Irish sheriffs [*sic*], seneschals of liberties, serjeants, coroners, or keepers of the peace': R. Frame, '"Leys Engleys nées en Irlande": the English political identity in medieval Ireland', *Transactions of the Royal Historical Society* (6th ser.) 3 (1993), pp 83–103, at 92.

[26] NAI, RC 7/3, p. 355. 'T' and 'C' in medieval script are difficult to differentiate. His name was probably 'Omaccus'.

[27] NAI, RC 7/3, pp 316–17.

[28] J. Mills (ed.), *Calendar of justiciary rolls, Ireland, 1295–1303* (Dublin, 1905), p. 394.

[29] See quote in note 25.

[30] There are numerous land grants which state that the land being granted formerly belonged to a certain Gaelic person. These appear to show that the Gael had died and the lord was choosing a new tenant. These records do not specify whether the Gaelic landholder had died without an heir or whether the lord was preventing the heir from inheriting in favour of a new English tenant; for example: C. McNeill (ed.), *Calendar of Archbishop Alen's Register* (Dublin, 1950), pp 14–15, 24–5, 31, 45, 46, 53, 64–5.

[31] K. Nicholls and P. MacCotter (eds), *The pipe rolls of Cloyne: rotulus pipae Clonensis* (Cloyne, 1996), pp 15, 178.

[32] Nicholls identified Glinshalewy as Clann Sealbaig in south-west Cork: Nicholls, 'Anglo-French Ireland', p. 384. MacCotter examined this area and its origins; he labelled it as C35 (cantred no. 35) in his geographical study: P. MacCotter, *Medieval Ireland: territorial, political and economic divisions* (Dublin, 2008), p. 154.

[33] NAI, RC 7/1, p. 246. No result was recorded, but the case may have been delayed (the surviving record does not state whether it was respited). In a later case, Robert and Raghnailt defeated an objection and won the case after they had alleged that her sisters were illegitimate because the latter were born before their parents were married. In the final court case—which may have been a continuation of the first—David, Dearbhorgaill, Thomas and Éadaoin sued Robert and Raghnailt for two-thirds of the cantred. Robert and Raghnailt claimed that her sisters were illegitimate, and the itinerant justices supposedly summoned the bishop of Emly, Gillebertus Ó Dubartaig, to decide the issue, but no answer was recorded. The plaintiffs then argued that when Alan de la Zouche was justiciar he was not in Ireland to make a ruling; that Geoffrey de St John, bishop of Ferns, had died on itineration as justiciar; that itinerant justice Hugh de Kingsbury could not rule without the other itinerant justices present; and finally that Lord Edward had mandated Stephen de Longespée, justiciar, and not the itinerant justices to certify the pleading from the case. No verdict survives, but both couples were allowed to use the royal courts and recovered other lands after the sisters were labelled illegitimate: ibid., pp 263, 282–3.

[34] C. Parker, 'The internal frontier: the Irish in County Waterford in the later Middle Ages', in T.B. Barry, R. Frame and K. Simms (eds), *Colony and frontier in medieval Ireland: essays presented to J.F. Lydon* (London, 1995), pp 139–54, at 140–2; P. Dryburgh and B. Smith (eds), *List and index society, cccxx: inquisitions and extents of medieval Ireland* (Kew, 2007), pp 7–8.

[35] NAI, RC 7/1, p. 61; RC 7/2, pp 61–2.

[36] E. St John Brooks (ed.), *The Irish cartularies of Llanthony Prima & Secunda* (Dublin, 1953), no. 34.

[37] *Irish cartularies of Llanthony*, no. 98, p. 301. These 'Okellis' were probably related to the Uí Cheallaigh lords of Brega who ruled before the advent of the English. Conell Mageoghagan, writing in 1627, believed that the 'Okellis of Brega' had been reduced 'to be mere churles' over the centuries. We should remember, however, that Congalagh Ó Ceallaigh was listed as the lord of Brega at his death in 1292—120 years after the invasion of Meath: D. Murphy (ed.), *The annals of Clonmacnoise: being annals of Ireland from the earliest period to AD 1408* (Dublin, 1896), pp 124–5; *Annals of the Four Masters*, iii, 454–5. John O'Donovan, editor of the *Annals of the Four Masters*, believed that Congalagh's title did not reflect his political power (or lack thereof) and the diminished size of the 'principality' of Brega. Many thanks to Katharine Simms for providing me with this reference.

[38] J. MacCaffrey (ed.), *The Black Book of Limerick* (Dublin, 1907), pp 55–6.

[39] E. Curtis (ed.), *The calendar of Ormond deeds* (6 vols, Dublin, 1932), i, no. 252.

[40] Ibid., i, nos 211, 218.

2

An Irish context to a Scottish disaster: James IV, the O'Donnells of Tyrconnell and the road to Flodden

Simon Egan
(2016 prize)

Introduction

On 9 September 1513 the Scots suffered one of their most catastrophic military defeats. At Flodden Field an army of 30,000 men under the command of James IV of Scotland was decimated by a smaller English force led by Thomas Howard (d. 1554), earl of Surrey.[1] The cream of the Scottish nobility was wiped out that day, including King James, three bishops, eleven earls, fifteen lords and thousands of rank-and-file pikemen.[2] English losses were minimal in comparison.[3] Traditionally, Flodden has been regarded as something of a fool's venture, and James IV's strategy for invading England as extending little beyond taking advantage of Henry VIII's absence in France.[4] Indeed, most historians have tended to view developments in England and on the Continent as the main dynamics driving the course of Anglo-Scottish relations during this period.[5] Aside from a few notable exceptions, very little work has been undertaken on the broader Gaelic dimension underpinning James IV's Flodden campaign.[6]

Over the course of the later Middle Ages the wider Gaelic world, or *Gaeltacht*, came to encompass nearly 50% of the British Isles. Despite this profound geopolitical recasting of much of late medieval Britain, the broader impact of the Gaelic resurgence has featured little in the historiography of late medieval Ireland, England and Scotland. Unfortunately, a short essay such as this is not the place for a detailed reassessment of how the resurgence of Gaelic power affected the political development of late medieval Britain and Ireland. The case-study of Flodden is useful, however, as it allows for a thematic overview of how the Stewart monarchy, during the late fifteenth and early sixteenth centuries, was able to draw upon considerable support from the Gaelic world, support which in turn could be used against England.

The origins of the O'Donnell–Stewart alliance

Over the course of the late fifteenth century the O'Donnells of Tyrconnell established themselves as one of the most powerful Gaelic dynasties within the wider Irish Sea world.[7] Under the leadership of Aedh Ruadh (d. 1505) and his son, Aedh Dubh (d.

1537), the O'Donnells created a large hegemonic empire spanning much of Ulster, Connacht and northern Leinster. The strategic position of their lordship on the north-west coast of Ireland, coupled with their ability to raise considerable military and maritime resources, made the O'Donnells ideal allies for the Stewart monarchs.[8] On one level they served as a counterbalance to the MacDonald lordship of the Isles. During the fourteenth century the lordship of Clan Donald emerged as a powerful, autonomous force in western Scotland.[9] Holding lands on both sides of the North Channel, in Antrim and the Hebrides, and often courted as allies by the Plantagenet kings, the lords of the Isles posed a significant threat to Scotland's western seaboard.[10]

The O'Donnell–Stewart alliance largely derived from this situation, and connections between the O'Donnells and the Stewarts can be traced to the late fourteenth century.[11] It is important to note that the earlier Stewart monarchs, Robert II (d. 1390) and Robert III (d. 1406), were highly attuned to the cultural and political nuances of the Gaelic world.[12] Originally hailing from the west coast of Scotland, these kings enjoyed considerable support from the Gaelic Scottish nobility, their chief supporters including the Campbells of Argyll and Clan Donnchaidh of Atholl.[13] These cultural and dynastic ties with Gaelic Scotland provided the Stewarts with a bridge into Gaelic Ireland, with which they could encircle the Clan Donald. Source material relating to Hiberno-Scottish connections for this period is often infuriatingly fragmentary. Nonetheless, it does appear that Clan Donald became increasingly concerned about the Stewart monarchy's influence with the O'Donnells during the first half of the fifteenth century. This is perhaps most obvious during the reign of James I (d. 1437).

Returning to Scotland in 1424 after eighteen years' captivity in England, James sought to establish strong personal rule over his kingdom.[14] Following the forfeiture and destruction of his kinsmen the Albany Stewarts, who ruled Scotland during his absence, James turned his attention westwards.[15] During the first two decades of the fifteenth century Clan Donald had expanded their territory across much of northern Scotland, most notably in the earldom of Ross. James unsurprisingly sought to reduce their hold on the earldom. Following a series of battles in 1429 and 1431, neither James nor the lord of the Isles, Alexander (d. 1449), was able to gain the upper hand. Based on evidence contained in Scottish and English chronicles and other governmental sources, it appears that James sought assistance from the then lord of Tyrconnell, Niall Garbh O'Donnell (d. 1439).[16]

In 1433 Niall Garbh moved eastwards against the MacDonald lands in Antrim.[17] Alexander and his kinsmen in Antrim were nonetheless quick to act. Allying himself with Eoghan O'Neill (d. 1455), the lord of Tyrone and the main regional rival of the O'Donnells, Alexander routed Niall Garbh's force in eastern Ulster before launching a two-pronged attack on Tyrconnell.[18] Eoghan's force marched into Tyrconnell, while Alexander's fleet landed at Inishowen. In the face of overwhelming numbers the O'Donnells were soon defeated. The hegemony that Niall Garbh had built across

Ulster and Connacht collapsed shortly afterwards in favour of the resurgent O'Neills. With his Irish option exhausted, James I had little choice but to make peace with Alexander and by 1436 the king had elevated Alexander to the coveted earldom of Ross, acknowledging Alexander's dominance in northern Scotland.[19] For the next few decades Clan Donald remained pre-eminent in the west, while the O'Neills emerged as the main power in Ulster. It is perhaps unsurprising that Edward IV of England (d. 1483) viewed both of these factions as potential allies for their ability to bolster English influence in regions where it was effectively non-existent.[20]

The O'Donnell resurgence, *c.* 1460–1500

Matters changed in 1461 when Niall Garbh's son, Aedh Ruadh, seized power within Tyrconnell.[21] A highly skilled politician and military commander, Aedh Ruadh was the mastermind behind the remarkable O'Donnell recovery. An alliance with the Clandeboy O'Neills drew the O'Neills of Tyrone's attention away from western Ulster, enabling Aedh Ruadh to lead a number of successful military hostings into Connacht.[22] Over the course of the 1460s Aedh Ruadh rebuilt his father's old alliance network, scoring a number of victories over the Burkes of Clanrickard, the O'Connors of Sligo and the O'Briens of Thomond, as well as propping up the Burkes of Mayo and the O'Connor Ruadh kindred in Roscommon.[23] By 1474 Aedh Ruadh had made peace with the O'Briens, marrying Fionnuala O'Brien, daughter of the clan chief, Connor (d. 1496).[24] The shifting balance of power in the west of Ireland formed the basis for further expansion into northern Leinster. In 1475 Aedh Ruadh marched eastwards, launching a devastating attack on the Pale and forcing black rent (tribute) from Dundalk.[25]

Similar developments were occurring in Scotland. Since the late 1460s the Scottish crown had pursued increasingly aggressive policies against Clan Donald. Through the promotion of loyalist kindreds such as the Campbells of Argyll, James III (d. 1488) hoped to break the power of the island lords.[26] The inability of John MacDonald (d. 1503), the fourth and last lord of the Isles, to control his kinsmen weakened the cohesion of Clan Donald and allowed James III to declare the earldom of Ross forfeit in 1475.[27] The political disintegration of the lordship soon followed: various island kindreds descended into fractious infighting during the 1480s and early 1490s, while the lordship itself was finally declared forfeit and seized by the Scottish crown in 1493.[28]

The extent to which developments in Ireland affected the collapse of the lordship of the Isles remains uncertain. The resurgence of the O'Donnell lordship in the west can hardly have been welcomed by Clan Donald, who were becoming increasingly caught on two fronts as the Scottish monarchy pushed westwards. The English government in Dublin was certainly fearful of royal Scottish intervention in Ireland at this time. In a panicked report sent to Westminster in 1474, the council went as far as to state that James III planned to 'reduce all thye land to the obeysuance of the king of Scotts'.[29] Though no such invasion occurred, the ascension of the Tudors eleven years later exposed Ireland to a far greater degree of foreign intervention.

James IV and Ireland

In the summer of 1495 Aedh Ruadh travelled to Glasgow. Upon arrival, he was greeted by the young king of Scots, James IV, and both men promptly entered into what the *Annals of the Four Masters* have dubbed a *comhaontu*, or alliance.[30] It is very likely that the issue of the Yorkist pretender Perkin Warbeck (d. 1499) was discussed during this meeting.[31] The threat of Yorkist pretenders such as Warbeck (and Lambert Simnel in the late 1480s) struck at the very heart of the fledgling Tudor dynasty. Though little became of this venture, Warbeck had for a time enjoyed the support of James IV, Margaret of Burgundy (d. 1503), the Holy Roman Emperor Maximilian I (d. 1519) and Maurice, earl of Desmond (d. 1520).[32] The fact that Warbeck had been able to move freely in Ireland throughout the 1490s highlighted the severe limitations of Tudor power in Ireland and the potential for foreign meddling therein.

Warbeck's capture in 1497 and execution in 1499 did little to reduce the security threat posed by developments in Ireland. During this time Henry VII had grown increasingly suspicious of his Irish lord deputy, Gearóid Mór FitzGerald, eighth earl of Kildare.[33] A known Yorkist sympathiser, Kildare had previously supported Lambert Simnel in 1487. He was arrested in 1495 at the height of the Warbeck crisis and, following a brief period of captivity in England, was released, returning to office in Ireland in late 1496.[34] Kildare, however, did little to actively increase the power of the Tudors in Ireland and there is evidence to suggest that he entered into some form of league with O'Donnell, placing his second-born son, Henry (d. 1514), into fosterage with Aedh Ruadh in 1499.[35] Moreover, following Aedh Ruadh's death in 1505, Kildare maintained this connection with his son and successor, Aedh Dubh.[36] Such was the ineffectiveness of Kildare's deputyship that by December 1506 Henry VII (d. 1509) considered leading a full military intervention to Ireland.[37] Only the fatal deterioration of his health prevented him from doing so.

The ambitions of his son, Henry VIII (d. 1547), for reviving Henry V's English empire in France exposed the Tudors to further Continental intrigue.[38] Fearing a French victory in the Italian wars of the early sixteenth century, Pope Julius II (d. 1513) created the Holy League, aligning the English, the Venetians, the Spanish, the Swiss cities and the Holy Roman Emperor against Louis XII of France.[39] Over the course of 1512 Henry VIII became increasingly entangled in Continental diplomacy, eventually committing to a full-scale invasion of France in the summer of 1513. Though James IV had renewed his alliance with Louis in 1512 and promised to attack England, the scale of the Scottish king's ambitions became clear in 1513. In early summer Aedh Dubh travelled to Edinburgh for a council of war with the Scottish king.[40] On 26 June they entered into a military alliance. Traditionally, historians have regarded James's treaty with Aedh Dubh as little more than a sideshow to his grander, Continental schemes.[41] Surviving Irish sources, however, suggest otherwise. The contemporary *Annals of Ulster* suggest that James IV originally planned a large military intervention in Ireland and that it was only on the advice of O'Donnell that James reconsidered.[42] Instead, a diversionary attack was launched against Carrickfergus in eastern Ulster, while James prepared his host for war in northern England.

Conclusion

Why O'Donnell cautioned against an intervention in Ireland remains uncertain. It is perhaps fair to suggest that both James and O'Donnell were confident that an invasion of England would prove successful. By early September it very much appeared that the Scots were in the ascendancy and that the English were surrounded on numerous fronts. Henry VIII was bogged down in an unsuccessful invasion of France, while King Louis had provided the Scots with arms, munitions, money and the promise of further aid.[43] French military advisers had been sent to train James IV's army in the art of Continental pike warfare, while the Scottish navy, one of the most advanced in northern Europe, posed a serious challenge to English sea power.[44] In Ireland, one of the most powerful Gaelic magnates stood poised to assist the Scots. For the first time since Robert Bruce, a Scottish king posed a serious challenge to English power within the British Isles. The O'Donnells had played no small part in this.

Notes

1 D.H. Caldwell, 'How well prepared was James IV to fight by land and sea in 1513?', *Journal of the Sydney Society for Scottish History* 14 (2013), pp 36–7.

2 J. Wormald, *Court, kirk and community: Scotland, 1470–1625* (Edinburgh, 1981), p. 7.

3 For a recent overview of the battle see G. Goodwin, *Fatal rivalry: Flodden 1513—Henry VIII, James IV and the battle for Renaissance Britain* (London, 2013).

4 A. MacDonald, 'Triumph and disaster: Scottish military leadership in the later Middle Ages', in A. King and D. Simpkin (eds), *England and Scotland at war,* c. *1296–1513* (Leiden, 2012), pp 255–82.

5 For example, see N. MacDougall, *An antidote to the English: the Auld Alliance, 1295–1560* (East Linton, 2001).

6 The exception being Stephen Boardman's work on the Campbells of Argyll; see S. Boardman, *The Campbells, 1250–1513* (Edinburgh, 2005), chapter 12; *idem*, 'Highland Scots and Anglo-Scottish warfare, *c.* 1300–1513', in King and Simpkin (eds), *England and Scotland at war*, pp 231–54.

7 For a broad overview of O'Donnell expansion in this period see D. MacGettigan, 'The renaissance and late medieval lordship of Tír Chonaill, 1461–1555', in W. Nolan, L. Ronayne and M. Dunlevy (eds), *Donegal: history and society* (Dublin, 1995), pp 203–24; K. Simms, 'Late medieval Donegal', ibid., pp 183–202.

8 For an overview of O'Donnell maritime power see S. Egan, 'By land and by sea: the role of the

maritime sphere in the expansion of O'Donnell power, *c.*1380–*c.*1500', *Journal of the North Atlantic* (forthcoming, 2018).

9 The last number of decades has witnessed a growing interest in Clan Donald and the lordship of the Isles. For which see A. Grant, 'Scotland's "Celtic fringe" in the late Middle Ages: the MacDonald lords of the isles and the kingdom of Scotland', in R.R. Davies (ed.), *The British Isles, 1100–1500: comparisons, contrasts and connections* (Edinburgh, 1988), pp 118–41; S. Kingston, *Ulster and the Isles in the fifteenth century: the lordship of the Clann Domhnaill of Antrim* (Dublin, 2004); *idem*, 'Trans-insular lordship in the fifteenth century', in T.M. Devine and J.F. McMillan, *Celebrating Columba: Irish–Scottish connections, 597–1997* (East Linton, 1999), pp 35–44; S. Boardman, 'The lost world: post-medieval accounts of the lordship of the Isles', in S. Duffy and S. Foran (eds), *The English Isles: cultural transmission and political conflict in Britain and Ireland, 1100–1500* (Dublin, 2013), pp 151–74; N. Murray, 'A house divided against itself: a brief synopsis of the history of Clann Alexandair and the early career of "Good John of Islay", *c.* 1290–1370', in C. Ó Baoill and N.R. McGuire (eds), *Rannsachadh na Gàidhlig 2000* (Aberdeen, 2002), pp 221–30.

10 For the Clan Donald's negotiations with the English crown in the late fourteenth and early fifteenth centuries see J. Munro and R.W. Munro (eds), *Acts of the lords of the Isles, 1336–1493* (Edinburgh, 1986), pp 1–12; D. MacPherson (ed.), *Rotuli Scotiae, 1292–1516* (2 vols, London, 1819), ii, pp 11, 45, 94–5, 155–6; the National Archives of the United Kingdom (hereafter TNA), E 101/315/23; T. Rymer (ed.), *Foedera* (20 vols, London, 1727–35), vii, pp 592, 622–9, 639–40, 656–8, 714–16, 777, 824; viii, p. 146; R.C. Fowler *et al.* (eds), *Calendar of patent rolls, 1405–8* (London, 1891–1916), pp 361, 487.

11 During the 1380s, petitions from Tyrconnell were being sent to Avignon via Robert II of Scotland; see W.H. Bliss (ed.), *Calendar of entries in the papal registers relating to Great Britain and Ireland: petitions to the pope, 1342–1419* (London, 1896), pp 559, 575–6. I am grateful to Mr Kenneth Nicholls for drawing my attention to this reference.

12 S. Boardman, 'The Gaelic world and the early Stewart court', in D. Broun and M. MacGregor (eds), *Mìorun Mòr nan Gall: 'The great ill will of the Lowlander'?: Lowland perceptions of the Highlands, medieval and modern* (Stornoway, 2006), pp 83–109.

13 Boardman, *The Campbells*, chapters 4–5; *idem*, *The early Stewart kings: Robert II and Robert III* (East Linton, 1997), pp 7–10.

14 For the best account of the kingship of James I see M. Brown, *James I* (East Linton, 1994).

15 For a reassessment of the governorship of the Albany Stewarts see K. Hunt, 'The governorship of the duke of Albany', in M. Brown and R. Tanner (eds), *Scottish kingship, 1306–1542: essays in honour of Norman MacDougall* (Edinburgh, 2008), pp 126–54.

16 For an overview of Niall Garbh's career see K. Simms, 'Niall Garbh O'Donnell, king of Tír Conaill, 1422–39', *Donegal Annual* 12 (1977), pp 7–21. For expansion into Connacht and Leinster during the 1420s and early 1430s see M. Freeman (ed.), *The Annals of Connacht, 1224–1554* (2 vols, Dublin, 1970) (hereafter referred to as *AC*), 1422–1430 (all annals references are given as the year rather than page number); J. O'Donovan (ed.), *Annals of the kingdom of Ireland: from the earliest times to the years 1616* (7 vols, Dublin, 1990) (hereafter *AFM*), 1422–1430; W.M. Hennessy (ed.), *The Annals of Loch Cé: a chronicle of Irish affairs from 1014 to 1590* (2 vols, London, 1939) (hereafter *ALC*), 1422–1430; W.M. Hennessy (ed.), *Annals of Ulster: a chronicle of Irish affairs from AD 431 to AD 1540* (4 vols, Dublin, 1887–1901) (hereafter *AU*), 1422–1430. See especially Niall Garbh's subjugation of the kindreds in northern Leinster and subsequent attack on the Pale in 1422 (*AC*, 1422; *AFM*, *AU*, 1423).

17 *AFM*, *AU*, 1433.

18 *AFM*, *AU*, 1433.

19 For the background to this see Brown, *James I*, chapter 7. See also S. Egan, 'The early Stewart kings, the lordship of the Isles, and Ireland, *c.* 1371–1433', *Northern Studies* 49 (forthcoming, 2018).

20 For Yorkist alliance with the O'Neills of Tyrone see K. Simms, '"The king's friend": O'Neill, the crown and the earldom of Ulster', in J. Lydon (ed.), *England and Ireland in the later Middle Ages* (Dublin, 1981),

pp 214–36. For Yorkist alliance with the Clan Donald see *Acts of the lords of the Isles*, pp 110–11; *Foedera*, xi, p. 486; *Rot. Scot.*, ii, pp 405–7. For a recent reassessment of Edward IV's treaty with the Islesmen see J. Petre, 'Domnall Balloch, the treaty of Westminster-Ardtornish and the MacDonald raids of 1461–3', *Historical Research* **88** (242) (2015), pp 599–628.

21 *AFM, AU, AC*, 1461.

22 Aedh Ruadh married his daughter, Iníon Dubh, to Conn O'Neill, lord of Clandeboy, *c*. 1465 (for her obituary see *AFM, AU, AC, ALC*, 1494). There is also evidence to suggest that Aedh Dubh supplied Conn with MacSweeny galloglass from Fanad; see *AFM, AU*, 1470.

23 For hostings into Connacht see *ALC*, 1467; *AFM, AU, AC*, 1468.

24 *AFM*, 1474.

25 *AFM, AU, AC*, 1475.

26 For an insightful overview of the crown's policy towards the lordship of the Isles see Boardman, *The Campbells*, chapters 7–8.

27 *Records of the parliaments of Scotland to 1707*, ed. K.M. Brown *et al.* (St Andrews, 2007–10; on-line resource, at http://rps.ac.uk; accessed 13 May 2016), 1475/26.

28 *Acts of the lords of the Isles*, lxxii; Boardman, *The Campbells*, chapter 10. John, the last lord of the Isles, was forced to surrender himself, becoming a crown pensioner and dying in ignominy in 1503.

29 TNA, C 47/10/29.

30 *AFM*, 1495; T. Dickson and J.B. Paul (eds), *Accounts of the lord high treasurer of Scotland* (4 vols, Edinburgh, 1877–1902), i, pp 227, 242.

31 N. MacDougall, *James IV* (East Linton, 1997), pp 116–17.

32 For an overview of Warbeck's unfortunate career see I. Arthurson, *The Perkin Warbeck conspiracy: 1494–1499* (Stroud, 1994).

33 D. Bryan, *The Great Earl of Kildare (1456–1513)*, *passim*; D.B. Quinn, 'The hegemony of the earls of Kildare, 1494–1520', in A. Cosgrove (ed.), *A new history of Ireland, ii. Medieval Ireland, 1169–1534* (Oxford, 1987), pp 640–1.

34 *AU*, 1495; A. Conway, *Henry VII's relations with Ireland and Scotland, 1494–1498* (Cambridge, 1932), pp 80–102.

35 *AFM, AU*, 1499.

36 For example, see *AFM*, 1507, 1510; *AU, AC, ALC*, 1510.

37 G.C. Bayne, *Select cases in the council of Henry VII* (London, 1958), pp 46–7.

38 For an overview of Ireland's place in Tudor foreign policy see W. Palmer, *The problem of Ireland in Tudor foreign policy, 1485–1603* (Woodbridge, 1994), chapter 2.

39 For the context of the Italian wars see M. Mallett and C. Shaw, *The Italian Wars, 1494–1559: war, state and society in early modern Europe* (London, 2012), pp 120–2.

40 *AFM, AU, AC, ALC*, 1513.

41 MacDougall, *James IV*, pp 266–70; Goodwin, *Fatal rivalry*, chapters 12–18; Wormald, *Court, kirk and community*, chapter 1; J. Dawson, *Scotland Re-formed, 1488–1587* (Edinburgh, 2007), pp 83–5. It is completely overlooked by Alastair MacDonald; see *idem*, 'Triumph and disaster', pp 255–82. For a more balanced view see Boardman, *The Campbells*, pp 330–2.

42 *AU*, 1513.

43 MacDougall, *James IV*, p. 270.

44 Though the level of Scottish proficiency in pike warfare remains debated, see MacDonald, 'Triumph and disaster', pp 280–1. For Scottish naval power see N. MacDougall, '"The greattest scheip that ewer saillit in England or France": James IV's "Great Michael"', in N. MacDougall (ed.), *Scotland and war: AD 79–1918* (Edinburgh, 1991), pp 36–60; S. Murdoch, *Terror of the seas? Scottish maritime warfare, 1513–1713* (Leiden, 2013), chapter 1; Goodwin, *Fatal rivalry*, chapter 13.

3

'It is easier to forgive an enemy than to forgive a friend': Barnaby FitzPatrick and Gaelic collaboration with the Tudor crown, *c.* 1535–81

Diarmuid Wheeler

By the dawn of the sixteenth century, and by the 1530s in particular, several Gaelic clans within the territories of Leix and Offaly faced a difficult dilemma. With the collapse of Silken Thomas FitzGerald's rebellion in 1535 and the imminent prospect of an English-born governor intervening in the affairs of the midland territories for the very first time, Gaelic chieftains were forced to make a difficult choice: to collaborate with this new administration or to resist it. For some chieftaincies, such as the FitzPatrick clan of Upper Ossory, the answer was relatively simple and straightforward. Occupying essentially a no man's land, wedged firmly between the two territories of Kilkenny and Leix, the FitzPatricks were forced to alter their allegiances in the wake of increasing Butler military power and the very real possibility of their territory being reshired as part of County Kilkenny.[1] The clan's chief, Brian FitzPatrick, was very aware of the crown's agenda to restrict Butler power as much as possible, all the while promoting them to higher office.[2] Thus he seized the initiative in an attempt to consolidate his family's position, making it clear to the administration that he and his family were capable, and more than willing, to serve as counterweights to Butler power in the south midlands.[3]

Brian met Lord Deputy Leonard Grey on 8 November 1537 and agreed to an early form of 'surrender and regrant', swearing to hold his lands of the king, to adopt the English tongue, to renounce the pope and to conduct himself and govern Upper Ossory in a similar manner to the feudal border lords of the Pale.[4] In return, the clan gained the protection of the crown and Brian secured his position as chieftain, safeguarding both parties against any Butler aggression in the future.[5] Brian embraced his newfound sense of loyalism to the Tudor crown and became the first Gaelic chieftain to be granted an English peerage, as baron of Upper Ossory, as well as the first to sit as a member of the Irish parliament in the House of Lords in 1541, subsequently travelling to London in 1543 to be knighted by the king in person.[6] Brian was adamant that his eldest son and heir, Barnaby, would continue in his footsteps, embracing not only collaboration with the crown but also English cultural assimilation, as well as continuing to resist Ormond claims upon Upper Ossory.[7] Over the course of this paper the life of Barnaby FitzPatrick will be analysed, in particular his decision to embrace not only collaboration with the crown but also

Anglicisation, his dedication to his role as a crown agent, his subsequent downfall and the impact his decisions had on Upper Ossory by the time of his death in 1582 and beyond.

Barnaby FitzPatrick was educated from an early age in the Pale, where within a year he learned to speak English fluently, eventually being sent by his father to London in 1542 to be raised as a courtier and challenge Butler court influence.[8] Upon his arrival in London, Anthony St Leger, lord deputy of Ireland, referred to the Gaelic youth as a 'goodly and proper child'.[9] His time in London quickly became an overwhelming success for father and son alike. Chosen to march in Henry VIII's funeral procession in 1547 carrying a 'banner of ancient arms', he quickly became a close friend of the young prince and eventual king, Edward VI, who, until his untimely death in 1553, allegedly spoke of Barnaby with 'an ease and informality suggesting a strong personal affection'.[10] During Edward's short reign Barnaby was made a gentleman of the king's privy chamber alongside Robert Dudley, and eventually carried out the same role from 6 December 1551 to 9 December 1552 for Henry II, king of France.[11] Acting as an undercover English crown agent, FitzPatrick served as Edward's eyes and ears in France during the Italian War of 1551–9 against the Holy Roman Emperor Charles V, reporting regularly to the young king about events on the European mainland.[12] Before his departure from France, Barnaby secured glowing recommendations from prominent figures such as Henry II and Anne de Montmorency, king and constable of France respectively.[13] In addition, upon his return to England Barnaby played an active part alongside his cousin, Thomas Butler, 10th earl of Ormond, in crushing Thomas Wyatt's rebellion of 1554, receiving further high praise and recommendations from Queen Mary I of England and King Philip II of Spain.[14]

By 1554 Barnaby was back in Upper Ossory, where he quarrelled with his father Brian and his wife, Elizabeth O'Connor, whom he referred to as 'the most naughty and malicious creature alive'.[15] Barnaby seemed particularly vexed at his father's apparent unwillingness to assist the government in its efforts to establish the Leix and Offaly plantation or to sufficiently suppress the rebellious O'More and O'Connor clans.[16] Even at this early stage it appeared clear that Barnaby was unwilling to allow his father to jeopardise all that he had achieved in England and abroad.[17] Barnaby offered his support to the crown once again in 1556 and was appointed to lead a band of his clan's horsemen and kern on a government expedition into Ulster to dispel the Scots there.[18] Further assignments followed, such as his participation in the unsuccessful defence of English-held Calais in 1557–8.[19] When Barnaby was appointed by Queen Mary to crush O'More and O'Connor resistance in March 1558, unlike his father he seized with open arms the opportunity to prove his loyalty to the crown.[20]

A dynastic struggle quickly ensued between Brian and Barnaby, who, backed by government support, gradually eclipsed his father as chieftain of the FitzPatrick clan.[21] Meanwhile, Barnaby served as lieutenant to Sir George Howard, general of the men-at-arms and demi-lances, at the Siege of Leith in 1560.[22] His bravery earned him the recognition of the crown and he was subsequently knighted at Berwick on 18 July by the duke of Norfolk.[23] In 1564 he garnered high praise for bringing yet another O'More and O'Connor rebellion in Leix and Offaly to an end.[24] He further assisted the crown in a northern expedition against Shane O'Neill in 1566 and was subsequently referred to by Sidney as 'a gentleman of noble service and valour'.[25]

Later that same year he appealed for Upper Ossory to be shired as part of the Queen's County, in an attempt to avoid the territory being absorbed within the Ormond palatinate.[26] The tumultuous latter half of the 1560s and the 1570s as a whole provided Barnaby with an opportunity to prove his worth to the crown even further. Thus, reinforced with powers of martial law and whilst serving as sheriff of the Queen's County, Barnaby launched a relentless assault on the O'Mores and O'Connors.[27] In 1577, having killed several members of both groups, Barnaby informed Sir Francis Walsingham: 'I doubt not with the help of God to kill or banish the rest in short time'.[28] Arguably, his greatest achievement during this period occurred in July 1578, when he succeeded in hunting down and killing the formidable Gaelic rebel Rory Óg O'More, referred to as 'the only Robin Hood of all Ireland', essentially putting an end to one of the most dangerous Gaelic rebellions for the crown in the midlands.[29] According to Lord Deputy Henry Sidney, when offered the reward of the bounty on O'More's head of £1,000, Barnaby was content to accept a mere £100 for his services.[30]

For the duration of his career, however, Thomas Butler, 10th earl of Ormond, had been a thorn in Barnaby's side. Upon hearing that the baron of Upper Ossory granted Sir John FitzGerald hospitality in Coulkill Castle at the height of the Desmond revolt in 1579, combined with the defection of Barnaby's two half-brothers to the rebels, Ormond accused Barnaby of treason, for which he was eventually jailed in Dublin Castle on 14 January 1581.[31] Sir Henry Wallop, vice-treasurer of Ireland, eventually secured Barnaby's and his wife's release from prison when both fell ill after some four months in captivity, persuading the queen to relocate them to a house in the city.[32] Although his wife made a full recovery, Barnaby was not so lucky and succumbed to his illness that November, dying at the age of just 46.[33]

There can be no doubt that Barnaby's brief but industrious career ultimately ended in failure, accused of treason and dying as a result of time spent in captivity. Historians such as David Edwards argue that Barnaby's sole achievement was that he managed to retain Upper Ossory's 'independence, an accomplishment which had cost him his life in the end'.[34] Edwards also argues that, at the 'peak of his career', Barnaby received just one significant appointment within the new administration, as 'lieutenant to the lord deputy' of the forts in King's County and Queen's County.[35] One could argue, however, that this is an unfair assessment of what Barnaby had truly achieved through collaboration with the crown. By embracing the process of cultural assimilation to a greater extent than his father had, he rose to become a valued confidant of King Edward VI, a position that few sons of Old English lords—never mind Gaelic chieftains—ever experienced. He also fulfilled his father's wish for greater court influence in London, securing the backing not only of the young King Edward himself but also of Secretary of State William Cecil and Lord Deputy Henry Sidney, among others, in addition to glowing recommendations from the French king, Henry II, as well as Queen Mary I and King Philip II of Spain. He succeeded in every role bestowed on him, whether on expeditions in Queen's County and King's County crushing O'More and O'Connor resistance or on crown assignments in Ulster and in Scotland, for which he eventually received a knighthood. It is also highly probable, despite his leaving no religious testament behind, that Barnaby was one of the first native Irish lords to embrace Protestantism, as it seems highly unlikely that it would have been possible for him to get so close to Edward, or indeed to be held in such favour, had he been an openly professing Catholic.[36] This is even more noteworthy and significant when one considers the high praise and support he received from the staunch Catholic monarchs Queen Mary and King Philip.

Barnaby also laid the groundwork for his successors to inherit, as was the case with his younger brother, Florence FitzPatrick, who continued his clan's collaboration and eventually secured lucrative monastic land grants from the queen, as well as the formal shiring of Upper Ossory to the Queen's County in 1600, thus freeing it from any future Butler attempts to absorb the territory within County Kilkenny.[37]

Regarding Edwards's argument that Barnaby received just one significant appointment during his lifetime, it could be argued on the contrary that he in fact held several significant positions, often at the expense of his new English counterparts. According to Jon G. Crawford, the structure of the English military establishment after 1556 centred around three distinct positions or posts, of which Barnaby held all three: first, the role of captain over a band of soldiers;[38] second, the constableship of forts and wards with both civil and military authority;[39] and, third, the position of seneschal.[40] Barnaby was also appointed to the position of sheriff of Queen's County from 1568–9 onwards.[41] He held the position of commissioner of musters for Queen's County in 1572 and 1573, commissioner for the conduct of military upper affairs in Munster and Connaught in 1576, 1577 and 1580, and commissioner for ecclesiastical causes in the latter year.[42]

In conclusion, there can be no doubt that collaboration offered the FitzPatrick clan a means of overcoming the Butler stranglehold on Upper Ossory, but, as highlighted throughout this paper, in the case of Barnaby collaboration meant so much more. It seems apparent that Barnaby genuinely embraced the process of English cultural assimilation and throughout his career incessantly fought to prove himself to the Tudor government which had placed so much trust in him. Although we will never truly know his mind-set or the real reasons for his fervent collaboration, his efforts were unquestionably invaluable to the crown during times of war and rebellion, which seemed relentless throughout the sixteenth century. Barnaby's actions, one could therefore argue, ensured that the crown administration retained a foothold and a presence within the midlands, the shires of King's County and Queen's County and the territory of Upper Ossory well into the seventeenth century. In turn, it could be argued that the clan became a symbol and model for other chieftaincies of the benefits of embracing cultural assimilation, Anglicisation and the overall policy of 'surrender and regrant'.

Notes

1 C.A. Empey, 'The cantreds of the medieval county of Kilkenny', *Journal of the Royal Society of Antiquaries of Ireland* (hereafter *JRSAI*) **101** (2) (1971), pp 128–9; J. Buckley (ed.), 'A viceregal progress through the south and west of Ireland in 1567', *Journal of the Waterford and South-East of Ireland Archaeological Society* **12** (1909), p. 184; L. Price, 'The armed forces of the Irish chiefs in the sixteenth century', *JRSAI* (7th ser.) **2** (2) (1932), p. 202; H.F. Hore and J. Graves, *The social state of the southern and eastern counties of Ireland* (Dublin, 1870), pp 98–121; D. Edwards, 'The MacGiollaPhádraigs of Upper Ossory, 1532–1641', in P.G. Lane and W. Nolan (eds), *Laois: history and society: interdisciplinary essays on the history of an Irish county* (Dublin, 1999), pp 331–2.

2 Edwards, 'The MacGiollaPhádraigs of Upper Ossory', pp 331–2.

3 Ibid., p. 331.

4 *Letters and papers, foreign and domestic, Henry VIII* (21 vols, London, 1862–1932), xii (ii), nos 1046, 1537.

5 Edwards, 'The MacGiollaPhádraigs of Upper Ossory', p. 335.

6 *L. & P. Hen. VIII*, xvi, no. 935; B. Bradshaw, *The Irish constitutional revolution of the sixteenth century* (Cambridge, 1979), pp 238–40.

7 Edwards, 'The MacGiollaPhádraigs of Upper Ossory', p. 341.

8 *L. & P. Hen. VIII*, xvi, no. 552; Edwards, 'The MacGiollaPhádraigs of Upper Ossory', p. 341.

9 *L. & P. Hen. VIII*, xvii, nos 688, 761.

10 Order of ceremonies to be observed at the funeral of Henry VIII, 15 February 1547, the National Archives of the United Kingdom (hereafter TNA), SP 10/1/16; K. Eisenbichler, *The premodern teenager: youth in society, 1150–1650* (Canada, 2002), pp 140–1; W.K. Jordan, *Edward VI: the young king* (Cambridge, 1968), p. 44.

11 J.G. Nichols, *Literary remains of King Edward the sixth: edited from his autograph manuscripts, with historical notes and a biographical memoir*, part 2 (London, 1857), p. 64.

12 Ibid.

13 Henry II, king of France, to King Edward VI, 8 December 1552, TNA, SP 68/10/589; Constable Montmorency to King Edward VI, 8 December 1552, TNA, SP 68/10/590.

14 M. Archdall (ed.), *Lodge's Peerage of Ireland*, vol. ii (1789), p. 335; J.T. Gilbert, *Facsimiles of the national manuscripts of Ireland* (London, 1884), p. 171; C. Giblin, 'Catalogue of Irish material in the Nunziatura di Fiandra', *Collectanea Hibernica* **1** (1958), p. 46; Edwards, 'The MacGiollaPhádraigs of Upper Ossory', p. 343.

15 Gilbert, *Facsimiles of the national manuscripts of Ireland*, p. 172.

16 Ibid.; Edwards, 'The MacGiollaPhádraigs of Upper Ossory', p. 343.

17 Edwards, 'The MacGiollaPhádraigs of Upper Ossory', p. 343.

18 Charles Haliday, *Acts of the privy council in Ireland, 1556–1571* (London, 1897), p. 18.

19 BL, Cotton MSS, Caligula E.I., ff 28–55.

20 Queen Mary to Barnaby FitzPatrick, 12 March 1558, TNA, SP 62/1/18.

21 Essentially, Barnaby succeeded his father as captain and chief ruler of Upper Ossory by 1566 but did not officially succeed him as baron of Upper Ossory until his father's death in 1575: Haliday, *Acts of the privy council in Ireland, 1556–1571*, pp 4–18; C.L. Kingsford, *Report on the manuscripts of Lord de l'Isle & Dudley*, vol. ii (London, 1925), pp 366, 376 and 384; Edwards, 'The MacGiollaPhádraigs of Upper Ossory', p. 344; J.S. Brewer & W. Bullen (ed.), *Calendar of the Carew Manuscripts, 1515–74*, vol. i (2nd edn, London, 1974), no. 215; Lord Justice and council to Upper Ossory, 5 August 1564, TNA, SP 63/11/61; Lord Deputy Sidney and council to the privy council, 13 April 1566, TNA, 63/17/79; Petition of Sir Barnaby FitzPatrick to the privy council, 1566, TNA, SP 63/19/329; Elizabeth to Sidney, June 1568, SP 63/25/12; *The Irish fiants of Tudor sovereigns during the reigns of Henry VIII, Edward VI, Philip & Mary, and Elizabeth* (4 vols, Dublin, 1994), iii, nos 953 and 1329.

22 G.E. Cokayne, *The complete peerage of England, Scotland, Ireland, Great Britain, and the United Kingdom* (2nd edn, Gloucester, 1987), vol. vi, pp 184–5; *Holinshed's chronicles of England, Scotland, and Ireland* (London, 1807–9), vol. iv, p. 189; *Calendar of the patent rolls, Elizabeth I, vol. ii, 1562–1563* (London, 1948), p. 17.

23 Cokayne, *The complete peerage*, p. 185.

24 J. O'Hanlon and E. O'Leary, *History of the Queen's County*, part ii (Dublin, 1907), p. 450.

25 Haliday, *Acts of the privy council in Ireland, 1556–1571*, p. 167; Lord Deputy Sidney and council to the privy council, 13 April 1566, TNA, 63/17/79.

26 Petition of Sir Barnaby FitzPatrick to the privy council, 1566, TNA, SP 63/19/329; D. Edwards, 'Collaboration without anglicization', in P.J. Duffy, D. Edwards and E. FitzPatrick (eds), *Gaelic Ireland* c. *1250–1650* (Dublin, 2001), p. 86.

27 *Fiants, Eliz.*, nos 953, 1329.

28 Upper Ossory to Walsingham, 30 January 1577, TNA, SP 63/57/8.

29 Nicholas Malby to Burghley, 26 July 1578, TNA, SP 63/61/41; Lord Deputy Sidney to the privy council, 1 July 1578, TNA, SP 63/61/29; Sir Edward Fitton to Burghley, 1 July 1578, TNA, SP 63/61/31; Mr Edward Fitton to Burghley, 6 July 1578, TNA, SP 63/61/32.

30 H. Hore (ed.), 'Sir Henry Sidney's memoir of his government of Ireland', *Ulster Journal of Archaeology* 8 (1860), p. 189.

31 Ormond to Lord Grey, 28 August 1580, TNA, SP 63/75/73; Ormond to Walsingham, 28 May 1580, TNA, SP 63/73/30; Treasurer Wallop to Walsingham, 14 January 1581, TNA, SP 63/80/5; Ormond to Wilson, 15 January 1581, TNA, SP 63/80/11; Offenders indicted by Ormond, 15 January 1581, TNA, SP 63/80/12; *Calendar of the Carew Manuscripts, 1515–74*, no. 489.

32 Wallop to Walsyngham, 23 April 1581, TNA, SP 63/82/47; Edwards, 'The MacGiollaPhádraigs of Upper Ossory', p. 349.

33 Lord Deputy Grey to the privy council, 6 November 1581, TNA, SP 63/86/51; James Morrin (ed.), *Calendar of the patent and close rolls of chancery in Ireland, Henry VIII–Elizabeth I*, vol. ii (London, 1862), pp 89–90.

34 Edwards, 'The MacGiollaPhádraigs of Upper Ossory', p. 349.

35 *Fiants, Eliz.*, nos 2843–4; Edwards, 'The MacGiollaPhádraigs of Upper Ossory', p. 347.

36 Edwards, 'The MacGiollaPhádraigs of Upper Ossory', p. 342.

37 Queen Elizabeth to Lord Deputy Mountjoy and the council, 21 July 1600, TNA, SP 63/207/41; *Fiants, Eliz.*, nos 4640, 6493, 6610; Edwards, 'The MacGiollaPhádraigs of Upper Ossory', pp 349–50.

38 Barnaby had been in charge of a band of kern since 1558: J.G. Crawford, *Anglicizing the government of Ireland* (Dublin, 1993), pp 277–8; Queen Mary to Barnaby, 12 March 1558, TNA, SP 62/2/18; An estimate of the debt due to the garrisons in Ireland at Michaelmas 1567, 30 September 1567, TNA, SP 63/21/531; Book of the establishment of the Irish garrison in November 1568 and on 20 March

1569, 20 March 1569, TNA, SP 63/27/361; The monthly charge of the queen's army and garrisons, 1 April 1571, TNA, SP 63/32/1; Book of the garrison discharged and those remaining in pay, 1572, TNA, SP 63/36/275.

39 A post to which he was essentially appointed when undertaking the role of lieutenant of the forts in 1576: *Fiants, Eliz.*, nos 2843–4.

40 A position he held in Queen's County in 1572: Lord Deputy FitzWilliam and council to Queen Elizabeth, 27 June 1572, TNA, SP 63/36/275.

41 *Fiants, Eliz.*, no. 1329.

42 Ibid., nos 2117, 2345, 2862, 2884, 3047, 3667, 3668.

4

Burning their bridges: the opposition of the Gabhal Raghnaill and Feagh Mac Hugh O'Byrne to the process of Anglicisation during the long sixteenth century

Chris Lawlor
(2013 prize)

For many people, the name Feagh Mac Hugh O'Byrne is synonymous with County Wicklow, and they allude to him as one of the first leaders in that county to oppose British rule.[1] This essay traces the rise of the O'Byrne clan, and particularly the Gabhal Raghnaill sept, during the long sixteenth century, outlining the resistance of Feagh and some of his forebears to the crown. The essay then seeks to evaluate Feagh's contribution to Irish affairs during the sixteenth century, with emphasis on his roles during both the Baltinglass rebellion and the Nine Years War. The latter was primarily a revolt by Ulster chieftains under Hugh O'Neill, the earl of Tyrone, but there was also a Wicklow theatre, where Feagh Mac Hugh's resilience and tenacity in the face of adversity demonstrated why he had earned the sobriquet 'the Firebrand of the Wicklow Mountains'.[2]

By Feagh's final year (1597) Lord Deputy Russell had identified him as 'the cheife rebel of Lynster',[3] indicating how much progress had been made by the Gabhal Raghnaill sept of the O'Byrne clan as the sixteenth century progressed. During the early part of that century Leinster was identified with the governorship of the Kildares. Garret Mór ruled with an iron hand, especially after his victory over the rebellious Burke and his allies at Knockdoe on 19 August 1504.[4] The influence of the Kildares continued to spread, and in 1518 the 'Duties upon Irishmen' in their rental, listing Gaelic leaders from whom they received tribute, included all the major chiefs of Leinster, with the O'Byrnes prominent among them.[5] Garret Mór died in September 1513, however, and his successor, Garret Óg, did not exert the same control. He suffered some embarrassing defeats at the hands of the native Irish,[6] and the success of the O'Byrnes' raid on Dublin Castle in 1533 underlined both the decline of the earls of Kildare and the advancement of the Wicklow clan.[7] In 1534 the two factions actually joined forces during the revolt of Silken Thomas, but this was ultimately crushed and Thaddeus, the chief of the O'Byrnes, submitted to Henry VIII in 1535.[8] In 1536 he promised to be a faithful subject, not to maintain rebels, and to pay monies to the king in return for possession of his lands and the protection of the lord deputy.[9] The Henrican Reformation represented a sea change in political as well as religious relationships on the island of Ireland, however, and the issues involved in the Kildare revolt indicated that there was a large cohort of Irish (and Anglo-Normans or later Old English) whose Catholicism could be invoked to erode loyalties to the English monarchy[10]—a theme which will resurface later in this work in relation to Feagh Mac Hugh O'Byrne.

The mid-sixteenth century saw a game of cat and mouse regarding such loyalties being played out between the English authorities and the Gaelic chiefs. At one stage Thaddeus O'Byrne even requested that his territory be shired. As Sir John Davies recalled: 'the Byrnes of the mountains, in the thirty-fourth of Henry the Eight [1542], desired that their country might be made shire-ground and called the county of Wicklow'.[11] The clan rejected this proposal, however, removed Thaddeus from the leadership and elected a new chief, Shane Mac Redmond, who opposed the scheme. The middle third of the century witnessed continuing sporadic clashes between the O'Byrnes and the authorities. In 1548, for example, Shane's son, Hugh Mac Shane O'Byrne, threatened the Boystown area, occupying it with 60 kernes for three days.[12] In 1566 Hugh Mac Shane raided Ballymore Eustace, which lay on the very boundary of the Pale, and exacted black rents there.[13] These actions pointed to Hugh's belligerent intentions and increased the rising power of the Gabhal Raghnaill sept, which emerged as the leading branch of the O'Byrne clan during this time.[14] Hugh's Gabhal Raghnaill was a formidable force, and they regularly embarked on raids and expeditions against contiguous English settlements.[15] Edmund Spenser's *View of the state of Ireland* confirmed the improved fortunes of the clan under Hugh's leadership.[16]

It was Hugh's son Feagh, however, born *c*. 1544, who truly figured among the foremost Gaelic leaders of his age.[17] As a young man, Feagh was involved in Sir Edmund Butler's escape from Dublin Castle in 1569, and was implicated in the murder of Robert Browne in Wexford in 1572.[18] Crucially, he grew to maturity at a time when his clan's fortunes were waxing. Elizabeth I was crowned in 1558, however, and the Elizabethan administration was the principal agency of Anglicisation in Ireland.[19] Such a policy was opposed to the Gaelic way of life practised and the social control wielded by the O'Byrnes and other clans. The stage was thus set for further conflict.

Feagh proved to be a thorn in the side of the Dublin administration throughout the 1560s and 1570s. In 1563 Feagh and his father captured two captains, Henry Davells and George Harvey, probably with the intention of holding them for ransom.[20] The prisoners were eventually released and the abductors pardoned, but Feagh's lengthy campaign of resistance had begun. Kinship bonds and close family loyalties were a significant feature of Gaelic Ireland,[21] and in 1572 Feagh joined his brother-in-law, Rory Óg O'More of Laois, in attacking the Pale.[22] Later in that decade, on 21 September 1578, Feagh submitted to Lord Justice Drury at Christ Church Cathedral.[23] The game of cat and mouse with the authorities continued; in all, Feagh was pardoned seven times for treachery against the crown.[24] By the beginning of 1580, Rory Óg had been killed (but not before he had burned Naas in retaliation for the massacre of Mullaghmast in 1577)[25] and Feagh and his followers had been pacific for a little over a year. This situation changed dramatically with the outbreak of the Desmond rebellion in Munster, an event that received papal support.[26] In Wicklow, Feagh supported the rebellion of Viscount Baltinglass, and this support culminated in the heavy defeat of English forces at Glenmalure on 25 August 1580.[27] Baltinglass was a religious zealot, channelling Gaelic resentment in the name of the Catholic faith; although Feagh does not seem to have shared his religious convictions,[28] Catholicism had been invoked once again and Feagh rallied to the cause. He may not have fully shared the fundamentalist Catholic zeal of the viscount but he was not unaware of the Counter-Reformation ideas entering Ireland at the time,[29] and he ensured that the papal standards were raised in Leinster during the insurrection,[30] hoisting the papal banner over the still-smouldering castle of Newcastle McKynegan in 1580.[31] Feagh was now well on his way towards attaining the height of his power, and his crushing victory over Lord Arthur Grey de Wilton at Glenmalure marked the zenith of his military achievements.

Defeat at Glenmalure was a huge setback for the authorities. The event had all the hallmarks of a total rout, and casualties were very high. One source estimates the number of English casualties at 909.[32] Another source states that:

> A hosting was made by the Lord Justice and Captain Malby, to scatter and disperse these warlike plunderers. When the insurgents had heard of the approach of such an overwhelming force, they retreated into their fastnesses in the rough and rugged recesses of Glenmalure. The Lord Justice then selected the most trustworthy and best tried captains of his army, and despatched them, at the head of eight or nine companies of soldiers, to search and explore Glenmalure; but they were responded to without delay by the parties that guarded the valley, so that very few of these returned without being cut off and dreadfully slaughtered by the Irish party. On this occasion were slain Peter Carew, Master Moor (John), and Master Frans, with many other gentlemen who had come from England in the retinue of the Lord Justice. When this news reached the Lord Justice, he left his camp.[33]

Glenmalure was one of the heaviest defeats ever suffered by crown forces in Ireland. It caused panic within the Pale and on the streets of the capital, where a follow-up attack by Feagh's forces was expected almost hourly once the calamitous news had come through. Feagh, however, did not possess the military strength for such a risky undertaking, so he remained in the mountains awaiting developments. Victory was sweet but short-lived. The rebellion ultimately failed, but highland

Wicklow was still firmly in O'Byrne's possession. It is true that Sir William Stanley burnt Feagh's settlement at Ballinacor in April 1581,[34] but its remote nature made it difficult to hold and Feagh and his followers soon reoccupied the area. Throughout most of the 1580s and '90s, the highland Wicklow region was referred to as 'O'Byrnes' Country' or 'Feagh Mac Hugh's Country', and the chief's presence so close to Dublin was both an embarrassment and a challenge to the authorities.[35] The suitability of the Ballinacor site for defence meant that the O'Byrnes had no need to construct a stone-built fortification within its fastnesses, and a wooden fort was deemed sufficient for their needs.[36] From Glenmalure the clan had access to Glendalough and the Glen of Imaal, providing channels towards both the Pale and lowland Leinster, with an emergency escape route via the plateau atop Table Mountain to the north-west.[37]

The 1590s witnessed an escalation of hostilities. Red Hugh O'Donnell and Art O'Neill escaped from Dublin Castle in 1591. One source informs us that they headed towards Glenmalure,

> the place where Fiach Mac Aodha was. This was a secure, impregnable valley, and the English of Dublin were accustomed with their instruments of battle to besiege and assault it in order to plunder and lay it waste. This Fiach maintained it valiantly against them, so that many heads were left behind with him, and they could do nothing against him; but though their attacks were many and various, and though great were their seizures of battle, he was not submissive to them as long as he lived. Every hostage and every prisoner who escaped from them did not go past him, but towards him, and the first place he would head for was Glenmalure, the place where Fiach was, as we have said, for it was his home fort.[38]

After great hardship, which caused the death of O'Neill in the Wicklow Mountains, O'Donnell reached O'Byrnes' country.[39] It is perhaps simplistic to assume—and there is no documentary evidence to support the premise—that local mountain-dwellers aided the escape, as any loyalties owed by Wicklow peasants to a prince from Donegal were, at the very least, probably quite tenuous.[40] Nonetheless, the event created a bond of sorts between Feagh and Red Hugh, possibly forged through the ideas of Gaelic identity and Counter-Reformation Catholicism.[41]

In May 1593 Red Hugh O'Donnell, with the help of Archbishop Magauran, instigated a confederation; later that year Hugh Maguire began his military campaign.[42] O'Donnell joined him in 1594 and, crucially, O'Neill did likewise in 1595.[43] In that same year Feagh was declared a traitor and a large reward was offered for his capture or his head.[44] In 1596 Feagh formally allied himself with Hugh O'Neill and took the field on 9 September,[45] gambling on a successful Spanish landing, but the shipwreck of the 'second armada' off La Coruña on 13 October sealed his fate. Following news of the ships' destruction, Lord Deputy Sir William Russell returned to Wicklow to put Feagh and his army to flight. The old chief was discovered in a cave in Glenmalure and was killed by a Sergeant Milburne (under the command of Captain Thomas Lee) on 7 May 1597.[46] Hostilities continued briefly under the leadership of Feagh's son and successor, Phelim Mac Feagh O'Byrne,[47] but by the dawn of the new century this revolt had also been crushed and the Wicklow region was at last ripe for plantation.

From the late 1570s onwards Feagh Mac Hugh O'Byrne was the foremost Gaelic chief in Leinster, ably succeeding his brother-in-law Rory Óg O'More in that role after the latter's death. Feagh's participation in the Baltinglass revolt, and his resounding victory at Glenmalure in 1580, raised his profile considerably and catapulted him to national prominence.[48] Feagh's use of Gaelic identity, his adherence to Catholicism, his record on the field of battle and his complex relations with other Gaelic chiefs and with Baltinglass all point to diplomatic adroitness, military skill, political adaptability and a keen instinct for survival. His involvement in the Nine Years War, and the longevity of his military operations in highland Wicklow, drained the resources of the crown forces, which needed to maintain a constant military presence to protect areas of adjacent lowland Leinster and the Pale from attack. Feagh's death was a severe blow to O'Neill's cause, and in 1598, when the earl was most in need of the O'Byrnes to keep the forces of the Pale occupied, it deprived the Great Earl of support and the use of highland Wicklow as a diversionary theatre. In the final analysis, Feagh's military operations were a diversion within a larger conflict and his standing was not on a par with that of Tyrone; nevertheless, as the earl's powerful Leinster ally, his support aided the rise of Hugh O'Neill and his attempt to defeat English forces—an attempt that almost succeeded.

Notes

1 Later Wicklow leaders might include Michael Dwyer and Charles Stewart Parnell, embodying the physical-force and constitutional nationalist traditions respectively.

2 C. Lawlor, '1597–1997—the Firebrand and the Wicklow legend that's still burning', *Dunlavin–Donard–Davidstown Parish Link* 3 (6) (1997), p. 7. See also C. Lawlor, 'Some Wicklow history—originally recorded', *Dunlavin Festival of Arts Brochure* 21 (Naas, 2003), pp 49–52, *passim*.

3 D. Edwards, 'Feagh McHugh O'Byrne: forgotten leader of the Nine Years War', http://homepage.eircom.net/~nobyrne/Feagh_McHugh_%20Forgotten_Leader.htm (accessed 1 April 2013).

4 A. Cosgrove, *Late medieval Ireland, 1370–1541* (Dublin, 1981), p. 103.

5 Ibid., p. 104.

6 H.A. Jefferies, 'The Kildare revolt: accident or design?', *Journal of the County Kildare Archaeological Society* 19 (3) (2004–5), p. 447. See also H.C. Hamilton (ed.), *Calendar of state papers relating to Ireland, of the reigns of Henry VIII, Edward VI, Mary and Elizabeth, 1509–1573* (London, 1860), i, entry 10, p. 2, where it was alleged as early as 1515 or 1516 (when the complainant died) that Kildare was unable to stop lands 'falling into the hands of the wild Irishmen', and that the lands of Rochford of Kilbride are

'made waste by daily oppression of coin and livery'.

7 This nocturnal raid was led by Edmund Oge O'Byrne: D. Byrne-Rothwell, *The Byrnes and the O'Byrnes, i. A new insight upon Irish history* (Isle of Colonsay, 2010), p. 82.

8 County Wicklow Heritage Project, *The last county: the emergence of Wicklow as a county 1606–1845* (Wicklow, 1993; repr. 2006), p. 10.

9 M. MacCurtain, *Tudor and Stuart Ireland* (Dublin, 1972), p. 42.

10 Jefferies, 'The Kildare revolt', p. 456.

11 Sir John Davies, *A discovery of the true cause why Ireland was never entirely subdued nor brought under obedience of the crown of England until the beginning of his majesty's reign* (London, 1612), pp 267–8.

12 E. O'Byrne, 'The rise of the Gabhal Raghnaill', http://homepage.eircom.net/~nobyrne/Rise_of_Gabhal_Raghnaill.htm (accessed 12 March 2013). Boystown is adjacent to the present settlement of Blessington.

13 Catalogue of the battles of Hugh O'Byrne by Ferganainm McKeogh (TCD, Tales and poems, transcribed by Hugh O'Daly in the year 1750, MS 1288, f. 91). Black rents were a form of protection money.

14 This topic is treated in some depth in sections vii, viii and ix of O'Byrne, 'The rise of the Gabhal Raghnaill'.

15 C. O'Brien, 'The Byrnes of Ballymanus', in K. Hannigan and W. Nolan (eds), *Wicklow: history and society* (Dublin, 1994), p. 306.

16 E. Spenser, *View of the state of Ireland written dialogue wise between Eudoxus and Irenus by Edmund Spencer Esq. In the yeare 1596* (repr. Dublin, 1809), p. 186. Spenser wrote:

> Hugh Mac Shane, the father of this Feagh, first began to lift up his head, and through the strength and great fastnes of Glan-Malor, which adjoyneth unto his house of Ballinecor, drew unto him many theeves and out-lawes, which fled unto the succour of that glynne, as to a sanctuary, and brought unto him part of the spoyle of all the countrey, through which he grew strong, and in short space got unto himselfe a great name thereby amongst the Irish, in whose footing this his sonne continuing, hath, through many unhappy occasions, increased his said name, and the opinion of his greatnes, insomuch that now he is become a dangerous enemy to deale withall.

17 For a brief but concise treatment of Feagh's career see C. Crampton, 'Wicklow biographies, no. 8: Feagh Mac Hugh O'Byrne', *Journal of the West Wicklow Historical Society* 3 (1989), p. 15; also Lawlor, 'Some Wicklow history—originally recorded', *passim.*

18 Lawlor, '1597–1997—the Firebrand', p. 7.

19 C. Lennon and R. Gillespie, 'Reformation to Restoration', in S. Duffy (ed.), *Atlas of Irish history* (Dublin, 1997), p. 56.

20 B.C. Donovan, 'The rise of Feagh McHugh O'Byrne in Gaelic Leinster', http://homepage.eircom.net/~nobyrne/The_rise_of_Feagh_macHugh_OByrne_in_Tudor_Leinster.htm (accessed 23 March 2013).

21 M. de Paor and L. de Paor, *Early Christian Ireland* (London, 1958; repr. 1978), p. 184.

22 Lawlor, '1597–1997—the Firebrand', p. 7.

23 H.C. Hamilton (ed.), *Calendar of state papers relating to Ireland, of the reign of Elizabeth, 1574–1585* (London, 1867), ii, entry 17, p. 143. The actual submission reads as follows:

> To the right honourable the Lord Justice.
> With all due obedience & humilitie ffeagh m'hue That where he came unto your honor simpley and dutifully submittinge him self to hir majesties grace & mercy havinge sought for nether pardon nor proteccon And albeit that sundry men would saye and judge of him to be a disturber of the common weale which brutes proceded rather of malice then for any juste cause, for he did

nothinge butt stode in defence of his countrie agayniste those which allwayes sought his distruccon, yet repentinge such as in times paste have been by him dowen. And meaninge henceforth to live in due obedience to his prince & hir governor here for time beinge, he thought good to repayer unto your honor aswell to shew his greeffe as to make all the world understand how he is bente to loyaltie & dutifullnes henceforth to continue so as his adversaries be stopped ffrom annoyinge of him and notwithstandinge in [?] of his fformer doinges butt referringe himself to hir majesties moste gracious favour & clemencie. The causes whye he made any stirre heretofore were to tediouse in particulars to reherse butt in generall he protesteth before God & your honor it was through the manifould enjuries done unto him by his neighbors whoe killed his uncle, prayed his countrie & sought his owen death diverse wayes, and ffor no other desire he had to live otherwise then become a true and fayethfull subjecte. And when he hath putt his pledges into the hande of Sir Henrie Harrington knight (whome he taketh to be his Capten) ffor kepinge of the peace he thinketh himself oppressed that his adversaries viz Thomas Masterson & Peter Carewe esquiers are not compelled to put in theire pledges all so, he hath allso at comandmente of his sayed Capten refrayned to comitt any hurte or seke any revenge uppon those which annoyed him since the time that your honor receved the sword albeit that three severall prayes have bene taken ffrom him by Mastersons men and others since your honour receyved the sworde viz the laste thursdaye after his cominge oute of newe castle ffrom his sayed Capten iiii`[80] stod mares were taken ffrom him that night and uppon ffryday after mastersons men came to his countrie & toke v [100] stod with xl [40] markes worth of houshould stuffe from him and allso at annother time the toke iii [60] kine owte of your suppliants countrie in profe wherof parte of your supliants men followed the pray to Rissellage & in rescuinge some of both sides were sleine. ffor theise and many other owtrags your Supliant hath omitted to seeke any revenge bycause he gave his word to his sayed Capten who promised him to have redresse uppon his comminge to your honor humblye cravinge her majesties pardon ffor the hurte paste and to cause the sayed parties to put in securitie hencefourth not to annoy yor Supliant or his termants. In so doinge he will undertake to kepe himself and all his hence forth in dutifull sorte not comittinge any spoyles or hurte uppon any hir majesties subjects and besids will do such service to hir majestie as shall be acceptable to your honor iff it shall please your Lordship or his sayed Capten to command him therunto.

(Ffeough m' Hughes Submission in Cristes churche in Dublin the xxi of September 1578, National Archive of the United Kingdom (hereafter TNA), SP 63/62/17).

24 County Wicklow Heritage Project, *The last county*, p. 11.

25 S. Hickey, L. Kenny and P. Behan (eds), *Nás na Ríogh: from Poorhouse Road to the Fairy Flax … an illustrated history of Naas* (Naas, 1990), p. 142.

26 Pope Gregory XIII granted a plenary indulgence to 'all who take up arms against Elizabeth': MacCurtain, *Tudor and Stuart Ireland*, p. 79.

27 For a concise account see E. O'Byrne, 'The battle of Glenmalure, 25 August 1580: cause and course', http://homepage.eircom.net/~nobyrne/Battle_of_Glenmalure.htm (accessed 15 February 2013).

28 C. Maginn, *'Civilizing' Gaelic Leinster: the extension of Tudor rule in the O'Byrne and O'Toole lordships* (Dublin, 2005), pp 178–9. In west Wicklow, Edmund of Tubber (Tober) also supported Baltinglass. Edmund was the viscount's younger brother and succeeded to lands in Tober, where there had been a settlement in medieval times: J. Lynott, 'The parish of Tober', *Dunlavin Festival of Arts Brochure* 12 (1994), p. 61. Following eventual defeat, Edmund fled to Scotland and was attainted in 1585. He went to Spain and served with the Spanish Armada before dying in Portugal in 1594: C. Chavasse, *The story of Baltinglass* (Kilkenny, 1970), pp 32–3.

29 It has been suggested that one reason for the failure of the Anglican Reformation in Ireland was that the Counter-Reformation actually preceded it, thus strengthening the resolve of the native Irish to defend the old religion with which they identified: T. Bartlett, '"What ish my nation?": themes in Irish history,

1550–1850', in T. Bartlett *et al.* (eds), *Irish studies: a general introduction* (Dublin, 1988), p. 48.

[30] Edwards, 'Feagh McHugh O'Byrne: forgotten leader of the Nine Years War'.

[31] O'Byrne, 'The battle of Glenmalure, 25 August 1580: cause and course'.

[32] *The Annals of Loch Cé, s.a.* 1580. The annals state that 'nine captains were slain and with each perished one hundred men'. An on-line version of the *Annals of Loch Cé* is available at http://www.ucc.ie/celt/published/T100010A/index.html (accessed 15 August 2012). One account has actually placed English losses at 'over a thousand': E. O'Byrne, 'The battle of Glenmalure', in C. O'Brien (ed.), *Feagh McHugh O'Byrne: the Wicklow firebrand* (Rathdrum, 1998), p. 179. However, another study argues that 'it is unlikely that English losses exceeded one hundred': C. Maginn, 'The Baltinglass rebellion, 1580: English dissent or a Gaelic uprising?', *Historical Journal* **47** (2) (2004), p. 221. It is perhaps probable that the true figure lies somewhere in between.

[33] *Annals of the Four Masters* (on-line version), http://www.ucc.ie/celt/online/T100005E/text008.html (accessed 5 September 2012).

[34] H. Long, 'Three settlements of Gaelic Wicklow, 1169–1600', in K. Hannigan and W. Nolan (eds), *Wicklow: history and society* (Dublin, 1994), p. 245. A contemporary poem laments the destruction of 'the lios of the hostages, the lios of the women, the bright bank of thin spears and the guest house': S. MacAirt (ed.), *Leabhar Branach: the book of the O'Byrnes* (Dublin, 1944), p. 146. I am indebted to Ms Crona Cassidy MA for this translation.

[35] Crampton, 'Wicklow biographies, no. 8', p. 15. For an excellent treatment of this subject see Maginn, *'Civilizing' Gaelic Leinster, passim.*

[36] Long, 'Three settlements of Gaelic Wicklow, 1169–1600', p. 248.

[37] D. Somers, *Endurance: heroic journeys in Ireland* (Dublin, 2005), p. 49.

[38] L. Ó Cléirigh, *Beatha Aodha Ruaidh Uí Dhomhnaill* (on-line version translated by P. Walsh), http://www.ucc.ie/celt/published/T100080.html (accessed 4 January 2013).

[39] Lawlor, '1597–1997—the Firebrand', p. 7.

[40] Somers, *Endurance*, p. 30.

[41] D. Mac Eiteagáin, 'Feagh McHugh O'Byrne and the Ulster princes: his role in their castle escapes', http://homepage.eircom.net/~nobyrne/Dublin_Castle_escape.htm (accessed 2 March 2013).

[42] MacCurtain, *Tudor and Stuart Ireland*, p. 84.

[43] Lennon and Gillespie, 'Reformation to Restoration', p. 60.

[44] Lawlor, '1597–1997—the Firebrand', p. 7. The reward stemmed from Feagh's audacious attack on Piers Fitzgerald's lands near Athy in 1594, which convinced the authorities of the necessity to pacify highland Wicklow and prevent the threat of attack through large areas of lowland Leinster and the Pale.

[45] This in spite of the fact that Feagh had sought another pardon earlier in the year. His request read:

> Right honorable, my humble dewtie remembred. Ffor asmuch as through my owne wickednes and bad behavior many waies, I have purchased her Majesties greate indignacon and hatred towards me, which no waie can be excused, havinge wowrthely deserved the same in the highest degree. Notwithstandinge, as her highnes of her most graciouse goodnes hath heretofore delt mercyfully with me so likewise I partely understand nowe of her graciouse inclynacon towardes me in grauntinge me her most gracyous pardon, the benyfytt whereof I can not receave unles I should forgoe my lyvinge and content myself with a pencon, which I presume is no parte of her majesties meaninge. although the curse of my lyffe hathe ben such hetherto, as in no waie is wowrthy of so greate a favor, but rather deservethe to be utterly subverted and overthrowen, yet presumynge of yor honorable favor I have ymboldened myself to lay oppen unto yor honnor my poore distressed estate, lyvinge in her majesties disgrace and contempned of all men, which two poinctes very much disquyetinge my mynde, hathe urged me at this presente humbly to crave yor honnors, furtherance in obtayninge for me her majesties most gracyous favor aswell for my

pardon as also to be restored to my poore lyvinge, beinge suche as is not to be accompted of for badnes of soyle, as is sufficiently knowen to divers and sundry. W it shall please her majesty to extend so much of her gracyous goodnes towards me, I would soner like yt by grant from her highnes, than hold yt as heretofore I have done, yeildinge thereout yerely unto her highnes and her successors for ever such rent as other gentlemen borderinge nere me dothe; protestinge that duringe my lyffe, I will never attempte any thinge that shall offend her majesty but with all dewty will serve in every respecte as becometh a subiecte, utterly renouncinge to ioyne or take parte with any other in this Realme or elswhere that shall goe about to disturbe this state, but to the uttermost of my power will adventure my lyffe in defence thereof. And for assurance of my faithfull meaninge in performinge the same, I will deliver a sufficient pledge for my obedience from tyme to tyme to answere all sizes and sessions when I shalbe called upon, as other gentlemen of this country dothe, and to performe what els shall be requysted. Most humblie besechinge yor honnors favor and furtherance herein, otherwise I shall not be able to lyve and mayneteyne my people but by hurtinge and spoilinge the subiecte, which can not be but to my utter undoinge. chosinge rather som other kind of lyffe than to live any more in that manner. And for that I greately desyre to submytt my selfe to her majestie and to acknowledge the heynousnes of my offences, I humbly beseche yor honnor before her highnes, which I now desyre, then anythinge in the world. Thus cravinge pardon for my overmuch boldnes herein, I humbly take leave. Rannellagh the xvth of Aprill 1596.

Yor honnors most humbly to be comanded
Ffeaghe Mchughe.

(Feagh McHugh to Lord Burghley [Elizabeth I's treasurer], 15 April 1596, TNA, SP 63/188/37).

46 Edwards, 'Feagh McHugh O'Byrne: forgotten leader of the Nine Years War'. Feagh was decapitated and his head presented to Russell. His corpse was quartered, and the head and quarters hung on pikestaffs over the drawbridge of Dublin Castle. Aonghas Ó Dálaigh composed a lament for Feagh. Desmond O'Grady's English translation is available at http://www.munsterlit.ie/Southword/Issues/17A/Poetry/ogrady_desmond.html (accessed 4 April 2013). The poem outlines very well the role of a Gaelic chief in charity, patronage and hospitality.

47 A. O'Brien, 'Phelim MacFeagh's revolt', *Journal of the Wicklow Historical Society* 2 (4) (1998), pp 78–86.

48 The term 'national' is used in the context of islandwide. Whether an Irish nation existed and, if it did, of what exactly it consisted are moot points in relation to this essay.

5

Russell's grudge: the demise of Feagh McHugh O'Byrne

Stephen Kestell

Introduction

The chief residence of the O'Byrnes of Gabhal Raghnaill was 'Balliena Cora',[1] at the mouth of the deep glacial valley of Glenmalure. The natural fortress protected the clan from any significant encroachment until 1546.[2] Successive Tudor governments then attempted to Anglicise Wicklow through their rogue 'seneschals'.[3] This oppressive regime threatened the Raghnaill (Ranelagh) lordship of Feagh McHugh. Ultimately, it transformed him 'from a local clan warlord in the 1560s to the status of regional Gaelic rebel leader in the 1580s'.[4]

In July 1580 Arthur Grey de Wilton was appointed lord deputy. He focused his attention on the rebellion in Leinster, and on 25 August he entered Glenmalure with 2,000 men to confront Feagh.[5] Grey made a critical error by entering the natural fortress, however, and it resulted in a catastrophic defeat for the English.[6] Sir William Stanley stated that 'it was the hottest piece of service for the time, that ever I saw in any place'.[7] Moreover, one of Grey's officers, Sir Peter Carew II, was killed during the battle,[8] and this death would prove to be significant.

The battle soured the English attitude towards Feagh McHugh.[9] Glenmalure had damaged the confidence of their military, while equally 'legitimizing the desire for revenge among others'.[10]

In the summer of 1594 Queen Elizabeth appointed Sir William Russell as lord deputy. Russell's previous time in Leinster had had a profound effect on him. He took a particularly dim view of Feagh,[11] whose success in 1580 was not going to be forgiven or forgotten.[12]

The fall of Ballinacor

In January 1595 Russell 'took a hunting journey to Ballinecor'.[13] During the assault on Ballinacor, Feagh's wife, Rose O'Toole, was 'wounded in the breast'.[14] Feagh retreated to Dromkilt and Russell immediately prepared to pursue 'the wolf out of his den'.[15] On 17 January 'Feagh McHugh, Rose his wife, Walter Reagh, and all their sons and followers were proclaimed traitors'.[16]

It is argued that Feagh rose in rebellion against the crown as early as 1594 at

Feagh's victory at Ballinacor

Despite Russell's intentions, Feagh defeated the garrison at Ballinacor. Initially, English officials on their way to the fort with provisions were ambushed by Feagh's son Redmund.[49] At the same time, Feagh successfully attacked Ballinacor and 'raised it to the ground and departed'.[50]

It was a crucial victory for Feagh. The attack had to succeed, for he was more than likely aware that Russell had sent 200 soldiers and 40 horses from Dublin that day to reinforce the fort. The English soldiers *en route* reversed course upon hearing 'word the fort was lost'.[51]

War in the Glens

As a result of Feagh's actions, Norris now had to support Russell's campaign in Wicklow.[52] On 24 September Russell went on the offensive. He set out towards Ranelagh at dawn and engaged in a ferocious encounter near Ballinacor hill. His men later entered Feagh's village of Fananerrin and burnt it.[53]

The lord deputy continued his offensive through night marches, cattle raids and prisoner executions. The English also came close to capturing Feagh. It was claimed that 'had a cry not been too soon raised' they would have 'captured Feagh and his wife, and the rest of the women in their cabins'.[54] Feagh responded by using his snipers to fire into the English camp at Rathdrum.[55] Despite the numbers at his disposal, Russell's actions had little impact, but on 14 December 1596 Feagh was dealt a significant military blow.

The ambush

Feagh's men laid an ambush for the English as they travelled from Wicklow to Rathdrum with provisions. Snipers lay in wait at a river about a mile from Rathdrum, but the ambush was a disaster. Captain Lee with the assistance of 'horsemen of the O'Byrne's country' killed over 30 of Feagh's men, including two of his best men, 'Morris Duffe his nephew & secretary, and Edmund McShane'.[56] After the failed ambush the momentum was with Russell. On 15 December he received '17 of the traitors heads' from Lee.[57] The loss of prominent clansmen would have serious implications for Feagh's military capabilities over the coming months.

Russell's agenda

Russell should have remained in Dublin in order to address issues such as Tyrone's camping 'within a mile of the Newry with 5,000 men', and O'Donnell 'burning and spoiling' Connaught with a strength of over '3,000 foot and 200 horse'.[58] Instead, his next move was to proceed south.

On 4 March 1597 the true nature of Russell's agenda was demonstrated. The lord deputy and his men marched over the mountain 'into the deepest bottom of' Glenmalure and completed a ceremony for the knighting of 'Serjant Major Sir John Chichester'.[59] The significance of knighting Chichester in Glenmalure cannot be overlooked. On that day, Francis Mitchell in Russell's journal states that Glenmalure was 'the place where Sir Peter Carew was slain in the Lord Grey's time'.[60] Mitchell's mention of Carew reveals why Russell knighted Chichester in the valley. It was the place where his friend Sir Peter Carew II died in 1580.[61] Ultimately, Russell's agenda was to avenge Carew's death by subduing Feagh.

On 15 March the lord deputy returned to Dublin, while Feagh came under increased pressure from Russell's captains, making little response in return. After the ambush Feagh was vulnerable, and Tyrone attempted to obtain him a pardon from the queen 'on such conditions as should be thought fit'.[62] His vulnerability, combined with English pressure, resulted in Feagh's demise on 8 May 1597.[63]

The death of Feagh

On 7 May Russell journeyed towards Wicklow in order to finish Feagh. He made his way to Rathdrum, where he was met by companies of soldiers who 'were in readiness there'.[64] With guidance from an informer,[65] the English were able to make their way on foot into Feagh's camp and apprehend him as he fled into a cave, 'where one Milborne, serjant to Captain Lee, first lighted on him, and the fury of our soldiers was so great as he could not be brought away alive'.[66]

Feagh was killed, but within a year his sons Phelim and Redmund were on the warpath and held 'the same course they did in his time'.[67] Moreover, by 1600 the English still needed 'a fort in Feagh McHughe's country'.[68] The O'Byrnes of Ranelagh were far from finished despite Feagh's demise. Russell's time in Ireland was finished, however, and Elizabeth recalled him to England soon after the death of Feagh McHugh.

Conclusion

After 1580 Feagh was predominantly concerned with ruling his lordship and was not a formidable danger to Pale security. He was a nuisance who needed strong alliances to survive, but that was the limit of his threat. Feagh was a victim of his own success in 1580 and of the resulting personal grudge held by Russell. It is not surprising that Russell was recalled to England, considering that he spent a significant portion of his tenure in Wicklow when he should have been in Ulster. He eventually subdued Feagh, but the Ranelagh O'Byrnes remained formidable. Nevertheless, Russell set sail for England on 25 May 1597, safe in the knowledge that he had exacted his personal revenge on Feagh McHugh for the killing of Sir Peter Carew II at the battle of Glenmalure.

Notes

1 H. Long, 'Settlement and social life in Feagh McHugh's Ballinacor', in C. O'Brien (ed.), *Feagh McHugh O'Byrne: the Wicklow firebrand* (Rathdrum, 1998), p. 251.
2 C. Maginn, *'Civilizing' Gaelic Leinster: the extension of Tudor rule in the O'Byrne and O'Toole lordships* (Dublin, 2005), p. 85.
3 B.C. Donovan, 'Tudor rule in Gaelic Leinster and the rise of Feagh McHugh O'Byrne', in O'Brien (ed.), *Feagh McHugh O'Byrne*, p. 146.
4 Ibid., p. 118.
5 Maginn, *'Civilizing' Gaelic Leinster*, p. 160.
6 Ibid., p. 161.
7 Sir W. Stanley, 'A calendar of manuscript material relating to Ireland, 1580–1602; Letter of Sir William Stanley, 31 August 1580', http://www.ucc.ie/celt/published/E580000-002/text002.html.
8 E. O'Byrne, 'The battle of Glenmalure, 25 August 1580—cause and course', in O'Brien (ed.), *Feagh McHugh O'Byrne*, p. 178.
9 Maginn, *'Civilizing' Gaelic Leinster*, p. 165.
10 Ibid., p. 164.
11 'Russell's Journal', in D. Edwards (ed.), *Campaign journals of the Elizabethan Irish wars* (Irish Manuscripts Commission, 2014), p. 190.
12 *Calendar of the state papers relating to Ireland, of the reign of Elizabeth* [hereafter *CSPI*], *1588–1592* (London, 1885), p. 610.
13 Edwards (ed.), 'Russell's Journal', p. 203.
14 *CSPI, 1592–1596*, p. 292.
15 Ibid.
16 Edwards (ed.), 'Russell's Journal', p. 203.
17 D. Edwards, 'In Tyrone's shadow: Feagh McHugh O'Byrne, forgotten leader of the Nine Years War', in O'Brien (ed.), *Feagh McHugh O'Byrne*, p. 214.
18 Maginn, *'Civilizing' Gaelic Leinster*, pp 160–1.
19 *CSPI, 1592–1596*, p. 286.
20 Edwards (ed.), 'Russell's Journal', pp 204–5.
21 Ibid., p. 207.
22 Edwards, 'In Tyrone's shadow', p. 232.
23 *CSPI, 1592–1596*, p. 91.
24 Edwards, 'In Tyrone's shadow', p. 244.
25 Edwards (ed.), 'Russell's Journal', p. 210.
26 Edwards, 'In Tyrone's shadow', p. 232.
27 Edwards (ed.), 'Russell's Journal', p. 211.
28 *CSPI, 1592–1596*, p. 311.
29 Edwards (ed.), 'Russell's Journal', p. 216.
30 Edwards, 'In Tyrone's shadow', p. 233.
31 K. Nicholls, 'The genealogy of the O'Byrnes of Ranelagh', in O'Brien (ed.), *Feagh McHugh O'Byrne*, p. 113.
32 *CSPI, 1592–1596*, p. 330.
33 Nicholls, 'The genealogy of the O'Byrnes of Ranelagh', p. 112.
34 E. O'Byrne, *War, politics and the Irish of Leinster, 1156–1606* (Dublin, 2003), p. 227.

[35] *CSPI, 1592–1596*, p. 374.
[36] Ibid., p. 383.
[37] Edwards (ed.), 'Russell's Journal', p. 232.
[38] Edwards, 'In Tyrone's shadow', p. 234.
[39] Ibid., p. 235.
[40] Ibid., p. 236.
[41] Edwards (ed.), 'Russell's Journal', p. 255.
[42] Edwards, 'In Tyrone's shadow', p. 237.
[43] Ibid., p. 238.
[44] J.S. Brewer and W. Bullen (eds), *Calendar of the Carew manuscripts preserved in the archiepiscopal library at Lambeth, 1515–1624* (6 vols, London, 1867–73), iii, document 247.
[45] Edwards, 'In Tyrone's shadow', p. 238.
[46] Ibid., p. 239.
[47] *Cal. Carew MSS*, iii, document 248.
[48] Edwards (ed.), 'Russell's Journal', p. 257.
[49] Ibid., p. 240.
[50] Ibid.
[51] Ibid., p. 257.
[52] Edwards, 'In Tyrone's shadow', p. 240.
[53] Edwards (ed.), 'Russell's Journal', p. 259.
[54] E.G. Atkinson (ed.), *Calendar of the state papers relating to Ireland, of the reign of Elizabeth, 1596, July–1597, December* (London, 1912), p. 156.
[55] Edwards (ed.), 'Russell's Journal', p. 263.
[56] Ibid., p. 267.
[57] Ibid.
[58] Ibid., pp 268–70.
[59] Ibid.
[60] Ibid.
[61] Ibid., p. 190.
[62] *CSPI, 1596–1597*, p. 278.
[63] Edwards (ed.), 'Russell's Journal', pp 274–7.
[64] Ibid., p. 279.
[65] C. O'Brien, 'Feagh McHugh O'Byrne', http://www.historyireland.com/early-modern-history-1500-1700/feagh-mchugh-obyrne/.
[66] Edwards (ed.), 'Russell's Journal', p. 279.
[67] *Cal. Carew MSS, 1597*, document 268.
[68] *Cal. Carew MSS, 1600*, document 515.

6

The strange tale of Mary Bux: ethnicity and identity in 1641

Gordon Bond

For those with an interest in Irish history, the ongoing 'decade of commemorations' is a bonanza. The Irish public is being treated to memorials, lecture series, television documentaries, museum exhibitions and magazine articles about any number of events and personalities of 100 years ago. We have already had remembrances and re-enactments connected to World War One and the Battle of Clontarf, while memories of 1913 have already faded from sight in the rear-view mirror. Easter 2016 was preceded and followed by probing questions about the legitimacy of the Rising, the worth of the Proclamation and the experiences of people other than the rebels themselves, whose stories long overshadowed those of their contemporaries.

While the Clontarf millennium certainly gave rise to renewed debates about the notion of the 'Irish' versus the 'foreigner', the most obvious effect of the centenaries has been to focus attention once more on the history of Ireland's relationship with Britain, colonialism and the continued legacy of partition. All this has recently been thrown into even sharper relief by the Brexit bombshell, and we are again in the midst of protracted re-examinations both of the Republic's relationship with Britannia and of the events which led to the establishment of that Republic in the first place.

In keeping with this theme, and using the 1641 depositions collection for Kildare as evidence, this essay attempts to offer a word on the history of this relationship with reference to the events of that year. The conflict that began in the winter of 1641 will not feature in any of the decade's commemorations, yet its violence—characterised as it was by a clash between Catholic and Protestant communities—set a tragic pattern of enmity and mistrust which was to endure for centuries, and which must continue to be regarded as fundamental to any analysis of Irish history up to independence. By analysing the ways in which members of these communities perceived one another, the essay will try to illustrate the existence and extent of cultural divisions between the apparently 'Irish' Catholic community and the apparently 'English' or 'British' settlers. Based on differences of language, religion and ethnic heritage, these divisions had a fatal effect on the relationship between Ireland's two communities, and they found their personification in the form of Mary Bux.

Even the most cursory examination of the 1641 depositions—statements taken both during and after the period of warfare lasting from 1641 to 1649—will quickly reveal the ubiquitous presence of the terms 'English', 'Protestant', 'Irish' and 'papist'. At first glance, these terms appear to function as synonyms, 'English' being easily interchangeable with 'Protestant', and the same being true for the labels 'Irish' and 'papist'. In some cases the equation of Protestantism with English identity was made explicit by proximity: Thomas Huetsonn, John Drake, Thomas Carpenter and William Ashley all referred to themselves in their statements to the commissioners as English Protestants.[1] In others, particularly in accounts concerning the attitudes of the rebels, this equation was implied rather than openly expressed: 'that night, when *the English* were rifled by the garrison soldiers and others . . . he there saw Peter Higgins now in restraint . . . encouraging the soldiers and pillagers . . . wishing them to proceed valiantly, *for the cause was for their faith or religion* [my italics]'.[2] Even more striking are several deponents' representations of themselves as 'British' Protestants, a term wholly unique to the deponents in that there are no references to 'British' settlers made by the Irish.[3] In one isolated case a distinction is made between Protestantism and English identity in reference to one John Murphy, 'a zealous and honest Protestant and a man much endeared to the English nation'.[4] The implication of this passage, taken from a deposition made in 1645, is that Murphy was of the Protestant religion and pro-English, but not of a strictly English background. The distinction is given even more weight thanks to the survival of a 1642 deposition made by the same man, John Murphy of Athy, who identified himself as 'an Irish Protestant all his lifetime'.[5] Clearly, Protestants living in Kildare were at least *aware* of differences between themselves in terms of religious identity and national or ethnic heritage. Nevertheless, that this sense of difference was articulated on just two occasions, and in reference to just one person, implies that members of the Protestant community also held a certain sense of overall homogeneity regarding both their religious and political identities.

This ability to differentiate between one another did not manifest itself in the deponents' descriptions of their aggressors. Instead, the deponents characterised the insurgents variously as 'Irish', 'papist' and, indeed, 'Irish papists'.[6] More often the insurgents were referred to simply as 'the rebels', but even this term could be linked to their ethnicity in the formulations 'Irish rebels' and 'the Irish army'.[7] The historian and geographer William Smyth has pointed out that the term 'Irish papist' was in the first instance an English 'colonial' creation, intended not only to marginalise the Irish as an 'idolatrous, barbaric' people but also to eliminate the distinctions between native Irish and Old English.[8] Indeed, on only one occasion does a deponent display any appreciation of the existence of that hybrid group which had lately compromised its 'colonial identity': 'and he also saith that all the gentry of the counties of Meath and Kildare *that are English Irish* are at this instant in open rebellion [my italics]'.[9] The general Protestant view of the Irish as a monolithic group whose ethnicity was synonymous with its Catholicism is therefore self-evident.

The information on Mary Bux comes from a series of four depositions taken during the period of judicial trials in the 1650s but relating to events which took place in Kildare in 1642. The most important point of note emerges in the deposition of Mary Sutton, who informs us that Bux was 'of English parents, but could speak Irish'.[10] There is an immediate implication that such cultural mixing was to some extent unusual. Mary Bux was 'left behind' by a Mr Parker, who, having suffered robbery at the hands of a group of insurgents which included one Ambrose Connor, hoped that she might 'discover who the robbers were'. As a result, these men made several attempts to murder her, prompting George Fitzgerald, the husband of the aforementioned Mary Sutton, to take Bux to an English garrison for her safety. Unfortunately, she 'would not be received into the garrison because she had been a long time with the rebels'.[11] Instead, the Fitzgeralds (who as an Old English family were Catholic and presumably safe from insurgent aggression) allowed her to live in their home until the day when Connor and two others descended on the house. Fitzgerald himself was away, leaving Bux, his wife and their servant Jane Lawlor alone in the house. With the aid of his accomplices, Connor took Mary from the house, dragging her through the fire as he did so, ignoring the lady's plea 'for Christ's sake to let her alone'.[12] Having been taken to a nearby wood, Mary was murdered—probably hanged—and her body cast into a bog pit. The particulars of the murder, already known to the Fitzgerald couple and their servant, were further corroborated by the evidence of another local woman, Rose Halgan.[13] The evidence against Ambrose Connor and the context in which it was given are fraught with the usual problems associated with the 1650s depositions. It is both strange and convenient, for example, that neither of his alleged accomplices was named, and that both were by that time apparently 'killed or dead'.[14] Far more important here, however, are the brief but revealing details of cultural complexities personified in the form of Mary Bux.

Although Bux may have possessed the *cúpla focal*, it is significant that Mary Sutton felt her English parentage to be equally worthy of note. Not so the English garrison, whose suspicion of her loyalties demonstrated that for them her blood was already tainted by having been too long among the savages. Thus Mary Bux emerges from the sources as a woman trapped between two worlds, one who moved within both communities but failed to *belong* to either of them. Like Kipling's musings on East and West, Irish was Irish while English was English, and never the twain should meet. When these two cultures did come together in the person of a single individual the contradictions proved too much, and Bux's failure to be accepted by her parents' countrymen ultimately cost her her life. There are further examples of bilingualism (and the lack thereof) to be found among the depositions, particularly in the interrogations of prisoners from the castles of Rathcoffey and Clongowes Wood, who had to be questioned through interpreters.[15] But for every Mary Bux who managed to cross the linguistic divide there was also a John Harrison, a man not trusted by the insurgents among whom he lived, who 'whenever this examinant came near . . . left off speaking English and turned it into Irish'.[16]

Whatever level of accommodation or toleration had been reached in Kildare by 1641, the cultural divisions that separated the two communities had not gone away. Instead, they continued to endure, and were perhaps made all the more volatile for being buried below (albeit not very far below) the surface. While an Englishman was selling livestock to an Irish buyer, or an Irish tenant was handing over his rent to an English landlord, all might appear normal. Yet how many English landlords locked their doors at night for fear of the Catholic savages who peopled their newly acquired land? How many Irish Catholics nursed quiet grudges against the settler community that had brought new ways of living and a new economic order in its wake?[17] Certainly, once the conflict began there were those within the Irish camp who wanted no part of it. At least two deponents, John MacGawly of Kildare and Nicholas O'Kenaght of Naas, claimed to have served as rebel soldiers against their will, with John MacGawly in particular claiming that the lives of his wife and children were threatened in order to force him to take part. These claims, made at a time when both men had been captured and were facing execution, must certainly be treated with a cautious scepticism, but given that both identified the same commander, Thomas Wogan, as the man who had dragged them into service, it seems reasonable to conclude that some level of press-ganging was being employed by some commanders in order to artificially swell the rebel ranks.[18] Nevertheless, the general presence among the 'common people' of a hatred for 'all things English' seems undeniable.[19]

In the coming months and years, it is likely that many of the more unsavoury aspects of the historical relationship between Ireland's communities of Catholics, Protestants, nationalists, unionists or any combination of the same will be played down or perhaps airbrushed out of the picture altogether, in an attempt to make the decade of commemorations palatable for as many people as possible. Nevertheless, as we continue to move forward on the path of reconciliation, of new eras of understanding and of reciprocal state visits, it is also important to face the realities of that history, to acknowledge the genuine divisions and enmities which have previously existed, and in doing so to take further important steps towards overcoming what is still for many a challenging and uncomfortable historical legacy.

Notes

1 Deposition of John Drake, TCD MS 813, f. 289r; Deposition of Thomas Carpenter, TCD MS 813, f. 290r; Deposition of Willyam Ashley, TCD MS 813, f. 296r; Deposition of Thomas Huetsonn, TCD MS 813, f. 260r.

2 Deposition of Thomas Greames, TCD MS 813, f. 015r; see also Deposition of Patricke Gosson, TCD

MS 813, f. 250r.

3 Deposition of Ellinor Lee, TCD MS 813, f. 224r; Deposition of Roger Pickering, TCD MS 813, f. 242r; Deposition of John Samme, TCD MS 813, f. 239r; Deposition of William Harrison, TCD MS 813, f. 268r; Deposition of James Garstang, TCD MS 813, f. 270r.

4 Deposition of James Peirsy, TCD MS 813, f. 302r.

5 Deposition of John Murphy, TCD MS 813, f. 328r.

6 Deposition of Richard Clarke, TCD MS 813, f. 292r; Deposition of Robert Browne, TCD MS 813, f. 343r; Deposition of Thomas Huetsonn, TCD MS 813, f. 260v; Deposition of Mary Viscountess Netterville, TCD MS 813, f. 398r.

7 Deposition of Richard Pickering, TCD MS 813, f. 242r; Deposition of Samuell Jefferies, TCD MS 813, f. 248r; Declaration of Thomas Farback, TCD MS 813, f. 252v.

8 W. Smyth, *Map-making, landscapes and memory: a geography of colonial and early modern Ireland, c. 1530–1750* (Cork, 2006), p. 124; see also K. Noonan, '"The cruell pressure of an enraged, barbarous people": Irish and English identity in seventeenth-century policy and propaganda', *Historical Journal* 40 (1998), pp 157–61.

9 A. Clarke, 'The genesis of the Ulster rising of 1641', in P. Roebuck (ed.), *Plantation to partition: essays in Ulster history in honour of J.L. McCracken* (Belfast, 1981), p. 45; Information of Walter Hussey, TCD MS 813, f. 048r.

10 Deposition of Mary Sutton, TCD MS 813, f. 115r.

11 Deposition of George Fitzgerald, TCD MS 813, f. 118r.

12 Deposition of Jane Lawlor, TCD MS 813, ff 114r–114v; Deposition of Mary Sutton, TCD MS 813, ff 115r–115v.

13 Deposition of Rose Halgan, TCD MS 813, f. 116r.

14 Deposition of Jane Lawlor, TCD MS 813, f. 114r.

15 Examination of Hugh Cullen, TCD MS 813, f. 078v; Examination of Marrogh Malone, TCD MS 813, f. 078r; Information of James Slevin, TCD MS 813, f. 076v; Information of Nicholas Noland, TCD MS 813, f. 076r.

16 Examination of John Harrison, TCD MS 813, ff 028r–028v; see also Deposition of Elizabeth Bradley, TCD MS 813, f. 304r—'and used some words unto them in Irish, which the deponent understood not'.

17 Smyth, *Map-making, landscapes and memory*, p. 126; J. Kenyon and J. Ohlmeyer, 'The background to the civil wars in the Stewart kingdoms', in J. Kenyon, J. Ohlmeyer and J. Morrill (eds), *The civil wars: a military history of England, Scotland, and Ireland, 1638–1660* (Oxford, 1998), pp 29–30.

18 Information of John Macgawly, TCD MS 813, ff 057r–058r; Examination of Nicholas O'Kenaght, TCD MS 813, f. 079r.

19 M. Perceval-Maxwell, 'The Ulster rising of 1641, and the depositions', *Irish Historical Studies* 21 (1978), p. 164.

Part II: Chiefs and clans

7

A gallowglass clan: the Mac Cabes in Ireland

Brian McCabe

The late Gerard Hayes-McCoy, when referring to the gallowglass families in his ground-breaking work on Scots mercenary forces in Ireland, described the Mac Cabes as 'the most enigmatical of all',[1] and this is indeed true of the early history of the name. Most accounts follow the noted sixteenth-century genealogist Duald Mac Firbhis in ascribing Scottish—and earlier Norse—origins to the name.

Accepting this as likely, it is not clear exactly when the Mac Cabes first made their appearance in Ireland. Both Hayes-McCoy and John Marsden, writing more recently on 'Galloglas', deal with the early references to *galloglach* (or *Gall Gaeidhel*) in Ireland in the mid- to late thirteenth century.[2] Other accounts—and family traditions—refer to the Mac Cabes coming to Ireland with Edward Bruce's expedition of 1315. It is likely that the fame earned by this new type of full-time warrior in notable Scottish military victories such as the battle of Largs and, later, Bannockburn would have prompted the Irish chieftains to employ them for their own battles, whether dynastic or in their ongoing war against the Anglo-Normans.

What is certain, however, is that by the 1350s the Mac Cabes had become sufficiently well established in Ireland, and sufficiently renowned in warfare, to warrant the first of many specific references in the ancient annals. The first of these is for the year 1358, when the annals record a defeat by O'Neill of the Oirgialla and the Fir Manach, where 'Aedh Mac Cába was killed therein and the son of the Bishop O Dubhda'.[3] This early reference places the Mac Cabes firmly in the geographic area that was to become their home ground over the following centuries, and illustrates how their fortunes were to become closely entwined with those of the hereditary clan chieftains in these border territories, represented by the modern counties of Monaghan, Cavan, Leitrim and Fermanagh. It would seem to suggest that their first area of operation was 'Oriel' (modern Monaghan); indeed, a later entry, for 1394, records the death of Brian Mac Cába, who is clearly described as 'Constable of Oirgialla'. This would have made him head of the gallowglass of the Mac Mahon chieftain, and it is likely that the Thomas Mac Cabe who accompanied Philip Mac Mahon when he went to Dundalk to pay homage to King Richard II the following year was Brian's successor in that role. The official record of these submissions also supplies evidence for their territory when it identifies Thomas as 'MacCabe of Clogher diocese'.[4]

Their role with the Mac Mahons would also seem to have led to the Mac Cabes becoming involved in the dynastic struggles in the neighbouring kingdom of Breifne (modern Cavan). Annalistic entries for 1369, for example, refer to the imprisonment of Philip O'Raighilligh (O'Reilly) 'by his own brethren' in Clough Oughter and his displacement by Maghnus O'Raighilligh. Not surprisingly, 'a very great war occurred in the Breifne through this capture and a great army was assembled by Annadh O'Raighilligh'. This army included Mac Mahon and 'the rest of the Airghialla', and the annals go on to record that a great defeat was subsequently inflicted on Maghnus by Mac Mahon and the 'Clann Chába'.[5]

By 1392 at least some of the Mac Cabes were venturing further afield. In that year an O'Neill army invaded Tirconnell (Donegal), and O'Donnell prepared to defend his territory. The annals record that O'Donnell's forces attacked and defeated the invading army, killing many, including 'Donough MacCabe'.[6]

The early fifteenth century finds the Mac Cabes heavily involved in the Breifne wars, particularly the battles between the O'Reillys and their former overlords, the O'Rourkes—and, indeed, in internecine struggles within those clans. In 1402, for example, we find a record of Fergal, the son of Aedh O'Rourke, 'son of the king of Breifne and royal heir of the Ui Briuin', being killed 'in his own house' by Lochlainn Mac Cába.[7] Another source adds that this deed was done 'at the instigation of Eoghan O'Ruairc'.[8] The following year sees the wounding of Mahon (son of Gillachrist, son of Flaithbhertach) Mac Cába by the O'Rourkes in an attack on the O'Reilly stronghold of Cavan.[9] The assassin Lochlainn 'Colach' pops up again in 1405, when he is mentioned as accompanying Tadhg Mac Dermott of Moylurg on a tribute circuit of Roscommon, where 'a great defeat was inflicted by Mac Domhnaill' (Mac Dermott's constable) aided by Lochlainn and 'the recruits of Moy Lurg'.[10] It would seem that Mac Dermott felt a need for additional recruits for a difficult mission, and by then the Mac Cabes had clearly built up a reputation as military muscle. This may have been a temporary assignment, however, as a few years later (1413) we find Lochlainn Mac Cába (presumably the same man) amongst those killed on an O'Reilly–Mac Cabe raid into the Pale territory of Meath. This seems to have been a particularly bloody affair, as it also records the overtaking of the expedition by the 'Foreigners' and the killing of Mathgamhainn Mac Cába, as well as Lochlainn and 'many of his people'.[11]

Three years later (1416) the annals record another raid by the O'Rourkes and 'Clann-Cába', this time into Fermanagh.[12] This one seems to have been more successful and displays some evidence of military strategy, as it involved not just the usual 'hit-and-run' tactics but also an initial feint, followed up by an ambush of the pursuing party of Fermanagh men. The same annals record the death, a few years later (1419), of 'Áine, daughter of Henry Mac Cába, mother of the children of Thomas the Abbot [of Lisgabhail]'.[13] Clearly the Mac Cabes now had enough status to be marrying into the major families of the district. Perhaps Áine was the daughter of the then Mac Cabe chieftain?

Mac Cabe power and influence were growing, and the death notice of Mael Shechlainn (or Melaghlin) Mac Cába in 1424 describes him as 'Constable of the two Breifni and of Fir-Manach and of the Oirgialla'.[14] He is recorded as dying of the plague rather than in battle.

Five years later the Mac Cabes were again involved in the O'Reilly–O'Rourke struggles, this time also involving the O'Neills. They appear to have come off worst on that occasion, and the annals record 'the Baron of Delvin . . . and Henry Mac Cába . . . and other persons' being either captured or slain in the pitched battle, which took place at Aughakilmore, near Cavan.[15]

A very interesting entry in the *Annals of Ulster* for 1433 gives us some more detailed information on the genealogy of at least one branch of the Mac Cabes at this point. The entry concerns another internecine dispute—this time between two branches of the Mag Raghnaills (Reynolds)—in which the sons of Mahon Mac Cabe were taken into service and, once again, suffered casualties while holding off a pursuing force after a raid. Three of the sons (Ross, Donnchadh and Brian) were slain, while their elder brother, Eogan, is recorded as being taken prisoner 'when he was half dead'. The entry also records that their mother, Una, was the daughter of Seán O'Reilly, underlining again the close Mac Cabe–O'Reilly associations, and intermarriages, at this point.[16]

A decade or so later we get a look at the Mac Cabe hereditary succession stakes, which are now important enough in themselves to warrant annalistic comment. The *Annals of Ulster* for 1447 record that 'Mac Cába, the Breffnian, died this year—namely Cormac, son of Gilla-Crist, Mac Cába, and Henry Mac Cába, his brother, was chosen by the Sil-Raighillaigh and by the Clann-Cába also as Constable in Breifni'.[17]

Another decade on (1455) the annals record the death of Maine, son of Maelseachnaill Mac Cába, who is described as 'one fit to be a Constable of the two Breifni and Oirghialla and Fir-Manach for hospitality and prowess'.[18]

The year 1460 was an eventful one for the clan. The *Annals of Ulster* record, in some detail, the death of the aforesaid Henry, who is described as 'a Constable eminent for generosity and for prowess and for devotion. And full was Ireland [of the fame] of his goodness.'[19] The Four Masters' entry records that he died 'of a short fit of sickness' at the O'Farrell seat at Lissardowlin, in Longford. It goes on to describe what must have been a very impressive funeral procession, in which his body was accompanied by no less than 280 gallowglass, armed with battleaxes, back to Cavan for interment[20]—probably in the old Franciscan abbey there. One can only imagine the impact of such an imposing show of power and strength on the inhabitants of the territories through which the cortège passed!

Henry would seem to have been succeeded by his son Mathgamain (Mahon), whose death is recorded by the annalists in 1464.[21] A further entry for that year, however, records the death of another Mahon, 'son of Toirdelbach the Freckled', who was 'slain by the Foreigners', so perhaps one—for a short period—succeeded the other.

Other sons of Toirdelbach feature again in the annals in 1485, this time in a battle between the O'Reillys and McGoverns. On that occasion one of these sons, Gillacrist, was killed, along with an Alexander Mac Cába of another branch of the family, while another three of Toirdelbach's sons (Redmond, Donchadh and Maelsechnaill) were taken prisoner.[22] Maelsechnaill features again the following year, when he takes part in an expedition to aid one faction of the Reynolds against another and is killed in the process.[23] Clearly, being a gallowglass was a very hazardous occupation! Indeed, evidence of just how dangerous it could be—and how you could even end up fighting against others of your clan—is found a few years later (1489), when the annals record the killing by Toirdelbach's sons of two sons of Maine 'the Tawny' Mac Cába, and Aedh (Hugh) the son of Glaisne Mac Cába.[24]

Entries continue, with great regularity, through the remainder of the fifteenth and sixteenth centuries, featuring the involvement of the Mac Cabes in the various clan struggles and disputes, as well as the (occasional) deaths of Mac Cabe leaders away from the field of battle.

A more pleasant record, and another indication of how the Mac Cabes continued to gain status and marry into the older ruling dynasties, can be found in an entry for 1527, which records the death of Mór, daughter of Maelechlainn Mac Cába and wife of O'hAinlighe (Hanley). She seems to have been a particularly remarkable woman, and the scribes (mostly clerical) who compiled the annals—and who are not generally noted for their sympathetic treatment of women (when they mention them at all)—are compelled to wax lyrical about her many qualities. She is described thus:

> The best woman that ever came into Cenel-Doffa-mic-Aenghusa for a long time; the nurse of the learned and destitute of Erinn; the equal of Mór Mumhan in reputation, piety and good will; the woman who gave most in offerings and alms of food and clothing to the poor and to the orphans of the Lord, and to everyone who would require to receive them, died in the middle of her own residence in Port-Locha-Leise, et sepulta est in Oilfinn, under the protection of God and Patrick.[25]

This (necessarily) short history of the Mac Cabes in Ireland gives, I hope, a picture of how an outside group—albeit probably from a similar Gaelic-speaking background—managed to carve out a role for themselves, largely through military prowess, and to integrate relatively quickly into medieval Irish society along the Ulster border territories. Adapting to circumstances, they extended their power and influence by providing services to the ruling clans in this area, and so successful were they at doing so that ultimately they became recognised as a 'clan' in their own right, warranting references in the historic annals almost on a par with those of the older ruling regional dynasties.

Notes

1 G.A. Hayes-McCoy, *Scots mercenary forces in Ireland, 1565–1603* (Dublin, 1937), p. 34.

2 J. Marsden, *Galloglas: Hebridean and West Highland mercenary warrior kindreds in medieval Ireland* (East Linton, 2003), p. 22.

3 *Annála Uladh, annals of Ulster; otherwise Annála Senait, annals of Senat: a chronicle of Irish affairs, 431–1131, 1155–1541* (hereafter *AU*), ed. W.M. Hennessy and B. MacCarthy (4 vols, Dublin, 1887–1901; repr. 1998), ii, p. 507.

4 Marsden, *Galloglas*, p. 74.

5 *The annals of Loch Cé: a chronicle of Irish affairs, 1014–1590* (hereafter *ALC*), ed. W.M. Hennessy (2 vols, London, 1871; Dublin, 1939), ii, p. 41.

6 *Annála ríoghachta Éireann: annals of the kingdom of Ireland by the Four Masters from the earliest period to the year 1616* (hereafter *AFM*), ed. J. O'Donovan (7 vols, Dublin, 1851; New York, 1966; 3rd edn, Dublin, 1990), iv, p. 725.

7 *ALC*, ii, p. 101.

8 *Miscellaneous Irish annals*, ed. Seamus Ó hInnse (Dublin, 1947), p. 169.

9 *ALC*, ii, p. 105.

10 Ibid., p. 115.

11 *AU*, iii, p. 65.

12 Ibid., p. 71.

13 Ibid., p. 83.

14 Ibid., p. 97.

15 Ibid., p. 107.

16 Ibid., pp 125–7.

17 Ibid., p. 161.

18 Ibid., p. 185.

19 Ibid., p. 201.

20 *AFM*, iv, p. 1007.

21 *AU*, p. 211.

22 Ibid., p. 295.

23 Ibid., pp 303–5.

24 Ibid., p. 339.

25 *ALC*, ii, p. 263.

8

'Sr Richard Burk of the Newtowne knight otherwise called MacWilliam Eighter'

Declan Keenan

In 1585 a tax agreement was negotiated in Connaught in order to curb the excessive powers of the Gaelic and Gaelicised magnates. The agreement, known as the Composition of Connaught, served to remove the customary exactions due to the magnates, abolished traditional titles of chieftainship and signalled the commencement of English law within the province. On examination, however, it becomes evident that the Composition had the opposite effect of that intended, serving rather to maintain the position of the magnates at the pinnacle of society. One such magnate who benefited significantly was Sir Richard FitzOliverus Bourke, MacWilliam Íochtair 1583–5.

The purpose of this paper is to examine Richard FitzOliverus Bourke's succession to the MacWilliamship and his subsequent role as a key negotiator of the terms of the Composition, which had far-reaching consequences for the Gaelicised and Gaelic septs of County Mayo. What makes his contribution even more curious is that his reign as MacWilliam Íochtair (chief lord of the Bourkes of Mayo) was quite limited at approximately two years. This paper will demonstrate the determination, foresight and political 'savvy' of Richard FitzOliverus Bourke in securing an inheritance for his heirs in an ever-changing world through his succession and role in the Composition.

Utilising the work of Dubhaltach MacFhirbhisigh, we can deduce that Richard FitzOliverus Bourke was a member of Sliocht Ricaird, a powerful sept of the Mayo Bourkes based in the barony of Tyrawley.[1] His father, Oliverus Bourke, held the title of MacWilliam Íochtair in the mid-sixteenth century.[2] Furthermore, Richard's brother, John MacOliverus, held the title between February 1571 and November 1580. This indicates that Sliocht Ricaird was at the summit of its power in Mayo in the late sixteenth century. Richard FitzOliverus would therefore in time have also had a strong claim to the chieftainship.

One of the earliest records available concerning Richard is to be found in a document entitled the 'Divisions of Connaught and Thomond', the results of a survey undertaken between 1570 and 1574. The survey was carried out to aid the shiring of Connaught into counties and baronies and included listings of the principal gentlemen within the province. Richard is described as Richard FitzOliverus holding the castle of Newtown (currently known as Deel Castle), one of the largest tower-houses within the barony of Tyrawley.[3] His occupation of this structure indicates his wealth and prominence within the sept.

Records concerning Richard FitzOliverus become more frequent after 1580 as a result of his brother John's death, following which Richard challenged Richard an Iarainn, husband to Grainne O'Malley, for the MacWilliamship. Richard an Iarainn had served as tanist to John MacOliverus, giving him significant footing to succeed.[4] Regardless, there appears to have been a great deal of contention between the pair. A short time after John's death, Nicholas Malby (lord president of Connaught) made numerous notes of the 'great controversy' between Richard an Iarainn and Richard FitzOliverus over the lordship.[5] Clearly, both factions were intensifying their campaigns. In fact, Richard an Iarainn rose out in 1581, allegedly concerned that Malby was going to gift the MacWilliamship to Richard FitzOliverus.[6] Nevertheless, Richard an Iarainn appears to have been favoured in the contest and held the chieftaincy from November 1580 to April 1583. This loss most definitely had a profound effect on Richard FitzOliverus and may have bolstered his determination to succeed. Malby was clearly aware of the impact of the loss and gave him compensation, including entitlements to chief rents in Tyrawley, besides appointing him sheriff of Mayo. This is a clear indication of the intensity of the contest and of the level of pressure applied by Richard FitzOliverus, which Malby felt obliged to appease. The animosity between the parties appears to have continued throughout Richard an Iarainn's reign. For instance, in May 1582 Richard FitzOliverus and his brothers were recorded as having slain some of Richard an Iarainn's men alongside some of Malby's while collecting crown rents.[7]

Shortly afterwards, in September 1582, Malby noted that Richard an Iarainn was near death and suggested that two individuals would likely contest the MacWilliamship, one of them most definitely being Richard FitzOliverus.[8] It would also appear that Richard FitzOliverus was aware of Richard an Iarainn's condition, as by June 1582 he is recorded in the English state papers as having gone to O'Donnell in Tyrconnell to gather Scots[9]—that is to say, he attempted to develop his armed capability by hiring gallowglass soldiers from Scotland, a typical undertaking for any Bourke with ambition. Richard FitzOliverus was most certainly aware that Richard an Iarainn was in a weakened state and sought to bolster his position as a potential candidate for the MacWilliamship. The drawing in of Scots was nothing unusual and served to consolidate the position of MacWilliam Íochtair. In April 1583, following Richard an Iarainn's death, Richard FitzOliverus finally succeeded to the title and would have been inaugurated in the traditional manner at Rausakeera.[10] In November 1583 his position was confirmed when he was received as captain of his country and knighted.[11]

The events recounted above clearly indicate the great lengths to which Richard FitzOliverus was prepared to go in order to secure the title of MacWilliam Íochtair. Of course, it was a highly prized title, and any candidate would typically have exerted as much pressure as possible. Nevertheless, the fact that Malby offered compensation to Richard FitzOliverus (an incident without precedent in Mayo) indicates that the crown was aware of his capability and exceptional determination.

One could certainly suggest that Richard FitzOliverus may have been acutely aware of the change that was looming over Connaught, particularly Mayo, under the Composition of Connaught, particularly in relation to succession. After all, he would have witnessed the surrender and regrant schemes of the mid-sixteenth century and was perhaps well versed in their political impact. He would also have witnessed the composition agreement made with the lesser lords and gentlemen of Mayo in 1577. He may therefore have been aware that the traditional customs and practices were under threat and that some sept would be endowed with the power, wealth and benefits of the MacWilliamship, something that was traditionally contested by all Bourke septs. Thus it is likely that Richard FitzOliverus resolved to propel his immediate heirs and his own sept to the pinnacle.

In his capacity as MacWilliam Íochtair, Richard was entitled to the use of the mensal castle and lands. These included the castles of Ballyloughmask, Kinlough and Ballinrobe and their associated demesnes in the barony of Kilmaine. In addition, he was also entitled to rents from all of the freeholders within the entire barony of Kilmaine. The MacWilliamship title and its trappings were thus highly prized, owing to the wealth accruing to the successful candidate. It is also worth noting that Richard was entitled to rents from the other baronies of Mayo in his capacity as chieftain, and also to extensive rents in the barony of Tyrawley, not to mention his personal lands at Newtown. It is little wonder, therefore, that Richard displayed such determination in contesting for the title.

In the 1580s the English government made an increased effort to regularise the position held by Gaelic and Gaelicised magnates in Connaught society in order to stabilise the province. Sir Nicholas Malby had succeeded Sir Edward Fitton as lord president in 1579 (having been chief commissioner of Connaught since 1576) and set about establishing fiscal and military control over the greater lords, which formed the basis for the 1585 Composition of Connaught agreement.[12] A revised version of the 1577 agreement, the Composition of Connaught was adopted in 1585 at the start of Sir Richard Bingham's lord presidency. Ultimately, the government wanted to curb or remove the excessive customs, exactions, 'coign and livery' and cess systems that existed. In place of these was to be a rent charge paid annually.[13] The alternative to the private armies controlled by the magnates was to be an English force under the control of the lord president, financed by the terms of the Composition of Connaught. Indeed, Richard FitzOliverus was a noted negotiator in the Composition, described as 'Sr Richard Burk of the Newtowne knight otherwise called MacWilliam Eighter'.[14]

An additional agreement outlined within the Composition was the adoption of English law by the magnates. This was significant, as it affected the traditional methods of succession and involved the abolition of the titles of chieftainship such as MacWilliam Íochtair. Following the death of the standing MacWilliam Íochtair, Richard FitzOliverus, the title was to be abolished by law.

The adoption of English law in relation to succession or inheritance was quite significant. Under the Composition, the rule of primogeniture was to replace the traditional practice of tanistry and election. Where once the land and titles could be contested by any senior male member of the leading septs, under the Composition the titles and lands would be transferred to the eldest son of the reigning title-holder at the time of the Composition—that is to say, the son and heirs of Richard FitzOliverus Bourke.

In recognition of its impact on the status or loss of titles of the magnates, provisions were made within the Composition to compensate for this in the form of freedoms or exemptions from Composition rents.[15] Furthermore, a yearly rent charge was also payable to Richard FitzOliverus out of all inhabited land to compensate for the traditional exactions.

Richard FitzOliverus received ten quarters (one quarter = 120 acres) surrounding Newtown free of the Composition rent charges. This was in addition to significant exemptions in the barony of Kilmaine in recognition of Sir Richard's place of dignity.[16] The exemption of charges on these lands would have given Richard FitzOliverus and his heirs an immense advantage over other landholders in attracting tenants and labourers to their lands. In lands where no exemptions were applied, the Composition charge was transferred onto the tenants. Sir Richard Bingham noted the effect of the Composition on the lands of those where the rent charges did apply: 'the husbandman doth choose rather to dwell upon the great freedoms', thus creating waste lands throughout some areas of the county.[17] It is therefore likely that reasonably sized settlements would have developed about Ballinrobe, Kinlough, Ballyloughmask and Newtown subsequent to the Composition.

Over the preceding centuries a variety of septs had provided candidates for the MacWilliamship. One could suggest that any number of these septs could have rightfully claimed the title prior to the Composition. Two of the last three MacWilliam Íochtair were of Sliocht Ricaird, the second-last holder (Richard an Iarainn) being of Sliocht Ulick of Carra and Burrishoole. With this in mind, one could suggest that Sliocht Ulick had as much a claim as Sliocht Ricaird. Yet the associated powers of the title were ordered to be given by letters patent to Richard FitzOliverus and his heirs, including the mensal properties of Kilmaine and rents in the other baronies of Mayo, including Tyrawley. Thus a significant proportion of the possessions and income that had once belonged to the *derbfine* (the patrilineal family group, extending back four generations, who had collectively held the lands of the territory) of the Bourke septs had in one stroke been effectively signed over to Richard and his heirs.

Bernadette Cunningham states that the 1585 Composition had the opposite effect of that intended and merely underpinned the position that the great lords had occupied previously, central to this being extensive lands free of Composition rents.[18] The rent charges in lieu of traditional exactions also ensured this position. The great magnates, Richard FitzOliverus included, therefore had an interest in the maintenance of peace in Mayo, the smooth operation of the Composition and the collection of its rents. Adherence to the Composition had made Richard FitzOliverus and his heirs some of the wealthiest and most powerful individuals in Mayo, despite the loss of titles and traditional exactions. Richard FitzOliverus, however, appears to have died shortly after the Composition in late 1585, the benefits of his foresight passing on to his son William.[19]

On the basis of the above, one could surmise that Richard FitzOliverus was an astute, far-sighted man determined to propel his immediate heirs and sept into a profitable and prestigious position above the other Bourke septs of Mayo. He may well have recognised the potential impact of advanced English administration and sought to salvage the MacWilliamship for his own sept. As a result of his actions, Richard and his immediate heirs enjoyed the possessions, wealth and power that the MacWilliamship title previously bestowed. It could also be surmised, however, that his manoeuvrings contributed to the poor economic conditions of the other Bourke septs in Mayo, which may have contributed to their revolts in the latter stages of the sixteenth century. His actions also ensured that his descendants served the crown in order to support their position. For instance, his grandson is recorded as having served Elizabeth I at the battle of Kinsale in 1601, when members of his own sept aligned themselves with the Gaelic confederacy.[20] It would appear that Richard FitzOliverus had achieved his objectives in making his sept and descendants some of the most powerful individuals in Mayo up to the 1641 rising.

Notes

1 N. O'Muraile (ed. & trans.), *Leabhar mór na ngenealach: The great book of Irish genealogies* (5 vols, Dublin, 2003–4), iii, p. 117 (801.1).

2 H.T. Knox, *The history of the county of Mayo* (Dublin, 2000), appendix x, table 1.

3 Divisions of Connaught and Thomond, Lambeth Palace Library, Carew MS 611, p. 234. See also D. Keenan, 'A case study of tower houses in County Mayo' (unpublished MA thesis, University College Dublin, 2012), p. 49.

4 *Calendar of state papers relating to Ireland* [hereafter *CSPI*], *1574–1585*, p. 222, no. 8, 9 May 1580.

5 Ibid., p. 270, no. 55, 24 November 1580.

6 Ibid., p. 294, nos 42 & 42.1, 23 March 1581.

7 Ibid., p. 372, no. 90, 28 May 1582.

8 Ibid., p. 397, no. 38, 12 September 1582.

9 Ibid., p. 379, no. 37, 21 June 1582.

10 Ibid., p. 443, no. 46, 30 April 1583.

11 Ibid., p. 477, no. 58, 7 November 1583.

12 C. Lennon, *Sixteenth-century Ireland: the incomplete conquest* (Dublin, 2005), p. 240.

13 B. Cunningham, 'The composition of Connacht in the lordships of Clanricard and Thomond 1577–

1641', *Irish Historical Studies* 24 (1984), p. 1.

[14] *The compossicion booke of Conought*, ed. A.M. Freeman (Dublin, 1936), p. 99.

[15] Cunningham, 'The composition of Connacht', p. 3.

[16] Ibid., p. 4.

[17] Ibid., p. 6 (quotation).

[18] Ibid., p. 5.

[19] Knox, *The history of the county of Mayo*, p. 207.

[20] *CSPI, 1601–3*, p. 321, no. 55, 9 March 1602.

9

Resurrecting an ancient chief

Gerry Moloney
(2014 prize)

On the first day of summer 1639, a 'wild goose' in Brussels passed away somewhat unexpectedly and was interred in the Church of St Gudula in that city.[1] His resting place and that of his noble wife, Marie Hannedouche, is now no longer marked, owing to reconstructions of the church in the intervening centuries, but a plaque still on the column of St John the Apostle within the church—now called the Cathedral of St Michael and St Gudula—records his interment there.

His name was Dermot O'Mallun and he was the last Irish-born chief of the O'Molony sept of Thomond. He was born *c.* 1570, about 30 years before the English finally gained the decisive victory at Kinsale and outlawed the Irish system of

Epitaph of Dermot O'Mallun on the pillar of St John the Apostle in the Cathedral of St Michael and St Gudula in Brussels, where Dermot was interred in 1639. (Copyright: Église et Tourisme Bruxelles/Kerk en Toerisme Brussel)

chieftaincy forever. He was forced to flee Ireland at the age of fifteen to the safety of Flanders,[2] probably in the aftermath of the second Desmond rebellion led by his kinsman Gerald Fitzgerald, the 15th earl of Desmond, his flight almost certainly being assisted by two other kinsmen, the two bishops of Killaloe, Malachy O'Molony and Cornelius Mulryan.

The events that led to the flight of this particular 'goose' centre around the bishopric of Killaloe and the Desmond rebellions. A brief glance at these events and the relevant characters gives some background insight into why flight to Flanders became his lot. Malachy O'Molony, a kinsman of the O'Molony chief and of noble birth, as represented by Cardinal Morono,[3] was appointed bishop of Killaloe in 1571 before being transferred to Kilmacduagh in 1576. He was already a suspect of the English and well known to them: he had been incarcerated in Marshallsea prison in London for eighteen months around 1570 but had escaped.[4] He lived in Limerick in the late 1500s and died in 1603 in the house of Conor MacBrody,[5] husband of his niece Margaret O'Molony, a sister of John O'Molony. This John, written of by James Hogan,[6] was at the time studying at the Sorbonne, where he held the chair of philosophy in 1615 and was later procurator of the *Nation d'Allemagne*.[7] Later still, in 1630, John would himself become bishop of Killaloe and would die during the Cromwellian siege of Limerick in 1651.[8]

Malachy was followed directly in the Killaloe bishopric by Dermot's uncle, Cornelius O'Mulryan, son of the chief of Owney, who held the bishopric until his death in 1617 in Lisbon. Cornelius was a particularly avid supporter of the earl of Desmond and a staunch enemy of Queen Elizabeth. In 1579 he was attempting to bring foreign aid to Desmond from Lisbon, where he had a ship and 300 soldiers ready to sail.[9] His being in regular contact with Rome, too, obviously didn't endear him to the ruling powers.[10] He was Dermot's uncle by virtue of his sister Una O'Mulryan's marriage to Dermot's father, Rory. Another sister, Honora, was married to Sir John Burke, who defied Elizabeth by supporting the earl of Desmond and had his lands laid waste by Sir George Carew, president of Munster.[11] Sir John, therefore, was a first cousin of Dermot's. Refusing to renounce his 'popish' religion, he was hanged on 20 October 1607. Burke's stepbrother Piers de Lacy, a stepcousin of Dermot's, was an active confederate soldier of James Fitzmaurice in the rebellions. The earl of Desmond himself, also a kinsman, had of course been killed by Elizabethan forces in 1583 to end the second Desmond rebellion. The earl's nephew, James Fitzthomas Fitzgerald, also Dermot's kinsman, died in the Tower of London and was likely buried in the chapel there in 1608.[12]

It is clear, then, that neither Dermot nor those writing in his support in Europe were exaggerating in claiming that his family had had their lands confiscated in Ireland, having taken up arms against England, that many had also lost their lives and that he himself had been forced to flee at fifteen years of age.

The ancient sept lands of the O'Molonys are located in the barony of Tulla, especially Kiltanonlea, now Doonass,[13] about halfway between Limerick and Killaloe. The lands border the shores of the River Shannon around where Doonass demesne is today and not far downriver from the ancient military headquarters of Brian Boru. The sept lands, consisting of at least thirteen quarters (2,080 acres) spread across the townlands of Doonass, Clonfada, Garanboy, Fenlemor, Gleanomalun and others, were transferred to Donogh O'Brien, earl of Thomond, in September 1606, the transactions being made by three leading men of the O'Molony sept.[14] At that time, however, Dermot had been in Spanish Flanders for approximately two decades and was unaware of the transactions.

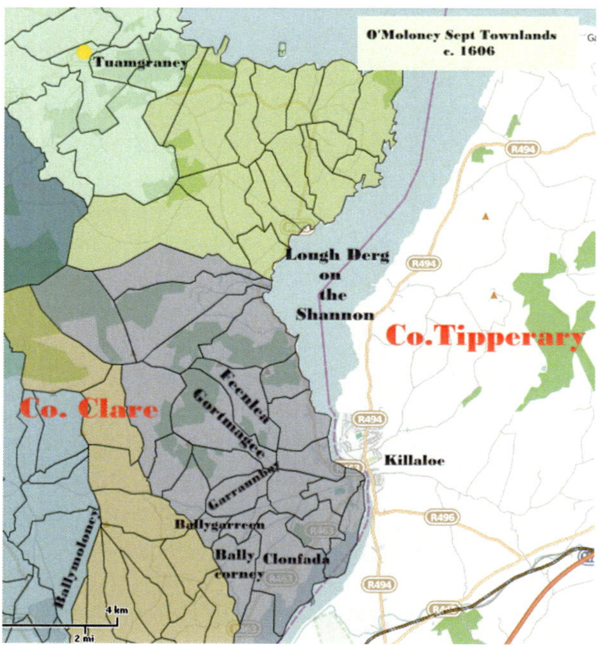

Townlands of the O'Moloney sept c. 1606.

Twenty-five years later, in 1631, by letter from Brussels, Dermot successfully renegotiated the return of the same O'Molony sept lands from Barnaby O'Brien, Donogh's son,[15] and in the English language too, in which he had little skill, by his own admission. The correspondence indicates that the earl of Thomond himself was also a relative of Dermot's, probably by virtue of his paternal grandmother Margarita O'Brien. The 1631 letter to Barnaby lists the lands which belonged to the sept and outlines the circumstances in which they had been transferred in 1606. Barnaby readily agreed to return the lands and, while noting that he was sure that his own father Donogh had dealt honourably with the O'Molonys back in 1606, he stipulated a price of £800 for their return. A legal contract transferring all the lands to Dermot for a price of £2,000 as the 'head and supreme of their sept' was drawn up by ten members of the O'Molony sept.[16]

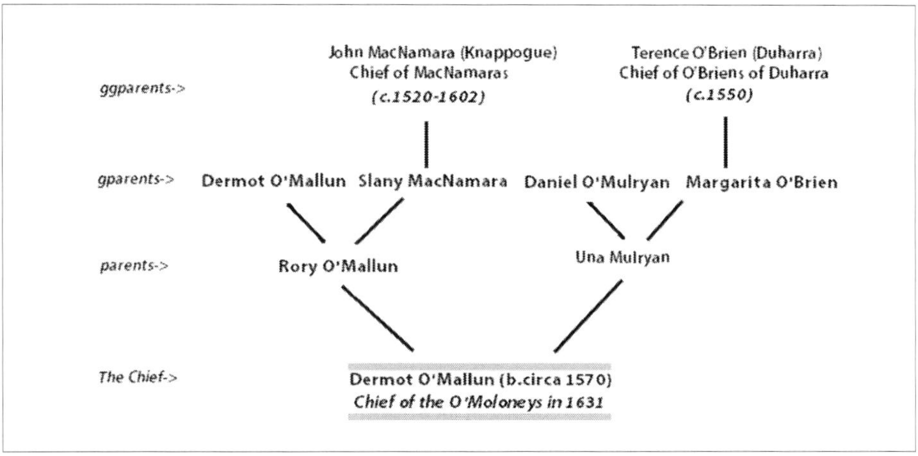

Genealogy of Dermot O'Mallun, showing connections to the chiefs of the Mulryans and the O'Briens.

By the time Dermot renegotiated the land transactions with Barnaby in 1631, however, he had gained much experience on the Continent in law and other matters. After his escape to Flanders, he enrolled in Law in the University of Douai, where he studied for twelve years.[17] In Douai he encountered Marie 'Dite De Hunctun' de Hannedouche, dame de Haguerne,[18] daughter of Sebastien Hannedouche, seigneur de La Haye, whom he married around 1610.[19] The Hannedouches were one of the many noble families of Flanders, and Dermot, Hugh Albert O'Donnell, Thomas Preston and others 'found brides in the Netherlands nobility'. Dermot's father-in-law was a man of standing in Flanders and with his support Dermot applied for legal positions in Douai and surrounding towns. Several correspondences to the Archduke Albert around this time are informative of Dermot's Irish past.[20] Sebastien wrote to Albert in support of Dermot on 6 March 1611, while the archbishop of Cashel, Dave Kearney, similarly wrote on 16 March and Christopher Cusack on 20 March. These letters show that Dermot's family possessions in Ireland had been confiscated and that he had come to Flanders over twenty years previously. He had already been in the archduke's employ for twenty years when the letters were written, was a licentiate in law, and was of such standing and character that he was suitable for any position for which the archduke would consider him. Furthermore, the letters confirm that the archbishop of Killaloe, Cornelius Mulryan, was his uncle.

To further consolidate their positions as persons of entitlement, many Irish applied for admittance to the Order of Calatrava, a military order of Spain. So it was with Dermot, as with Dermot O'Sullivan Beare, Hugh O'Donnell, Hugh O'Neill and others.[21] Admittance to one of these orders was not a trivial matter, as applicants were required to prove their suitability and to provide their genealogical credentials. The documents had to be submitted to an examining commission and the admission process could be lengthy. Dermot, however, was admitted in 1616, being sponsored by Donnacha O'Cleary, among others. His admission documents are still in the Archivo Histórico Nacional in Madrid, and clearly show his descent from other Irish sept leaders, including Torlough O'Brien, John McNamara and Daniel O'Mulryan. [22]

With a membership in the Knights of Calatrava under his belt, Dermot soon found favour with King James of England, who by letters patent on 5 October 1622 created him 'Baron of Glenomallun and Courchy' for life, with remainder to his son Albert O'Mallun and 'heirs male of his body'.[23] The Infanta Isabella used her influence in this regard too.[24] 'Courchy', however, is almost certainly a misprint or translation error in various documents and should be Quinche or Quinchy,[25] as it is in some documents, or, as in older Irish, Cuinché.[26] This is the modern parish of Quin or the 'barony of Quincé'. Indeed, Dermot's grandmother, Slany MacNamara, hailed from Knappogue (*Cnapóg* in Irish) in Quin, [27] which is probably the reason for its inclusion in the created title.

A series of correspondences between 1609 and 1631 reinforce for us Dermot's position in Flanders at the time and his past in Ireland. From Douai he wrote to the Archduke Albert on 12 August 1609, looking for the vacant post of bailiff of Douai and saying how he had to support two Irish students studying in the university. In a series of letters in 1618, referred to by Margaret MacCurtain in *Women in early modern Ireland*, he wrote how his loss of pension affected his ability to support his family and oversee his affairs.[28] In 1621 he wrote to the pope seeking a recommendation to the king of Spain. In the same year Lucio Sanseverino, internuncio at Brussels, corresponded with Cardinal Borghese in favour of 'Dermicius'. In that year also Dermot assisted at the funeral of Archduke Albert, who died on 13 July, as a conductor of the Cheval de Jouste.[29] On 24 February 1622 the Infanta Isabella wrote to Jehan de Pretz, treasurer of the Domains, ordering him to pay 200 florins, his yearly pension, to Dermot. On 4 September Count Gondomar corresponded with Isabella about Dermot.[30] In October 1623 George Chaworth, writing to the duke of Buckingham looking for a favour, used Dermot as an example of one who had 'obtained a title of honour' in Ireland through the influence of the Infanta.[31] In July 1626 Isabella instructed Diego de Messia to further the pension case of Dermot Omalun with his majesty. On 30 March 1629 a grant of 200 crowns yearly, for a further three years, was given to Baron Omalun (Albert), son of Dermot, 'lord and peer of the kingdom of Ireland, knight of the Order of Calatrava, and equerry to the Archduchess'. Again, on 29 May 1630 there are orders for the payment of 300 livres to Baron Gleanomalun. Finally, we see Dermot's son Albert writing on 6 November 1631 with these words: 'Albert Baron d'Omalun, godson of her Highness, son of the Baron of Gleanomalun and Guerchy, represents that although his Majesty, in consideration of the confiscation of his estates and baronies because his family had taken up arms against England . . .'—once again confirming the confiscation of Dermot's estates in Ireland.[32]

In family life Dermot was also active and had issue. Seven offspring were named Albert, Francis, Anne-Marie, Maria, Elizabeth, Jeanne and Isabella.[33] By 1631 Albert is being referred to as 'Dermot's only son', so it seems that Francis died between 1622 and 1631, as both had received letters of denizenship in 1622. Albert's son, called Dermot after his grandfather, sat in the Patriot Parliament of 1689 under the title 'Baron of Glenmalicre and Courchy', where, however, his name is erroneously spelt as Dermot Malune.[34] Anne-Marie, born in 1612, married Jacques de Quarré, seigneur de la Haye, in 1635 and had issue. Isabella became a nun of the Order of St Benedict at Arras.

The O'Molony surname, along with the more modern variants Moloney, Maloney and Mullowney, all derive from the Gaelic Ó Maol Domhnaigh, meaning 'descendant of a servant of Sunday'. The 'e' was inserted in the Molony surname in the 1700s to distinguish Catholic Molonys from their Protestant brethren. Omallun is another variant seen in the Petworth Archives and other documents. Dermot's Christian name, an Anglicised version of Diarmuid, was a common Anglicisation in the 1600s. Later it was more common to translate Diarmuid as Jeremiah—hence the 21st-century version of Dermot O'Mallun's name would probably be Jeremiah Moloney.

In conclusion, then, Dermot's main life events can be summarised as follows: Irish birth in the 1570s about the time of the Desmond rebellions, escape to Flanders in the 1580s, employment with Archduke Albert and the Infanta Isabella in the 1590s, legal studies in the University of Douai in the 1600s, marriage into Flanders nobility in 1610 with subsequent issue, admission to the Knights of Calatrava in 1616, creation as Baron Gleanomalun and Cuinché in 1622, recovery of the O'Molony lands in Clare in 1631, and finally death on 1 May 1639 with subsequent interment in Brussels. And so it can be seen that it is indeed possible to resurrect the life of a forgotten chief to an amazingly detailed degree, despite initial apparent absence of reference or record. Furthermore, on examination of his genealogical lines, it is now also possible to identify authentic living male descendants of Dermot—ready and willing to take up a rightful place on the modern Council of Irish Chiefs. Then might the spirit of Dermot O'Mallun, the last known Irish-born chief of the O'Molonys, be truly said to be resurrected. That, however, is a story for another day.

Notes

1 *Basilica Bruxellensis sive monumenta antiqua inscriptiones, et Coenotaphia . . .* (1743), p. 119; http://books.google.ie/books?id=6VZbAAAAQAAJ&pg=PA119&lpg=PA119&dq=don+dermicio+omallun&source=bl&ots=_Sm9kU-oIx&sig=Gt2jp0rCxqEiqU-lGGYn8ybaHJ4&hl=en&sa=X&ei=70gpU8P_OIu3hAeF0YCQBA&ved=0CDwQ6AEwBQ#v=onepage&q=don%20dermicio%20omallun&f=false (accessed December 2017).

2 B. Jennings (ed.), *Wild geese in Spanish Flanders, 1582–1700* (Dublin, 1964), p. 183; http://www.

irishmanuscripts.ie/digital/Wild%20Geese%20in%20Spanish%20Flanders%201582-1700/data/search.xml.

3 J. Frost, *The history and topography of the county of Clare, from the earliest times to the beginning of the 18th century* (Dublin, 1893), pp 162–3; http://www.clarelibrary.ie/eolas/coclare/history/frost/chap10_st_flannan.htm (accessed December 2017).

4 P. White, *History of Clare and the Dalcassian clans of Tipperary, Limerick, and Galway* (Dublin, 1893), pp 187–8; https://archive.org/details/historyofclareda00whit (accessed December 2017).

5 Frost, *History and topography of Co. Clare*, p. 163.

6 J. Hogan, 'Two bishops of Killaloe and Irish freedom: John O'Molony I (1630–1651)', *Studies: An Irish Quarterly Review* 9 (33) (1920), pp 70–93.

7 R. Hayes, 'Biographical dictionary of Irishmen in France', *Studies: An Irish Quarterly Review* 32 (127) (1943), pp 379–91, at p. 383.

8 W.M. Brady, *The Irish Reformation or the alleged conversion of the Irish bishops at the accession of Queen Elizabeth . . .* (5th edn, London, 1857), pp 144–5; https://archive.org/stream/irishreformation00braduoft/irishreformation00braduoft_djvu.txt (accessed December 2017).

9 R.J. Berleth, *The twilight lords: Elizabeth I and the plunder of Ireland* (revised edn, Lanham, Maryland, 2002), p. 86; http://books.google.ie/books?id=UyE5EiqGeZQC&pg=PA337&lpg=PA337&dq=daniel+o%27mulrian+margaret+o%27brien&source=bl&ots=P16sdS6S72&sig=XpAL0u9slXJE6a9nmofss2rmblo&hl=en&sa=X&ei=loNZU5OzC6aR7AaA6IDICA&ved=0CD8Q6AEwAw#v=onepage&q=O'mulrian&f=false (accessed December 2017).

10 W. Carrigan, *The history and antiquities of the diocese of Ossory* (4 vols, Dublin, 1905), i, p. 74.

11 See http://en.wikipedia.org/wiki/Sir_John_Bourke_of_Brittas (accessed December 2017).

12 See http://en.wikipedia.org/wiki/James_FitzThomas_FitzGerald (accessed December 2017).

13 Kiltonanlea, http://www.irelandxo.com/node/8552 (accessed March 2014; link no longer active).

14 L. McInerney, 'Documents from the Thomond Papers at Petworth House Archive', *Archivium Hibernicum* 63 (2011), 7–55, esp. pp 27–34; http://www.clarelibrary.ie/eolas/coclare/history/images/Thomond_Papers_from_Petworth_House_Archive.pdf.

15 Donough, the fourth earl of Thomond.

16 See note 14 above.

17 Victoria Sandoval Parre, unpublished Ph.D thesis, University of Murcia School of Law.

18 See http://gw.geneanet.org/gerardlpdupon?lang=en;pz=capucine+agnes+rolande;nz=perrier;ocz=0;p=dom+emilio;n=o+mallun (accessed March 2014).

19 J.J. Silke, 'The Irish abroad', in T.W. Moody, F.X. Martin and F.J. Byrne (eds), *A new history of Ireland, iii. Early modern Ireland, 1534–1691* (Oxford, 1991), p. 606.

20 Jennings (ed.), *Wild geese in Spanish Flanders.*

21 Spanish Wild Geese, http://indigo.ie/~wildgees/s-wgeese.htm (accessed December 2017).

22 Archivo Histórico Nacional, Madrid, Knights of Calatrava admission application documents.

23 *Irish patent rolls of James I: facsimile of the Irish record commissioners' calendar prepared prior to 1830*, with foreword by M.C. Griffith (Dublin, 1966), patent rolls 20th, James 1, p. 3, N.29.

24 Letter from Isabel to Conde de Gondomar (De Brusselas 12-II-1622) (Record no. 145178), https://realbiblioteca.patrimonionacional.es/cgi-bin/koha/opac-MARCdetail.pl?biblionumber=145178 (accessed March 2018).

25 N. Carlisle, *A topographical dictionary of Ireland* (London, 1810), under 'Quin, or, Quinchy'.

26 Frost, *History and topography of Co. Clare*, p. 51.

27 Knappogue Castle, http://en.wikipedia.org/wiki/Knappogue_Castle (accessed December 2017).

28 M. MacCurtain and M. O'Dowd (eds), *Women in early modern Ireland* (Dublin, 1991), p. 117.

29 Jean-Chrysostome Puslé de Montpleinchamp, *L'Histoire de l'archiduc Albert, gouverneur général et puis prince souverain de la Belgique* (1693), p. 367; http://books.google.ie/books?id=EAb6__77_2cC&pg=PA367&lpg=PA367&dq=albert+omallun&source=bl&ots=AL4hBD2xc0&sig=AnJ_4rH

bAVpaG1xl1ZyaEEgCYwk&hl=en&sa=X&ei=8F4sU_mID5OUhQfhj4GACw&ved=0CGYQ6AEwCQ#v=onepage&q=albert%20omallun&f=false (accessed December 2017).

30 Terms of Count Gondomar to Archduchess of Austria (London, 9-IV-1622) (Record no. 122054); http://realbiblioteca.patrimonionacional.es/cgi-bin/koha/opac-MARCdetail.pl?biblionumber=122054 (accessed December 2017).

31 A.J. Kempe (ed.), *The Loseley Manuscripts . . .* (London, 1836), p. 468; https://archive.org/stream/loseleymanuscrip00kempuoft/loseleymanuscrip00kempuoft_djvu.txt (accessed December 2017).

32 Jennings (ed.), *Wild geese in Spanish Flanders*, p. 275.

33 Albert O'Mallon; https://histfam.familysearch.org//getperson.php?personID=I158177&tree=Nixon (accessed March 2014; link no longer active).

34 J. D'Alton, *Illustrations, historical and genealogical, of King James's Irish army list, 1689* (Dublin, 1855), p. 692.

10

The unravelling of a Gaelic dynasty, 1446–1690

Eugene McMahon

By the late twelfth century the MacMahons had become the ruling family of Oriel, a kingdom roughly corresponding to present-day County Monaghan. Their dominance of this area continued until the seventeenth century, but long before that the unitary nature of their control had begun to unravel. When the powerful MacMahon chieftain Ruairí Mór died in 1446 he was survived by no less than seventeen sons. Complicating the issue of succession was the Gaelic system of tanistry, which determined inheritance by factors other than primogeniture. Individual ability, power and influence often played the decisive roles in determining who among the family would succeed to the title of 'The MacMahon'.

The MacMahon coat of arms.

Over the following two centuries the chieftainship rotated between the descendants of the three most influential of Ruairí's sons, namely Aodh Rua, Eoghan and Reamonn. The descendants of Aodh became the lords of Farney in the south, those of Eoghan lords of Dartrey in the west and those of Reamonn lords of Lucht-Tighe in the north. This geographic distribution is depicted below, together with that of the principal neighbouring lordships.[1]

As the sixteenth century advanced, this tripartite split ensured that the 'chieftainship' became increasingly nominal in nature, as no one faction proved consistently able to enforce payment of tribute by the others. Attempts by these factions to exact such tribute often entailed cattle raids on each other's territories. In this practice they would sometimes ally themselves with either neighbouring Gaelic lords or the English of the Pale.

Overriding all was the lumbering presence and competing claims to overlordship of the entire clan by both the English authorities in the Pale and the O'Neills of Tyrone. Nevertheless, these external threats were rarely sufficient to cause the MacMahon factions to unite in common cause. Instead, each faction dealt

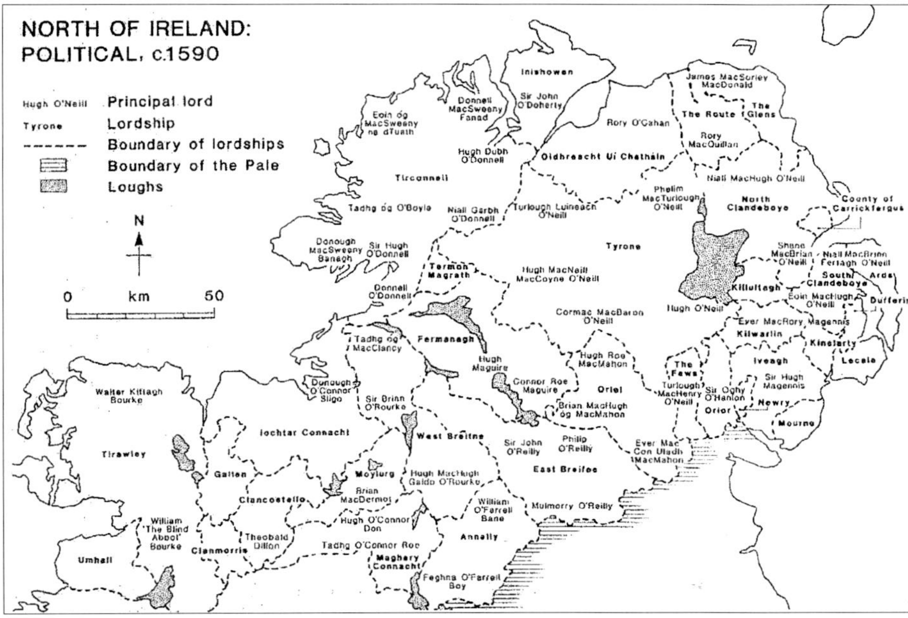

Gaelic chieftaincies in the late Elizabethan period. (After Hiram Morgan, 'Gaelic lordship and Tudor conquest, 1541–1603', *History Ireland* 13 (5) (2005).)

independently with these external powers and was more than ready to play one off against the other.

Ultimately, the greater threat was to emanate from the Pale, given the Tudor monarchy's determination to complete the conquest of Ireland. The various MacMahon lords, however, continued to treat the Pale administration as if it were but another competing lordship, and only belatedly came to recognise the serious threat that it posed to their very survival. Indeed, events following the death of the MacMahon chieftain Sir Ross Buí in 1589 could have left no one in any doubt as to the ambitions of the English administration in Dublin.

Normally, the chieftainship of the MacMahons would have been assumed by the tanist, Sir Brian Mac Aodh Óg of Dartrey. Ignoring this historical convention, Lord Deputy Fitzwilliam embarked instead upon a 'divide and conquer' strategy. This entailed a formal subdivision of all of the MacMahon lands, while providing guarantees of regional inheritance within the narrower framework of primogeniture. Not only would this have set aside the nominal unity of Oriel by abolishing the chieftainship itself but it would also have ended the more communal system of land-holding as practised by the clan. Henceforth all titles to land would be subject to English jurisprudence. Fitzwilliam's scheme soon stalled, however, given that at least four of the MacMahon lords were now laying claim to the chieftainship.

By default, Fitzwilliam opted to grant the chieftainship to Sir Ross Buí's brother, Aodh Rua of Lucht-Tighe. The other MacMahon lords now began to consider the possibility that such an English-appointed 'chieftain' would be deemed (under English law) to hold ultimate title to their own lands. In their eyes, this was clearly worse than Fitzwilliam's original proposal.

Although Aodh Rua was more than willing to avail of Fitzwilliam's support, it came at a steep price—namely, an annual tax of 700 cattle.[2] Aodh Rua, however, was unable to assemble such an exaction, unless he in turn could enforce payment of tribute from the other MacMahon lords, who were now (by virtue of an English fiat) nominally subject to him in his newly acquired role of 'chieftain'. To enforce payment of such tribute, Aodh Rua's forces invaded the lands of Eimhir MacMahon of Farney in 1590, whereupon the Farney MacMahons filed a strong complaint with the lord deputy. And so the trap was duly sprung! Fitzwilliam had Aodh Rua arrested on a trumped-up charge of treason—that he had attacked the queen's loyal subjects. After consulting the privy council, Fitzwilliam escorted Aodh Rua to his stronghold outside Monaghan Abbey. There he was arraigned before a packed jury and hanged from a tree outside his own door.[3]

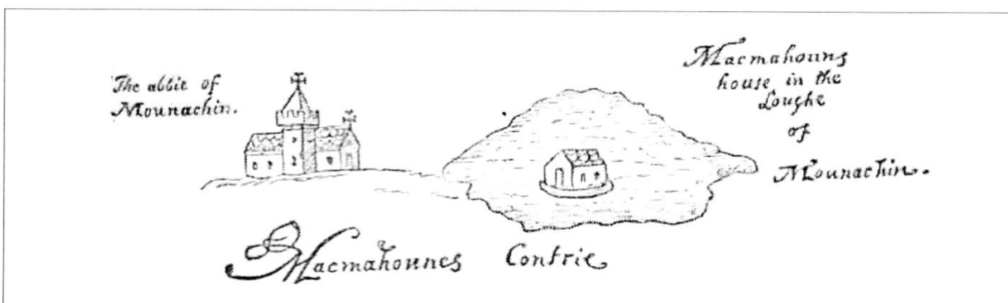

Aodh Rua MacMahon's crannog. (After Denis Carolan Rushe, *Historical sketches of Monaghan* (Dublin, 1895).)

Having deemed their so-called 'chieftain' a traitor, Fitzwilliam now saw his way clear to declaring all of the MacMahon lands forfeit to the crown. He then had these lands officially subdivided in 1591 and regranted to six Gaelic lords of his own choosing, five of whom were MacMahons. The manner in which he had brought this about, however, shocked the MacMahon nobles to the core. Fitzwilliam's treachery had finally convinced them that the lord deputy was bent on destroying their power and independence. Accordingly, most of them now swung their allegiance to Hugh O'Neill, earl of Tyrone, who was himself moving towards open rebellion.[4]

The earl of Tyrone

The long-standing relationship of the MacMahons with the O'Neills of Tyrone was based on a combination of political expediency and blood ties. This dynastic

Hugh O'Neill, Gaelic overlord of Ulster. (After Hiram Morgan, 'Gaelic lordship and Tudor conquest, 1541–1603', *History Ireland* **13** (5) (2005).)

connection was now further reinforced through the marriage of the earl's daughter, Máire, to Sir Brian MacAodh Óg, lord of Dartrey. By 1594 O'Neill had also proclaimed Sir Brian as clan chieftain, and this further cemented their alliance against the forces of the crown.

The ensuing Nine Years War saw a long and initially successful campaign by the Gaelic nobility of Ulster to preserve their lands, prerogatives, religion and culture. This winning streak ended in 1601, however, when the Gaelic forces were routed at the battle of Kinsale. Nevertheless, following the peace settlement of 1603, land ownership in Oriel was settled along lines similar to those previously imposed in 1591. In Dartrey, Sir Brian MacMahon was left in possession of 5,000 acres 'in respect of his dependencie in the country and hope of loyalty to her majesty'.[5] Meanwhile, in Farney Eimhir MacMahon remained as the dominant landholder, albeit on a leasehold basis from the earl of Essex.

Disregarding the terms of the peace settlement, English officials soon began to use whatever legal pretexts were available in order to chip away at the existing land titles and prerogatives of the native nobility. Both their power and their very sense of security were fast ebbing away from the Gaelic lords of Ulster. Finally, in a desperate attempt to secure Spanish assistance, the chief lords among them sailed for the Continent in 1607.[6]

Hugh O'Neill and Rory O'Donnell being rowed by some of their followers from the port of Rathmullan, Co. Donegal, to board their ship for Spain. (Drawing by Seán Ó Brógáin at http://www.askaboutireland.ie/learning-zone/secondary-students/history/tudor-ireland/the-flight-of-the-earls-1/)

The Flight of the Earls left a political vacuum throughout most of Ulster, with the exception of Monaghan, as the MacMahon lords had not joined in the Flight. At the time, it was observed that Sir Brian 'is best followed of any man in the country, and it were well he were not discontented',[7] and yet 'he will not stir unless there be a general revolt'.[8] Of course, any realistic prospect for such a 'general revolt' was entirely dependent on the earls returning in force with Spanish assistance.

In truth, effective political power in Monaghan had been lost by the former ruling family, and the MacMahons were now increasingly hard-pressed to maintain their economic status. Although Monaghan was largely spared the outright confiscations inflicted on much of Ulster, the MacMahons resented their loss of privilege as the natural ruling class. They objected even more to the heavy taxation required to pay for the newly imposed systems of administration and jurisprudence. In order to raise the cash entailed by these new obligations, many of them now had to mortgage much of their land. Indeed, over the following generation, the percentage of land in Monaghan (excepting Farney) still owned by those of Gaelic heritage declined from 78% to 55%.[9]

Because of their more southerly location, the Farney MacMahons had become increasingly Anglicised, although their living conditions did not necessarily match

The three-legged 'Tyburn Tree' (https://en.wikipedia.org/wiki/Tyburn).

those of the neighbouring Pale. In 1612 their houses were described as being 'of no reckoning, but for the most part built of roddes and covered with turves'.[10] With Eimhir's death in 1617 their situation deteriorated further, as Essex began to divide Farney up into smaller leaseholds.

When Sir Brian died in 1622 the title of chieftain died with him, in legal if not moral terms. His youngest son, Aodh Óg, eventually returned from service with the Spanish army to claim his inheritance. As a grandson of Hugh O'Neill and son of Sir Brian, Aodh Óg was very conscious of his noble heritage. In his own eyes, at least, he was now 'The MacMahon'.

Aodh Óg was soon drawn into plans for rebellion by the disaffected Gaelic lords of Ulster. He and Lord Maguire were assigned the task of seizing Dublin Castle. On the eve of the rebellion in 1641, however, they were arrested and imprisoned in the Tower of London. Two years later they managed to escape and went into hiding in the city. They were soon betrayed by their distinctive accents, re-arrested, tried for treason and hanged at Tyburn.[11]

Despite this setback the rebellion had gone ahead, and the pent-up fury of the dispossessed Gaelic gentry had led to the forcible ejection of the Protestant population from 'planted' lands throughout Ulster. In the aftermath, depositions by these ousted British colonists provided evidence of the many discontented MacMahons who had led factions in that disorganised uprising. These records contain accusations against 62 individuals from all three of the MacMahon factions.[12] This certainly indicated a widespread resentment of their lost status as the principal family of Monaghan.

During the subsequent Confederation Wars of the 1640s, the Gaelic forces of Ulster were commanded by Eoghan Rua O'Neill, nephew of the Great Earl and first cousin of Sir Brian MacMahon's wife. Meanwhile, two other prominent MacMahons, Bishop Eimhir of Farney and Colla Mac Brian of Cremorne, served on the Supreme Council of the Confederation in Kilkenny.[13] When Eoghan Rua died in 1649, the leadership of his army was assumed by Bishop Eimhir. The tide of war had turned by then, however, and Eimhir was captured and executed in 1650.

Following the defeat of the Gaelic forces, large acreages of MacMahon land were awarded to demobilised Cromwellian troops, many of whom then sold the land on to their officers. Meanwhile, the population had severely declined owing to famine and conflict throughout the previous decade. By 1659 the recorded population in County Monaghan was down to 4,084 heads of households, with 11% of these being British.[14] The resultant scarcity of labour allowed the MacMahons to remain on the land, albeit mostly as subtenants of smaller holdings. By 1663, when the Hearth Rolls listed the owners of the better class of houses, only 94 were MacMahons, with this number declining to 82 by 1665.[15] Rushe gives a greater total of 158, but this is likely a combination of the two poll totals, while making allowance for some double counting. That being said, Rushe also advances the plausible argument that the number of MacMahons being polled was undoubtedly greater still, given that many resorted to using their immediate patronymics, such as McArdle, McHugh, McAghey and others.[16]

The restoration of the monarchy in 1660 did nothing to slow down the confiscation of MacMahon land. In 1667, for instance, a royal grant of 4,150 acres in Dartrey was made to one Richard Dawson.[17] Fully half of the former fourteen owners of Dawson's acreage were prominent MacMahons, who were now expected to continue to farm the land but as tenants paying rent to their newly imposed British landlord.

In these reduced circumstances, what was left of the MacMahon élite was best represented by Colla Dubh MacMahon, who managed to retain significant leaseholds in Dartrey. As Colla Dubh's family tree below indicates, not only was he descended from the fifteenth-century MacMahon chieftain Ruairí Mór but his wife was a daughter of 'The O'Reilly' and a niece of Eoghan Rua O'Neill.[18] Here was royalty indeed, if such had still existed in Gaelic society!

Colla Dubh had inherited the lingering social status that had previously belonged to his cousin, Sir Brian. Colla's prestige was further buttressed in clerical terms by his brother, Arthur Augustine of Louvain, and later by his son, Hugh, the archbishop (primate) of Armagh. Yet Colla Dubh was thoroughly pragmatic when it came to matters of religion versus economic survival. Indeed, in his role as landlord he collected tithes for the established Anglican Church! Nevertheless, when the opportunity again arose to right past wrongs, two of Colla Dubh's sons, Padraig and Brian, fought and died in the Jacobite Wars.[19]

The Jacobite sympathies of the wider family were also evident in the fielding of two 'MacMahon Regiments' in 1689, as well as in the participation of two

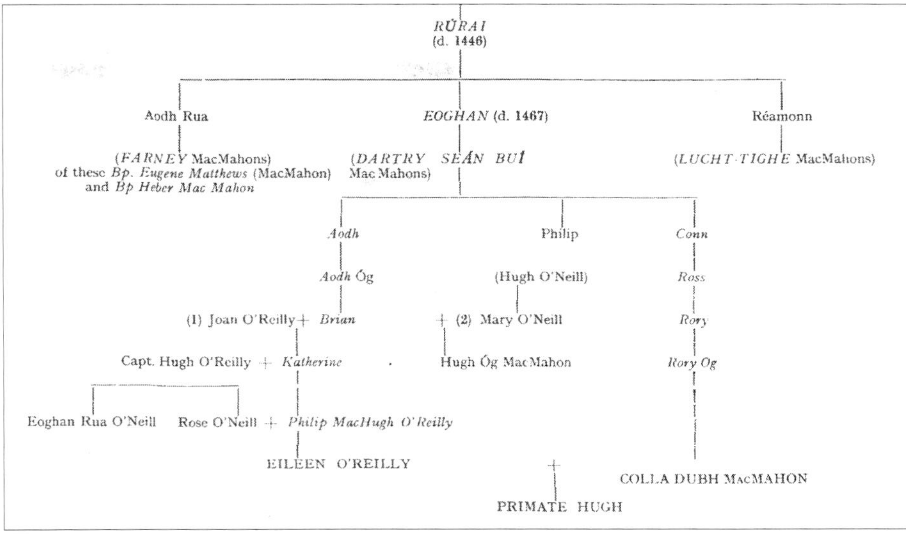

Colla Dubh MacMahon's dynastic pedigree. (After Laurence J. Flynn, 'Hugh MacMahon, bishop of Clogher 1707–15 and archbishop of Armagh 1715–1737', *Seanchas Ardmhacha: Journal of the Armagh Diocesan Historical Society* 7 (1) (1973).)

prominent MacMahons, Brian and Lt. Col. Hugh, in the Patriot Parliament that same year.[20] Indeed, it was hoped that this Jacobite parliament in Dublin would restore at least some of their lost birthright, but the Williamite victory soon decisively quashed any lingering hopes of reinstatement for the MacMahons of Oriel/Monaghan. What had once been a prominent Gaelic dynasty had been ultimately reduced, through both internal division and external assault, to a fading collective memory.

The putative MacMahon 'chieftaincy' devolved through four distinct, parallel lines of descent from Colla Dubh. The last historical references to these occurred in 1723, 1759, 1885 and 1892 respectively. Nevertheless, given that Ruairí Mór had seventeen sons and his own father, Ardghal, had thirteen, many other lines of direct descent from the former kings of Oriel clearly must exist and are simply awaiting discovery. With this in mind, the McMahon Surname Project is currently correlating the DNA records of those having the 'Colla gene', which purportedly traces the McMahon family's royal origins back to the fourth century.

Notes

1 H. Morgan, 'Gaelic lordship and Tudor conquest: Tír Eoghain, 1541–1603', *History Ireland* 13 (5) (2005), p. 2.

2 P. Mac Duinnshléibhe, 'The legal murder of Aodh Rua McMahon, 1590', *Clogher Record* 1 (3) (1955), pp 33–52.

3 D.C. Rushe, *Historical sketches of Monaghan: from the earliest times to the Fenian movement* (Dublin, 1895), pp 11–12.

[4] 'Plantations of Ireland' on Wikipedia: https://en.wikipedia.org/wiki/Plantations_of_Ireland.

[5] P. Livingstone, *The Monaghan story: a documented history of the County Monaghan from the earliest times to 1976* (Clogher Historical Society, 1980), p. 101; Mac Duinnshléibhe, 'The legal murder of Aodh Rua McMahon', p. 50.

[6] J. Bardon, *A history of Ulster* (Belfast, 1992), pp 116–17.

[7] D.M. Schlegel, 'Sir Brian and Lady Mary MacMahon', *Clogher Record* **15** (3) (1996), p. 141.

[8] Ibid., pp 133–44.

[9] Livingstone, *The Monaghan story*, p. 102.

[10] P.J. Duffy, 'Social and spatial order in the MacMahon lordship of Airghialla in the late sixteenth century', in P.J. Duffy, D. Edwards and E. FitzPatrick (eds), *Gaelic Ireland c.1250–c.1650: land, lordship and settlement* (Dublin, 2004), pp 115–37.

[11] P. Ó Mórdha, 'The MacMahons of Monaghan', *Clogher Record* **2** (1) (1957), p. 496.

[12] There may have been some overlapping of accounts, whereby individual MacMahon participants in the rebellion were named more than once.

[13] Livingstone, *The Monaghan story*, p. 117.

[14] Ibid., p. 124.

[15] D.C. Rushe, *History of Monaghan for 200 years, 1660–1860* (Dublin, 1921), pp 291–338; and http://www.failteromhat.com/monaghanhearth.php.

[16] Rushe, *History of Monaghan*, p. 21.

[17] J. Brown, 'Dartrey: the rise and fall of an Irish estate', *Clogher Record* **18** (2) (2004), pp 269–78.

[18] L.J. Flynn, 'Hugh MacMahon, bishop of Clogher 1707–15 and archbishop of Armagh 1715–37', *Seanchas Ardmhacha: Journal of the Armagh Diocesan Historical Society* **7** (1) (1973), 108–75.

[19] P.B. Ó Mórdha, 'Colla Dubh MacMahon, his ancestors and descendants', *Clogher Record* **8** (2) (1974), 194–206.

[20] T. Davis, *The Patriot Parliament of 1689* (London, 1893), p. 166.

Part III: Church, culture and craftwork

11
'From the cattle run to the Woods of Cluain': a king's circuit and the birth of an archdiocese

Ruairí Ó hAodha

Tuam owes its significance to its long history as an episcopal centre. Although it had been a noted monastic site since the 700s, an analysis of place-names in the native annals suggests that its choice as a metropolitan see in the twelfth century was no foregone conclusion but the result of a near-fatal attack on a young Irish king in the year 1115.

The victories of Brian Boru, which weakened the six-century domination of the Uí Néill over the northern half of the country, arguably played a role in stalling the emergence of a centralised monarchy in Ireland. His descendants were to reach impressive heights, but Brian's achievement served primarily to prove that Ulster was not invincible and that the crown of Ireland was there for the taking.[1] In the years before the Anglo-Norman settlement the country was given an alternative choice, and from an unexpected quarter, when Tairrdelbach Ua Conchobair inherited the title of king of Connacht. It was Tairrdelbach's grandfather who had asserted their family's influence throughout much of the west of Ireland, reducing the claim of the Uí Ruairc of Breifne to east Connacht and driving the Uí Briuin Seola (O'Flaherty)

Detail from the base of the Tuam market cross (after George Petrie, *Christian inscriptions in the Irish language* (1878)).

out of the great plain surrounding Tuam. With the gift of hindsight, the Four Masters referred to Tairrdelbach as 'the high-tide of national glory and splendour',[2] but the earliest account of his life is preserved in the much earlier Annals of Tigernach, which first began to be compiled in eleventh-century Clonmacnoise.[3] Their bias in his favour aside, they depict a man who made astute alliances to advance his cause, acquiescing to Ulster and concentrating his ambitions on subjugating the O'Briens of Munster.[4] Much of the late medieval art and archaeology of south Connacht—the Cross of Cong, the Romanesque cathedral and high crosses of Tuam—is a legacy of his patronage.[5] He was, however, overly violent and often failed to capitalise on victories, retreating as soon as tribute was given and using hostage exchange as his primary means of control.[6]

Tairrdelbach succeeded his father Ruaidhrí and took to the field in 1114, at the age of 26. He almost did not make it, as the following year he was the subject of a 'murderous' attack. He was so badly injured that the Annals of Loch Cé describe him as having been in *cru lige* (a 'gore bed'). Within a year, however, he recovered and came out fighting with a renewed sense of purpose. He made a pilgrimage to and bestowed thanksgiving gifts on the church of Clonmacnoise, before assembling a fleet to raid Limerick. He then marched an army into the midlands, where he divided the kingdom of Meath between the two sons of local dynast Domhnall Ua Maeleachlainn. According to the *Chronicon Scottorum* and the Annals of Tigernach, he was attacked by three of his own kin, and from the account of the episode recounted in the Annals of Ulster we know that he was attacked at a place named Áth (m)Bó.[7]

This name appears once again in a two-line reference to Tairrdelbach in the Annals of Tigernach for 1127. A brief but detailed entry, it has, perhaps through a lack of topographical investigation, been somewhat misunderstood. The episode in question recounts Tairrdelbach's granting of specific royal demesne lands (*ferainn*) to

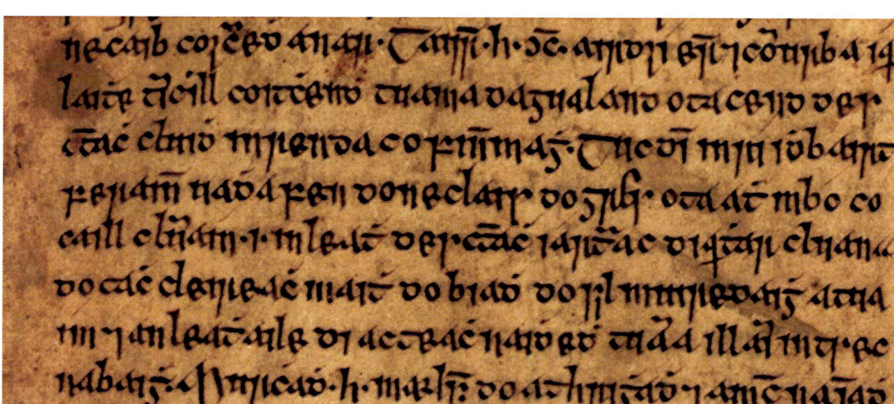

Detail from MS Rawlinson B 488, fol. 21v (Bodleian Libraries, University of Oxford).

the local church, following the proposal of Tuam as a diocese in 1111.[8] The entry does mark a new beginning, as a distinction is made within it between the older Christian community of Tuam, dating back to the eighth century, and the establishment of the town as a diocesan see, in line with the eleventh- and twelfth-century Gregorian reforms.[9] The Annals of Tigernach are best preserved today in a manuscript in the Bodleian Library, Oxford (MS Rawlinson B 488), and the passage in question is from folio 21 verso:

> Tairr.h.óc.airdrí erri 7 comurba íairlaithe timchill coitchend tuamadagualand ota cend desertach cluidh inrenda co finnmagh. Tuc di in rí iaidhbairt ferainn uadha fen don eclais do greas otá ath mbo co caill clumain .i. inleath desceach iarthac diaithar cluana do cach clerieach maith do biadh do silmuiredaigh atuaim 7 an leathaile di acteach na aidheadh tuama illaim in tseacnabaigh.[10]

It has been translated as:

> Toirdhealbhach Ó Conchobhair, overking of Ireland, and the successor of St Iarlaithe surround the (common) of Tuam from the southern end of Clad in Renda to Findmag. Then the king gave an offering of land from himself to the church in perpetuity from Áth mBó to Caill Clumain, that is, the south-western half of the western part of Cluain, to every good cleric of the Síol Muireadhaigh who should dwell in Tuam, and the other half of it, at the guesthouse of Tuam, into the hands of the prior.[11]

The passage has since been interpreted to infer that what was being described here was a short royal procession of sorts, in which the king and clergy traced out an area co-extensive with the current site of St Mary's Cathedral, or at most the extent of Tuam town.[12] Recent studies have also argued that the act marked the official handing over of the bishopric of Tuam to Ua Conchobair's Síol Muireadaigh allies, the O'Duffys, the 'archbishop of Connacht' then being Domhnall Ua Dubhthaigh (d. 1136).[13] Taking the word *coitchinn* in its wider sense ('general, whole, total'), however, *timchill coitchend tuamadagualand* might better be translated as meaning 'the king and comharb's circuit of all of (the lands/diocese of) Tuam'.[14]

Rawlinson B 488 states that the area in question extended from the 'southern head' of 'cluidh inrenda co finnmagh'. This suggests *clúid an reanna* ('the corner of the point'). An example that survived into modern times that suggests itself is Cluidranhy.[15] It is located exactly on the Galway boundary with Mayo, in Cappanacreha townland, on the western shore of Lough Mask. The south-eastern corner of this townland—perhaps the *cend desertach* referred to—forms a small rectangular point that juts into the lake.[16] The location of *Finnmagh* ('white plain')

Cluidh in renda—Cluidranhy on the Galway–Mayo border (© Ordnance Survey Ireland/Government of Ireland).

is well attested in the life of St Patrick written by the Tirawley native Tirechán in the latter half of the seventh century. It lay roughly twenty miles from Cluidranhy, as the crow flies, and was the location of a holy well, Slán Phádraic, which was until Reformation times the name for the modern parish of Manulla, near present-day Castlebar.[17] Following a retreat on Croagh Patrick, the saint performed a miracle before the local population, uncovering a spring that they had long revered as the abode of a deity, 'the king of the waters'.[18] Finnmagh, therefore, is the plain that long after marked the northern boundary of the Tuam diocese, understood to have terminated at Strade Abbey in Templemore parish, immediately north of Manulla.[19]

The personal offering of land by the king to the church, we are told, extended from 'ath mbó co caill clumain'.[20] In 1838 John O'Donovan recorded that *Beul-atha bo* was an 'ancient' name for the townland of Ballygaddy, immediately north of Tuam.[21] The 1840 OS maps show at least three fording points of the River Clare at the south-eastern entrance to Ballygaddy, the most prominent of which is now Ballygaddy Bridge.[22] This might also suggest that the 'gaddy' in the name did not come, as O'Donovan thought, from *Béal átha ghadaidhe* ('mouth of the ford of the thieves') but from *Béal átha ghadghaile* ('the mouth of the ford of the gadding', i.e. 'the furious running of cows').[23] The *iarthar cluana* ('west of the meadow') mentioned is therefore the adjacent townland of Airgloony, the piece of land in question extending from Ballygaddy Bridge to what must once have been a wooded area (*caill*) in the south-western corner of Airgloony.

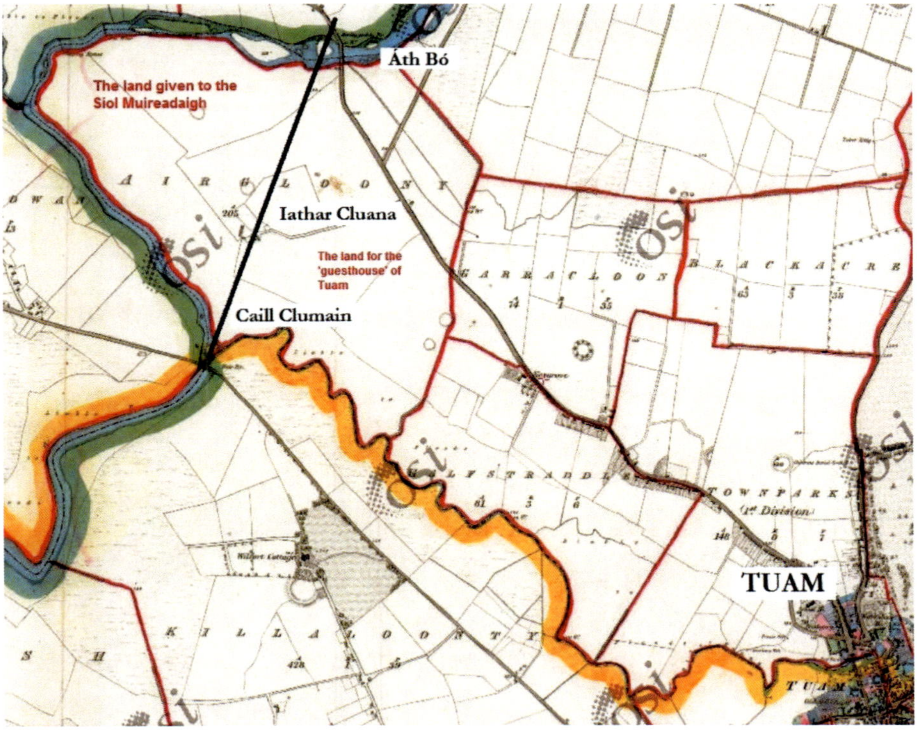

Áth mBó—part of Tairrdelbach Ua Conchobair's demesne lands and their division (© Ordnance Survey Ireland/Government of Ireland).

Áth mBó, looking south from Ballygaddy Bridge.

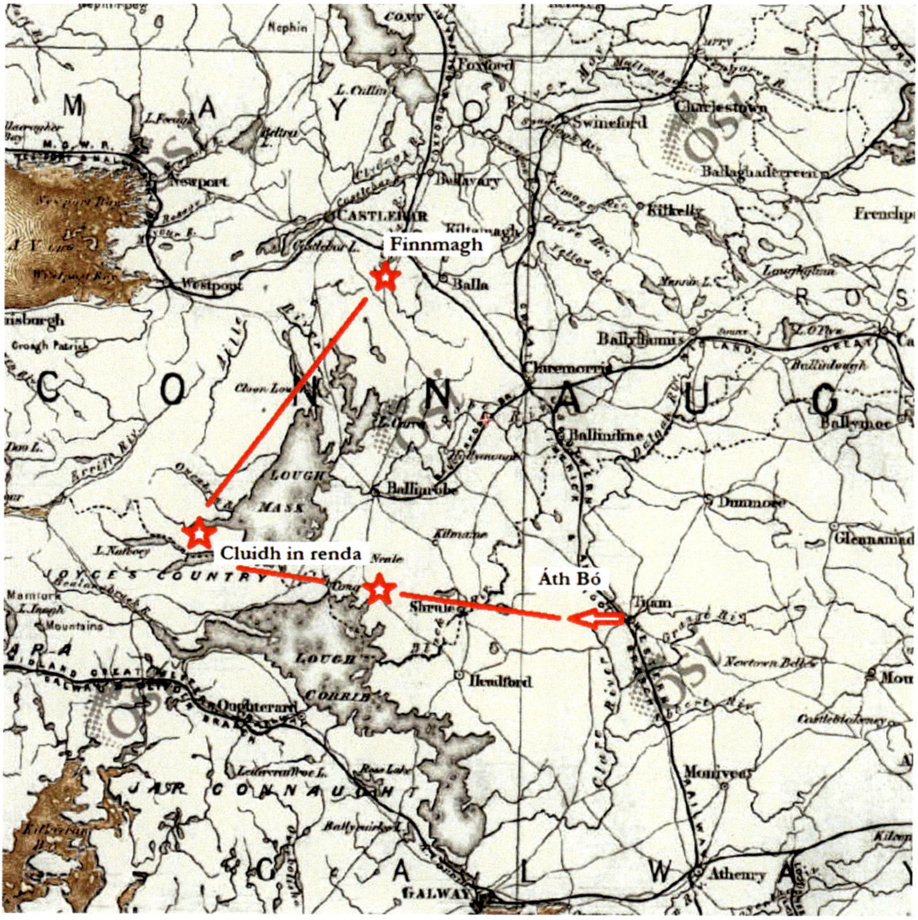

Timchill coitchend Tuama—the proposed route taken by Tairrdelbach Ua Conchobair and the successor of St Iarlath on their 'circuit' of the diocese (© Ordnance Survey Ireland/Government of Ireland).

The excerpt from the Annals of Tigernach might therefore be read today as:

Tairrdelbach Ua Conchobair, high-king of Ireland, and the comharb of Iarlath circuit all of Tuam [diocese], from the southern point of Cluidranhy to Finnmagh [Strade]. Then the king gave a permanent offering of his own demesne lands to the church, from Ballygaddy to the Woods of Cluain, that is, the south-western half of Airgloony, to every good cleric of the Síol Muireadaigh who would reside in Tuam, and the other half of it into the hands of the prior of Tuam's guesthouse.

When Tairrdelbach Ua Conchobair made a circuit of the proto-diocese of Tuam to Finnmagh he was at the height of his powers. John Ryan claimed that by 1127 he would have appeared in the eyes of his contemporaries as 'Toirdelbach the invincible'.[24] It was twelve years since he had almost lost his life at Áth mBó. Was his 'gore bed' in the nearby guesthouse of Tuam? If it was, this would explain his generosity to the community locally and the promotion of their comharb to higher office. Certainly, his granting of lands at the very place where he had been so seriously attacked cannot have been without significance. Their *timcheall* would have taken him and St Iarlath's successor on a circular journey from Tuam to the abbey of Cong, around the western shore of Lough Mask and to what they then demarcated as the northern boundary of the diocese. In the process, he would have not only given thanks for his survival and his many victories nationally but also laid long-lasting foundations for the future of Tuam town and the church in the west of Ireland.

Notes

1 J.H. Todd (ed.), *Cogadh Gaedhal re Gallaibh* (London, 1867), pp 100–204. Boru's grandson, Tairrdelbach Ó Briain, was addressed as 'King of Ireland' by the celebrated Pope Gregory VII; see A. Gwynn, *The twelfth-century reform: a history of Irish Catholicism*, ii, part i (Dublin, 1968), pp 29–33. For this article I also consulted C. Etchingham, 'Episcopal hierarchy in Connacht and Tairdelbach Ua Conchobair', *Journal of the Galway Archaeological and Historical Society* 52 (2000), pp 13–29.

2 AFM, 1156; Tairrdelbach's grandfather was Aedh *in gai bernaigh* ('of the cloven spear') Ua Conchobair. Ruaidhrí, his father, had ruled after Aedh, but his reign had been thwarted by his deliberate blinding by the O'Flahertys when he was still young.

3 K. Simms, *Medieval Gaelic sources* (Dublin, 2009), p. 30.

4 J. Ryan, *Toirdelbach O Conchubair (1088–1156): king of Connacht, king of Ireland co fresabra* (O'Donnell Lecture Series, Dublin, 1966), pp 3–25.

5 G. Murray, 'The establishment of Tuam as an archdiocesan capital in the twelfth century', in A. Tierney (ed.), *Glimpses of Tuam through the centuries* (Tuam, 2014), pp 15–17.

6 Ryan, *Toirdelbach O Conchubair*, pp 7–9.

7 See ALC, AT, CS, AU and AFM, 1115.

8 Tuam was proposed as a diocese at the Synod of Rath Breasail in 1111. It was only recognised as a metropolitan see by the papacy following the Synod of Kells–Mellifont in 1152; see Gwynn, *The twelfth-century reform*, pp 29–33.

9 AFM, 777.

10 Bodleian Library, Oxford, MS Rawlinson B 488, fol. 21v (http://image.ox.ac.uk/images/bodleian/msrawlb488/f21v.jpg; accessed 1 February 2016).

11 AT, 1127.

12 J.A. Claffey, *Tuam*, Irish Historic Towns Atlas no. 20 (Dublin, 2009), p. 2.

13 AFM, 1136. In 1123 a purported part of the True Cross was brought to Ireland, and Tairrdelbach, as 'king of Ireland', had unsurprisingly 'given great homage' (*Croch Crist a n-Erinn isin bliadain-sin, co tucadh mor-chuairt di laríg n-Erenn .i. la Tairrdelbach h-Úa Concobair*), requesting a piece for himself which he subsequently had enshrined at Roscommon in the reliquary now known as the Cross of Cong (AT, 1123). Tuam with the Cross, it has since often been argued, would become the Ua Conchobair's and Connacht's ecclesiastical capital, a rival to Cashel and a major site of pilgrimage in its own right; see especially Claffey, *Tuam*, p. 2, and G. Murray, *The Cross of Cong: a masterpiece of medieval Irish art*

(Dublin, 2014), pp 51–4.

[14] Where *timchill*, like the modern Irish *timpill*, can stand for either a nominative plural (lit. 'the encirclings') or, as in this case, a genitive singular of *timcheall*, and where 'Tuam' is also in the genitive (*Tuama*)—'the circuit *of* the lands of Tuam'; P. Ó Duinnín, *Foclóir Gaedhilge agus Béarla* (Dublin, 1927) (http://www.ucc.ie/celt/Dinneen1.pdf, pp 163–4; accessed 1 February 2016). In terms of the 'circuit', Tairrdelbach was following a tradition set by many others before him; in 1101, for instance, Muireachtach Ua Briain of Munster, after meeting with victory in Ulster, made a *timcheall* of his own, around 'all Ireland' no less, no doubt intending to make it clear to all in the process that it was he who was claiming the high-kingship:

> Do-chuaidh Muirchertach iarsin tar Fertais Camsa i n-Ultoibh, & tucc gialla Uladh, & táinicc **timchell** Erenn iomlán frí ré caeicthighisi ar mhís gan cath gan fuabhairt, & do-dheachaidh iar Slighidh Miodhluachra dia thigh. An slóighedh **timchill** ainm an t-sloighedh sin.
>
> Muircheartach after this went over Feartas-Camsa into Ulster, and carried off the hostages of Ulster; and he went **the round of** all Ireland in the space of a fortnight and a month, without battle, without attack, and he returned to his house by Slighe-Midhluachra. The expedition was called 'The **circuitous** hosting' (AFM, 1101).

[15] Cluidranhy was recorded as 'a village' by the OS surveyors in the nineteenth century, though it did not appear on their maps; see J. O'Donovan, Ordnance Survey Field Name Books (1838) (http://places.galwaylibrary.ie/asp/fullresult.asp?id=950; accessed 1 February 2016).

[16] In the civil parish of Ballinchalla but the ecclesiastical parish of Cong and Neale. Cappanacreha itself is overshadowed by the mountain of Binnaw, and the Bruin River flows through it into Lough Mask. According to Ruaidhrí Ó Flaithbheartaigh (1629–1718), by his era it still marked the northernmost extent of Connemara and Joyce's Country; R. O'Flaherty, *A chorographical description of West or H-Iar Connaught* (Dublin, 1846), pp 44–6; M. Herity (ed.), *Ordnance Survey Mayo* (Dublin, 2009), pp 207–9. It was also the 'corner' at which the medieval diocese of Tuam met that of Cong. According to Geoffrey Keating (*c.* 1569–1664), who drew much of his knowledge for the period from a now-lost Leinster chronicle known as the Annals of Clonenagh, Cong, like Tuam, had received recognition as a distinct diocese (under the archbishopric of Armagh) at the Synod of Rath Breasail. The church fathers who gathered at Rath Breasail in Munster in 1111 decided that the kingdom of Connacht should then contain only five bishoprics: Clonfert, Tuam, Cong, Killala and Ardcarne (Ardagh). No boundaries were outlined and a certain latitude was allowed for, however:

> 'If the clergy of Connacht agree to this division we desire it; and if they do not agree, let them divide it as they choose, and we approve of the division that will please them, provided there be only five bishops in Connacht' (see Gwynn, *The twelfth-century reform*, pp 29–33).

[17] Colourful as the later Lives of Patrick can be, Tirechán's account is significant, as it is specific as regards place-names and marks the first time (or possibly the second, the chronology of Tirechán's account making that somewhat uncertain) that Patrick returned to the region in which lay the *silvam Vocluti quae est prope mare occidentale* (generally identified with Foclut, south of Killala Bay), the dream-vision of which had prompted his return from Britain to evangelise the Irish; D. Conneely, *The letters of Saint Patrick* (Maynooth, 1993), p. 37.

[18] See 'Tírechán's text in English' (translated by L. Bieler) in *Ego Patricius* (http://www.confessio.ie/more/tirechan_english#; accessed 1 February 2016), and L. de Paor, *Saint Patrick's world: the Christian culture of Ireland's apostolic age* (Dublin, 1996), pp 168–9. 'He uncovered a dolmen built over the holy well at Manulla in the presence of a crowd of the Druids and heathen of the country who had

worshipped the well. It was called Slan, and from it the church and parish were called Slanpatrick down to the sixteenth century. The uncovering seems to have been a formal, prearranged act, that it might be seen whether the god of the well would punish the Christian who interfered with his altar, or a formal abolition of the worship. It seems clear that the Corcu Temne as a tribe, and their subjects, now generally adopted Christianity'; H.T. Knox, *The history of the county of Mayo: to the close of the sixteenth century* (Dublin, 1908), p. 47. The *Corca Theimhne* mentioned in Tirechán's and Knox's texts is generally thought to be the territory around Breaghwy, outside present-day Castlebar; see the very helpful recent study of Mayo place-names by Fiachra Mac Gabhann, 'The place-names of Mayo', in G. Moran and N. Ó Muraíle (eds), *Mayo history and society: interdisciplinary essays on the history of an Irish county* (Dublin, 2014), p. 103.

19 This was a significant border throughout the Middle Ages; it was often called *Áth Leathan* in the annals. That the northern boundary of Tuam diocese ended at Strade was attested to by John Lynch (1599–1674) in a passage where he was recounting the beginnings of the archdiocese in the twelfth century: *Diocesis vero Tuamensis XL mille passus ab Athenria ad Sradam, ac totidem latitudine ab Achayart ad insulas Aranas complectitur* . . . ('The actual/true diocese of Tuam extends 40 miles from Athenry to Strade, and the same distance from Aghyart [Ballinakill/Mountbellew, Co. Galway] to the Aran Islands . . .'); J. Lynch [1672], *De praesulibus Hiberniae*, ed. J.F. O'Doherty (Dublin, 1944), ii, p. 214.

20 A number of different locations have previously been proposed for where these places may have been. Dr Tony Claffey thought that it referred to some now-forgotten site to the west of St Mary's Cathedral in Tuam; Claffey, *Tuam*, p. 2. The archaeologist Griffin Murray recently suggested that Áth mBó might refer to the old fording point at Claretuam (where the current N17 road crosses the River Clare, four miles south of Tuam town). He suggested that this may have been the case in view of the number of surrounding townlands with *cluain* in their names, and because Claretuam marked the southern entrance and fording point to the Ua Conchobhair's new site of pilgrimage, land that the Ó Dubhthaighs and their lay and clerical allies would naturally want to control; Murray, *Cross of Cong*, p. 52.

21 '[T]he townland of Ballygaddy anciently *Beul-atha bo*'; M. Herity (ed.), *Ordnance Survey Letters, Galway* (Dublin, 2009), p. 25.

22 Ballygaddy Bridge, Mapviewer, *Ordnance Survey Ireland* (http://maps.osi.ie/publicviewer/#V2,542019,753809,10,7; accessed 1 February 2016).

23 Gadghaile—*gadding* being the 'furious running (of cows)'; Ó Duinnín, *Foclóir Gaedhilge agus Béarla* (http://www.ucc.ie/celt/Dinneen1.pdf, p. 323).

24 Ryan, *Toirdelbach O Conchubair*, p. 10.

12

A legacy of the munificence of Cathal Crubh Dearg O'Conor (1153?–1224) towards the Irish church: a women's story forgotten

Gerard Beggan

For the final few kilometres before it joins the River Suck,[1] the Shiven is a meandering, sluggish watercourse in north-east County Galway, flowing through flat land. A bizarre legend relates how Maine Mór was victorious over Cian, a Fir Bolg chief, following a conference of leaders of opposing forces in Mágh Seimhni, 'the plain of the Shiven', in ancient [Tuath] Seinchineoil—that being the archaic name of the region.[2] Maine's tribe, the Uí Maine or O'Kelly ancestry, thereby laid the foundation of the kingdom of Hy-Many in the period AD 327–57.[3] Occupied from very early times by the Uí Maine, the territory through which the Shiven passes subsequently became known as 'Cruffon',[4] its eponym allegedly being the chieftain Creamhan Caol, a grandson of Maine Mór. One concludes that 'Shiven' is a very old name.[5]

The 1840 six-inch OS map of County Galway reveals that the Shiven is comprised of two main tributaries. Its northern and lesser branch passes by the village of Newbridge, Co. Galway, where the bridge bears the sign 'R. Shiven'. Roughly 2km downriver from that village, however, this branch nowadays partially borders the townland of Killyan[6] and, for a distance on that map, is labelled the 'Killian River'. Almost the same distance downriver from Newbridge stand the structures of a former corn mill, a cloth mill and an eel-weir. Evidently, neither of these mills on the Shiven was the first to be erected at that place. Dr Petty's map shows that the riverside land near them was called 'Shanuallin',[7] meaning 'the old mill'[8]—a name

Dr Petty's map, showing the River Shiven, Shanuallin townland and the icon for a church ruin in 1633.

indicating that a long time previously a different mill had operated which had become old before 1633[9] and which possibly was not even still in existence by that year. What name this riverside land had before it was called 'Shanuallin' is long forgotten.

The Shiven forms pools as it nears Killyan townland. One pool is immediately upriver from the eel-weir, one is immediately downriver from it, and a third, far longer than either of these, is still further downriver. We shall call the lowest pool 'the long pool'. The 1840 OS map of County Galway (right)[10] shows all three pools in blue, and also shows the eel-weir and both mills.[11] On the road opposite the long pool the map shows an acute bend and an entrance. This was called *Bearna Buí*—'the yellow gap'—and gave access to this pool.[12] As ripe flax is yellow, the name suggests that the long pool was probably used for retting flax for weaving into coarse linen at the cloth mill.[13]

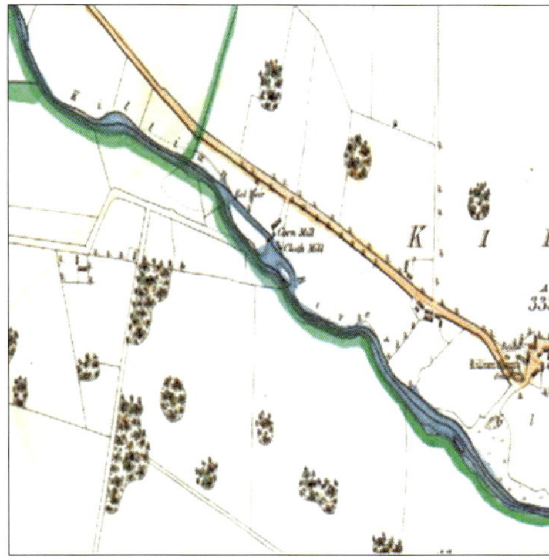

Pools on the Shiven River above Buncam and roadway entrance to the long pool.

Buncam, a small townland, borders the Shiven just below the long pool. The name *bun cam* means 'the bottom of the bends'. On this 1840 OS map one can discern five bends in sequence, resembling archery bows, all having the same orientation. Four are end to end below the eel-weir and are separated from the fifth, above the weir, by a short, straight stretch of river. The name *Buncam* establishes that these bends were of some significance to the local people and characterised this section of the Shiven in people's minds for a reason now forgotten.

The road from Newbridge to Ballinamore Bridge runs alongside the Shiven. Exactly at the aforementioned acute bend, it formerly passed between the long pool and the southern side of a cemetery, wherein there stands a medieval church ruin (see road-map, right).[14] Registered as 'Killethean' in Elphin diocese in the 1306

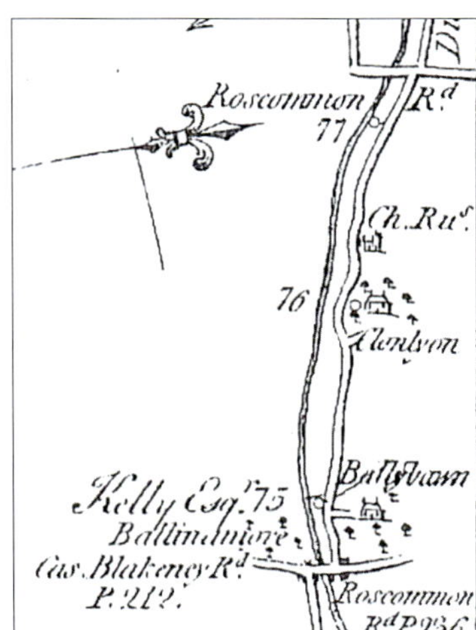

Taylor and Skinner's road-map, showing the road between the church ruins and the River Shiven in 1778.

Part of the south wall of Killyan nunnery.

A section of the old boundary wall.

'Church Taxation List',[15] and now called 'Killyan', this church is of unknown origin. So also are the ruins of a much larger and separate building near it within the cemetery.[16]

An ivy-clad broken wall in Killyan cemetery is 82ft long and runs east–west (above). Regarded from the exterior, the height of a window in this wall overlooking the river suggests that the building may originally have been two-storey. The remnants of two other walls establish a 22ft-wide area, subdivided into at least two rooms, though probably more. Round about lie mounds of rubble from fallen walls under swathes of grass and interspersed by graves. A remaining section of an old boundary wall varies between 7½ft and 8½ft high. Everything suggests that this was originally a monastic or conventual building occupied by some enclosed religious order.

A sketch of Killyan church doorway[17] is recorded in O'Donovan's Ordnance

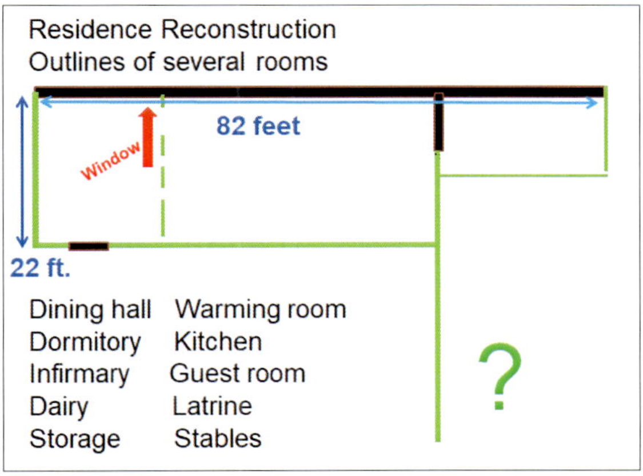

Sketch of the partial footprint of the Killyan monastic ruin today, with suggestions as to what rooms a medieval nunnery may have contained. Black lines denote walls still partially standing. Green lines denote ground evidence of fallen walls. The red arrow points at a window.

Killyan church door today.

Internal niches on the north side-wall.

Survey Letters.[18] Its arch is comprised of two arcs which seemingly form a semicircle. Measurement of the actual doorway from the springing points reveals, however, that these are arcs of different circles whose centres are about 4in. apart.[19] Of uniform width from these points to the ground, the doorway's ope, measuring 2ft 11in., seems narrow.[20] The whole seems to be a somewhat unsophisticated and amateurish specimen of a Gothic doorway of the early English school (i.e. 1180–1250).[21]

The chapel itself,[22] internally measuring roughly 24ft by 12ft, is windowless, apart from a small, high, narrow opening in the east gable,[23] overlooking the altar.[24] There are niches at waist height, two on each side wall, within the chapel (above, right), and an external niche above the doorway. A mortar-like holy-water stoup is plastered to the wall inside the door.[25]

In the century preceding the likely foundation of this establishment (i.e. in the twelfth century), the Irish church was undergoing a major reform. It was deemed to be backward, sinful and out of tune with the rest of Christendom, and strategies to renew it gave rise to at least seven conventions or synods at national or provincial level between 1100 and 1205.[26] Giants among reformers were Malachy of Armagh and Laurence O'Toole of Dublin, who realised that Irish monastic life had to be totally changed and brought under new rules of behaviour, preferably by introducing the way of life of the Cistercians and of the Augustinian Canons of the Arroasian Congregation.[27] At this time many Irish nunneries became revitalised by reforms, which included the introduction of Continental religious orders for both men and women. Gaelic kings showed renewed interest in including nunneries in their own reorganisation of local monastic houses.

The foundation of a monastic community at Killyan *c.* 1200 in that climate of reform would have depended on the benevolence of some wealthy nobleman. Though the Uí Maine were very early inhabitants of this territory, the Shiven region had over previous centuries become occupied by the Uí Briúin Aí tribes, who, expanding southwards from around Rathcroghan,[28] had pushed the Uí Maine south of Ahascragh as early as 600[29] and had contained them there. In contrast, by the twelfth century the O'Conor royal family had emerged from the Síol Muireadhaigh—a tribe which had become dominant among the Uí Briúin Aí—and were so powerful that they had gained not only the kingship of Connacht but also the high-kingship of Ireland.

In Connacht the spread of the reform of the Irish church was intertwined with the rise of the O'Conor dynasty, of whom it has been said that they were 'more concerned with the salvation of their souls than the grandeur of their residences'.[30] King Turlough Mór O'Conor became a most assiduous promoter of the Augustinian Canons, his patronage embracing several houses,[31] whereas, according to claims of a living kinsman,[32] his son Cathal Crubh Dearg O'Conor founded twelve abbeys in all. Knockmoy Abbey and Ballintubber Abbey[33] were among the more notable of these.

A major foundation in Connacht at this time was the O'Conor nunnery at Kilcreevanty, Co. Galway. It and its dependencies were well endowed with land and buildings, and it was staffed with women from the founders' families. On the Dalgan River near Tuam, Kilcreevanty was founded by Cathal Crubh Dearg *c.* 1200 for the noblewomen of the O'Conor household. Now in ruins, it was initially a Benedictine nunnery[34] but shortly after its foundation it became the mother house in Connacht for Canonesses Regular of the Order of Saint Augustine of the Arroasian Congregation,[35] probably owing to the decline of Clonard nunnery.[36]

Up to 1904, writers of Irish church history provided only a modicum of information about Kilcreevanty Abbey. In that year the publication of volume 5 of the *Calendar of entries in the papal registers* gave new insights.[37] A papal letter in that *Calendar* revealed that in 1223 Pope Honorius III placed Kilcreevanty Abbey and all its possessions under his protection, and that of St Peter, as a solution to a serious rift that had arisen between the archbishop of Tuam and the abbey's incumbent abbess, a feisty woman.[38] The former was prone to making random visitations to the nunnery, occasionally with friends, and taking goods from it, these on one occasion being valued at £100.[39]

The possessions of Kilcreevanty Abbey in 1223 included ten daughter houses in Connacht,[40] all called 'St Mary', plus the tithes of several townlands.[41] Two mills were listed.[42] Most of these daughter houses were in easily identifiable places, but the locations of three—St Mary Doryn with a mill, St Mary Cloonoghill and 'St Mary Kyllin with houses and appurtenances'—had proved elusive.

The 1904 *Calendar* was published just as historian Hubert Knox had completed for publication a history of three Connacht dioceses—Tuam, Killala and Achonry.[43] Its impact on him was such that he evidently updated his manuscript by writing 'additional notes and corrections' as a new final chapter.[44] In these 'additional notes' he reproduced the names of all the daughter houses of Kilcreevanty in 1223, identifying St Mary Doryn with Derrane, Co. Roscommon,[45] and St Mary Cloonoghill with a townland of that name in the parish of Taghmaconnell in Clonfert diocese.[46] He did not identify St Mary Kyllin.

In 1956 Revd Patrick Egan CC, in a published article concerning a Carmelite cell,[47] asserted that St Mary Kyllin was in Killinmulrooney, a townland now called 'Cuilleen' in the parish of Kilclooney and Creagh, near him in Ballinasloe.[48] Evidently Egan had read Knox's work[49] but seemingly had not yet consulted (or had not carefully consulted) volume 5 of the *Calendar*. In 1960 Fr Egan published a history of the parish of Ballinasloe.[50] Its bibliography included a reference to the aforementioned papal letter. Nonetheless, in that book he repeatedly recommitted himself to his earlier assertion that Killinmulrooney was a nunnery site—that of St Mary Kyllin. This information has been absorbed and used by several later researchers[51] and writers.[52] According to Fr Egan's investigations, all that remained of St Mary Kyllin were two little piles of stones in a field in Cuilleen.

No mention of a monastic settlement in the Killyan locality can be found in Archdall's history of the abbeys in County Galway;[53] neither does it arise in the *Monasticon Hibernicum* of Stephens and Moll.[54] Killyan does not feature in Gwynn and Hadcock's *Medieval religious houses: Ireland*,[55] nor in either the 1979 edition of the OS *Map of monastic Ireland*[56] or the scholarly pamphlet attached to it. None of a number of modern writers on Irish church history makes any mention of a monastic site at Killyan.[57] To this general omission there is a solitary exception: in the index to church names published in 1904 in volume 5 of the *Calendar of entries in the papal registers*, Kyllin is stated to be Killyan, Co. Galway.[58]

'Kyllin' is *Cill Linn*, meaning 'the church of the pools'. The name refers to the above-mentioned pools on the River Shiven, facing the nunnery and upstream from it, near the mills, whence this present research establishes that the medieval monastic ruins in Killyan, Co. Galway, are those of St Mary Kyllin. The name 'St Mary Kyllin' contains new information too: it implies that an ecclesiastical site must have pre-dated

St Mary's nunnery in Kyllin, its church being known as 'the church of the pools'.

Camnach was among the townlands which generated tithes for Kilcreevanty in 1223. *Camnach* translates as '(a place) having a set of bends'.[59] *Camnach* and *bun cam*[60] appropriately describe the riverside land called 'Shanuallin' in 1633. Both *Cill Linn* and *Camnach* identify those church, river and land features in the vicinity of Killyan medieval church and cemetery which formerly were significant for this local community.

In the papal letter, St Mary Kyllin was the only daughter house of Kilcreevanty Abbey that had 'houses' associated with it in 1223. When founding a new monastic site in medieval times it was not uncommon not only first to provide a church as a prerequisite for the arrival of the intended occupants but also to provide temporary accommodation for them, often wooden, until a permanent structure could be built.[61] The mention of 'houses' suggests that this situation obtained at Kyllin in 1223. Further, the fact that St Mary's church stood apart from the nunnery building would strongly hint that the original plan may have been to found a 'double' convent where Augustinian Canons, having their own separate accommodation, would be sited adjacently on the same complex and share the church, as was the case at Arrouaise in France and at several Irish monastic sites (e.g. seemingly also at Doryn).[62] Evidently this development never materialised at Kyllin.

In the papal letter, no mill was mentioned in connection with Camnach in 1223.[63] It is very likely that Kyllin was selected as a nunnery site because of the milling potential on this part of the Shiven.[64] As to who provided the site, the answer seems obvious. Over the centuries, the displaced Uí Maine were unable to return to their earliest homelands north of the Shiven. They were repeatedly in conflict with the Uí Briúin Aí, battles at Acadh Liag in 775 and at Rath Fhearaidh in 816[65] being just two of the defeats they suffered at the hands of the O'Conor ancestry. Rory O'Conor, last high king of Ireland, died in 1198; his brother, Cathal Crubh Dearg, established Kilcreevanty Abbey *c.* 1200, and in 1201 he became king of Connacht. It must therefore have been Cathal Crubh Dearg who, as founder of Kilcreevanty Abbey, provided the site and tithe support for that abbey's possessions,[66] including tithes out of Camnach.[67] Cathal Crubh Dearg O'Conor died in 1224, probably happy that Pope Honorius III had taken care of Kilcreevanty and its daughter houses the previous year. He is buried in Knockmoy Abbey.[68]

The tide of success for the Irish church's renewal of itself was already turning before Kilcreevanty Abbey was founded. The invading Normans made their first attempt to conquer Connacht in 1177.[69] From 1204 the O'Conors were losing territory to the king of England. O'Conor power was eventually sapped by the Anglo-Norman invaders.[70] O'Kelly power waxed and the O'Kellys made gains to the north of Uí Maine at O'Conor expense.[71] Thus in the early fourteenth century one finds the O'Kellys resettling in that northern part of their kingdom of Hy-Many which had become inhabited by tribes who were not Uí Maine people. An entry in the Annals of Loch Cé for the year 1337 illustrates the weakened state of the Síol Muireadhaigh/O'Conor condition.[72] William Buí O'Kelly, the eighth son of Donnchadh Muimhneach O'Kelly, chief of Hy-Many, established his claim over all Hy-Many in 1340.

The benefits which this nunnery brought to the local population can only be imagined. Medieval nunneries had to be self-sufficient. The nuns' lives revolved around (a) prayer; (b) work: embroidery, gardening and herb-growing, making their own clothes, perhaps even weaving linen, and sometimes including extra-mural community work such as tending to the sick; and (c) scholarship: copying sacred texts, illustrating books etc.[73] Nevertheless, its contribution to local development was somewhat short-lived. The 1306 'Church Taxation List' for Elphin diocese includes a church registered as 'Killethean'.[74] The name translates as *Cill Liatháin*, or 'Lidinia's church',[75] now corrupted to 'Killyan'.[76] It can be deduced that the St Mary Kyllin nunnery had ceased to function before 1306, its church becoming appropriated by the diocese.[77] Probably, like Clonard, it was unable to withstand the conditions of unrest, instability and wars caused by the Norman conquest in Connacht, and especially in the absence of O'Conor support owing to changed family fortunes and feuding.[78]

The ruin of the Gaelic nunnery 'St Mary Kyllin' today. A symbol of the Irish church renewing itself, its story is a women's story.[79]

In 1605 Cillian (*sic*) church (*alias* Killyan), together with 38 other Roman Catholic churches in Elphin diocese, was disposed of by John Lynch,[80] the incumbent Anglican bishop of Elphin. All had been suppressed in the Reformation. The recipient was Henry Linche (*sic*) of Galway. In 1611 this John, having as bishop greatly impoverished his diocese, resigned, declaring himself a Catholic![81] Killyan church fell to ruin. St Mary Kyllin had already fallen into oblivion.

Notes

1 Roughly midway between the Suck-side villages of Mount Talbot and Ballyforan in Roscommon, adjacent to the County Galway border.

2 J. O'Donovan (ed.), *The tribes and customs of Hy-Many, commonly called O'Kelly country*, pp 11 and 13, at CELT (Corpus of Electronic Texts), the on-line resource for Irish history, literature and politics (http://ucc.ie/celt/online/G105007.html; accessed 28 January 2017). [*Editor's note:* See Joseph Mannion, 'The Senchineoil and the Sogain: differentiating between the pre-Celtic and early Celtic tribes of central east Galway', *Journal of the Galway Archaeological and Historical Society* (hereafter *JGAHS*) **58**, pp 165–70.]

3 O'Donovan (ed.), *Hy-Many*, p. 2. O'Donovan herein revealed that, according to Denis Henry Kelly of Castle Kelly (d. 1877), Maine Mór acquired Imania in the south of Connacht and the county of Galway between AD 327 and 357, which his posterity greatly enlarged and extended beyond the River Suck to the Shannon, through the county of Roscommon.

4 According to D.H. Kelly, Cruffon incorporated the barony of Killyan and a large tract of the barony of Ballymoe and was celebrated for its coarse linen manufacture. See note 174 of *The tribes and customs of Hy Many*. Cruffon included the former parishes of Killian, Killeroran and Athleague, with part of Taghboy parish, Co. Galway; John O'Donovan, 'Castlekelly', in 'Ordnance Survey letters, Roscommon', p. 8 (typed version).

5 Ir. *Seimhin*, 'a bulrush'; the river abounds in bulrushes in its sluggish sections.

6 Many townland boundaries were readjusted in consequence of the first Ordnance Survey (1829–42).

7 Called 'Shanvallyline' in R.C. Simington, *Books of survey and distribution: being abstracts of various surveys and instruments of title, 1636–1703, iii: County of Galway* (Dublin, 1962), p. 258.

8 The mill may have been 'old' in design, i.e. of the horizontal type. An extremely well-preserved early medieval corn mill of horizontal design was recently excavated in County Roscommon: N. Jackman, 'Kilbegly Mill: the excavation of an early medieval mill in south Roscommon', *Journal of the County Roscommon Historical and Archaeological Society* (2012), pp 23–6.

9 In so far as it relates to Connacht, Dr Petty's map is based on the Strafford Survey of 1633–6.

10 Ordnance Survey Ireland map of County Galway (1840 six-inch), Galway County Council website (http://places.galwaylibrary.ie/maps/; accessed 6 June 2013).

11 Note: the Shiven was drained during the 1840s, with consequent alterations to some of its features.

12 The traffic path from road to pool is still noticeable, especially in very dry weather conditions, but access to it is no longer possible. This gap gave the name 'Barnaboy' to the immediate locality, and this name is shown on the modern Google map of the locality. Google 'Killian' or see on-line at https://www.google.ie/maps/place/Killian,+Co.+Galway/@53.4979303,-8.4109629,2001m/data=!3m1!1e3!4m5!3m4!1s0x485c1369221e1cb:0x60eedefed3be5b33!8m2!3d53.4994847!4d-8.401359.

13 Within living memory, elderly parishioners of Killyan parish spoke of local linen being brought to market in Mountbellew by their predecessors.

14 G. Taylor and A. Skinner, *Maps of the roads of Ireland* (London and Dublin, 1778), p. 80 (https://archive.org/details/TaylorSkinnerMapsOfTheRoadsOfIrelandSurveyed1777; accessed 28 January 2017).

15 *Calendar of documents relating to Ireland: 1302–1307* (London, 1886), p. 224.

16 The northern side of the nunnery site was in use as an animal pound in the 1840s. A new stretch of road now runs through it, allowing the acute bend to be used as a lay-by.

17 By George Petrie or William Wakeman.

18 J. O'Donovan, 'Ordnance Survey letters, Co. Galway', vol. 1 (typed version).

19 The photo shows that the door differs from its sketch. In the sketch, the wall is built of rectangular cut stone. In fact, the left arc is severed radially, through and through, and chipped at the cut.

20 For example, the width of Mungret Abbey church door, deemed to be twelfth-century, is 3ft 7in. at

ground level but tapers slightly inward as it rises. The doorway is lintelled, not arched.

21 Gothic design of the western school influenced church construction in Ireland at this time, as is evident in the chapel of St Lawrence O'Toole in Dublin's former Holy Trinity Cathedral.

22 The chapel was the Chevers burial ground *c.* 1690–1923. The grave shown centrally is that of Michael Chevers (d. 1889) and his wife, Annie French (d. 1898). Also within are the Chevers coat of arms (behind the grill) and Chevers' goats.

23 This design allowed the sun's rays to light the altar area directly. Possibly only the priest had reading matter in an era when books did not exist and only an élite few were literate.

24 The worshippers faced the rising sun.

25 Originally free-standing, the stoup has been associated with Killyan for as long as can be remembered. Viewed from overhead, four nodules give this vessel a cruciform appearance. A professional art designer suspects that a stoup of this design is not authentic but rather may be from some mortar-and-pestle set.

26 Fifteen councils at various levels convened between 1084 and 1205; J. Watt, *The church in medieval Ireland* (Dublin and London, 1972), pp 229–30.

27 St Laurence O'Toole was so impressed by the Arroasian house in France that he converted Holy Trinity Cathedral into an Arroasian congregation.

28 The Uí Briúin Aí were a Connacht dynasty named for the region they controlled, i.e. Mágh Aí—the lands around Cruachan, Co. Roscommon; see H.T. Knox, 'The early tribes of Connacht', *Journal of the Royal Society of Antiquaries of Ireland* (hereafter *JRSAI*) **10** (4) (1900), pp 343–56, at p. 352; *idem*, 'The expansion of two royal tribes of Connacht', *JGAHS* 4 (1905–6), pp 99–101. The Síol Muireadaigh became a dominant tribe and from these sprang the O'Conor kings of Connacht and of Ireland. Knox states: 'If we exclude the barony of Carbury and the Tri Tuatha, the diocese of Elphin defines the hereditary estates of the Silmurry at the succession of King Turlough Mor'. As for Silmurray incursion into Uí Maine, he states: 'The rest of the kingdom of Hy Maine was held by the Sodhans [Sogain] and the Corcamoe, except the part which had been taken from them by the Silmurray'. Note that the diocese of Elphin incorporated Cruffon and that Corca Mogha had a common boundary with ancient Cruffon. The registry of Clonmacnoise lists seventeen townlands which were bestowed on St Kieran (d. 549) by Cairbre Crom, king of Uí Maine (J. O'Donovan (ed.), 'The registry of Clonmacnoise, with notes and introductory remarks', *Journal of the Kilkenny and South-East of Ireland Archaeological Society* **1** (1857), pp 444–60, at pp 453–5). While many of these townlands were convenient to Clonmacnoise, there were four which lay north of the River Shiven, the most northerly being Creggs (barony of Ballymoe) and Aghagower (parish of Fuerty, from which Kieran is said to have come). Implicit in this is that Cairbre Crom was lord of these northern lands in St Kieran's time, and therefore in particular had dominion over Sliabh Fhorraidh, *alias* Sliaw-furri, Knocknaree, Slyewshannekuogh, Montescanchuach (i.e. *Sliabh Seana-thuath*—the mountain of the Old Tribes of ancient Seinchineoil; see G. Beggan, 'The Carmelite house of Holy Cross, Slewshancogh, diocese of Elphin', *Journal of the County Roscommon Historical and Archaeological Society* **13** (2016), pp 111–15). This expanse of high ground—the homeland of a number of ancient Tuatha Taidhean kings of Connacht (and possibly also of Tuatha Dé Danann?)—serves to help demarcate the ancient Seinchineoeil tribal lands to which Mac Firbis referred in the words '. . . Tuath Seincheinéil in northern Uí Maine . . .' (N. Ó Muraíle (ed. and trans.), *Leabhar mór na ngenealach: The great book of Irish genealogies*, compiled (1645–66) by Dubhaltach Mac Fhirbhisigh (5 vols, Dublin, 2003–4), §51.20) and which he distinguished from 'Tuath Cathraige in southern Uí Maine' (ibid., §51.18). By AD 600 the Uí Maine were constrained south of Ahascragh (G. Mac Niocaill, *Ireland before the Vikings* (Dublin, 1972), pp 36–7). The Uí Briúin controlled the land north of Ahascragh, from the Clare River to the Suck. MacNiocaill states: '. . . the lowland east of Lough Mask . . . and the gentle valley between the Clare and the Suck, was Uí Briúin land'. The battle of Acadh Liag was fought in 775 between the Uí Maine and the Uí Briúin (MacNiocaill, preface and p. 136). The site, only recently located, was in *Cluain Achadh Liag* (in Cruffon), a townland lying north of the River Shiven within the present borders of County Galway and now called 'Killeroran' but confused by O'Donovan ('The registry of

Clonmacnoise', p. 455, note 17) with the Suck-side townland of Cloonakilleg, Co. Roscommon (G. Beggan, 'Ballygar: the Hy Many royal seat', in K. Simms (ed.), *Gaelic Ireland (c. 600–c. 1700): politics, culture and landscapes* (Dublin, 2013), pp 87–95, at p. 92).

29 Mac Niocaill, *Ireland before the Vikings*, p. 36.

30 'O'Conors: Kings of Connacht', at clonalis.com/oconnor-kings-of-connacht/; Turlough Mór O'Conor was inaugurated as high king of Ireland in 1119 and died in 1156. Research by the present writer has established that there was a forgotten Cistercian abbey at Abbeygrey, Co. Galway, which was under the patronage of King Rory O'Conor in 1177; Beggan, 'The Carmelite house of Holy Cross', pp 111–15.

31 Turlough O'Conor's patronage embraced houses at Annaghdown, Clonfert, Roscommon, Cong, Tuam, Clonmacnoise and Cloontuskert (Co. Roscommon); Watt, *The church in medieval Ireland*, p. 46.

32 'O'Conors : Kings of Connacht', at clonalis.com/oconnor-kings-of-connacht/.

33 Founded in 1216, it is still functioning as a church.

34 M.A.M. Archdall, *Monasticon Hibernicum: or, a history of the abbeys, priories, and other religious houses in Ireland; interspersed with memoirs of their several founders and benefactors, and of their abbots and other superiors, to the time of their final suppression. Edited with extensive notes by the Right Rev. Patrick Moran, DD*, ii (Dublin, 1876), p. 220 (http://www.archive.org/details/monasrticonhiber01archgoog).

35 As early as 1146 the Augustinian Canonesses Regular had a nunnery in Dublin. Note: most nunneries in the thirteenth and fourteenth centuries followed the Order of St Augustine of the Arrouasian Congregation.

36 A nunnery was founded *c.* 1160 at Clonard by O'Malaghlin, king of Meath, and was the mother house of all Augustinian Canonesses Regular in Ireland down to 1223–4. From 1195 it was in decline and, according to Archdall, eventually was so reduced as to become a cell to the nunnery of St Brigid of Odra.

37 W.H. Bliss and J.A. Twemlow, *Calendar of entries in the papal registers relating to Great Britain and Ireland, v, 1398–1404* (London, 1904).

38 Ibid., pp 334–6.

39 The solution restricted the archbishop to making visitations only every three years, required that he be accompanied by the bishop of Limerick when doing so and, under severe penalty, limited him to taking from the abbey no more than three capons and a sextarius of wine (i.e. about 0.6 litres).

40 St Mary Achonry with its appurtenances, St Mary Annadown, St Mary Clonfert, St Mary Ardcarna, St Mary Drumcliff, St Mary Clonmacnoise, St Mary Roscommon, St Mary Doryn with a mill and other appurtenances, St Mary Kyllin with houses and other appurtenances.

41 The tithes of the lands of Crichbeg and Crichmore and the tithes of Mag[er] cassylederand Bechach, Suactardroura, Bylyscathayn, Syatilcomayn, Camnach, Cormayn, Hestiic, Corthet, Loug Frych, Kildeglan, Cluaincelnaid, Ardnabyr, Danalym, Ficlouatonn, Danaly Mugihmir, Baly Yuenne, Baly Ycollidy, Rosseach, Cluayngad, Balynyglayd, Brochscach, Leachraych, Raith Moechayn, Golwualy, Trybeth, Seanrayth, Rayth Achadallayn, Achraich; the lands of Cluayngad, Rosseach (or Rosscach), Urcludy, Ardfauir, Cloynmoyr, Ballayn Padryg, and Maddurad in Narmayl, Ardffassad and mill, and Tearmanduyamus, Druymalgath, Lysgeal, Lysintagat, and Eanach, Ochyllbeg, Leachat, Hyachareluana, Tamaynmayl, Druym Sulynd, Balynibealy, the tenement of Tuam with its appurtenances, and the lands of Rossyn with their appurtenances.

42 At Doryn and at Ardffassad (*sic*).

43 H.T. Knox, *Notes on the early history of the dioceses of Tuam, Killala and Achonry* (Dublin, 1904) (https://archive.org/details/notesonearlyhistOOknoxiala; accessed 28 January 2017).

44 Ibid., pp 383–8.

45 Though signposted 'Derrane', some locals still pronounce this name 'Doryn' (rhymes with 'foreign').

46 Barony of Athlone, Co. Roscommon.

47 P.K. Egan, 'The Carmelite cell of Bealaneny', *JGAHS* 26 (1–2) (1954–5), pp 19–25.

48 Fr Egan published forms of the name dating from as early as the ninth century and up to the Cromwellian

era; his results showed that the name always included the 'mulroney' element until the Cromwellian settlements. O'Donovan ('The registry of Clonmacnoise', p. 456, footnote 3) wrote: 'Coillin-Molruany ... alias Castle Park, the residence of O'Kelly of Turrock'. It had become known as 'Guillen' and 'Cuilleen' by the nineteenth century.

49 Fr Egan was critical of Knox's identification of some places.

50 Revd P.K. Egan, *The parish of Ballinasloe: its history from the earliest times to the present day* (Dublin, 1960).

51 For example, A. Kehnel, *Clonmacnoise: the church and lands of St Ciarán: change and continuity in an Irish monastic foundation (6th to 16th century)* (Vita Regularis 8, LIT-Verlag, Münster), p. 306 (https://www.google.ie/webhp?nord=1&gws_rd=cr,ssl&ei=QS6gVPiDE8re7Aa621GIDw#nord=1&q =Kehnel+Clonmacnoise); Diane Hall, *Women and the church in medieval Ireland* c. *1140–1540* (Dublin, 2008).

52 Killeenmulrooney is shown as a nunnery site on the 1979 Ordnance Survey *Map of monastic Ireland*. The Ohio State University Department of History website, *Monastic Matrix*, promotes 'Killinmulrooney' as the site of St Mary Kyllin (monasticmatrix.osu.edu/; accessed 28 January 2017).

53 Archdall, *Monasticon Hibernicum*, pp 170–227.

54 J. Stephens and H. Moll, *Monasticon Hibernicum* (London, 1722).

55 A. Gwynn and R.N. Hadcock, *Medieval religious houses: Ireland* (Dublin, 1988).

56 Ordnance Survey, *Map of monastic Ireland* (Dublin, 1979).

57 For example, F.M. Beirne (ed.), *The diocese of Elphin: people, places and pilgrimage* (Blackrock, 2000).

58 *Calendar of entries in the papal registers*, v, p. 704.

59 The Irish suffix '*-na*' converts *cam* into the collective form *camna*, meaning 'a set of bends'. *Camnach* therefore is '(a place) having a set of bends'. See '*cam*' and '*-na*' in P.S. Dinneen, *Foclóir Gaedhilge agus Béarla*.

60 Note that the local word used for 'river bend' was '*cam*' and not, for example, '*cor*', '*lúb*', '*uilleann*' etc.

61 See D.M. Robinson, *Tintern Abbey* (Cardiff, 1986), p. 16.

62 Stephens and Moll (*Monasticon Hibernicum*, p. 89) state that 'at Dhoran was a priory of regular Canons which was a cell to the Abbey of Roscommon and founded by one O'Connor, an Irish Nobleman'. Note: Roscommon Abbey, founded in the eighth century, survived as a house of Augustinian Canons into the fifteenth century but nothing remains of it today; 'The Dominican friary of Roscommon town', at www.cultural heritageireland.ie/.../98-the Dominican-friary-of-roscommon-town-co-ro...

63 There was a mill at Doryn and another in Ardffassad townland. No mill in Kilcreevanty or in its environs in 1223 was mentioned in the papal letter, but the 1840 OS map shows a corn mill on the Dalgan River at Kilcreevanty Bridge, near the nunnery ruins.

64 The arrival of the Augustinian canonesses in Kyllin corresponded with twelfth- and thirteenth-century technical advances in Europe, notably in the design of watermills, windmills, spinning-wheels etc. Watermills spread rapidly throughout Europe in consequence of the increase in numbers of monastic sites. It seems very likely that the Kyllin nuns were the first to construct a mill on the Shiven at a place which later gave rise to the townland name 'Shanuallin' on the riverside land shown on Dr Petty's map.

65 Rahara, a few miles east of Athleague, anciently in Dealbhna Nuadhat. Here Cathal Mac Murchadh, 29th king of Hy-Many, and many other nobles were slain by chieftains of Uí Briúin; Annals of the Four Masters, M816.5.

66 Some daughter houses already had some lands. St Mary Annadown held a small portion of ancient endowment which was absorbed with it eventually into Kilcreevanty; see Knox, *Notes on the early history of the dioceses of Tuam*, p. 255.

67 Tithes from a mill would have provided significant income.

68 Cathal O'Conor founded this abbey in 1189/90.

69 Annals of the Four Masters, pt 1, M1177.5. In early 1177, in an eight-day incursion into Connacht with 540 men at the invitation of Murrough O'Conor, Milo de Cogan and his first cousin Ralph Fitzstephen penetrated as far as Tuam, before taking flight and being driven from Roscommon by the men of

Connacht. Murrough had done this out of ill will towards his father Rory, high king of Ireland.

70 H.T. Knox, 'Occupation of Connacht by the Anglo-Normans after A.D. 1237', pt iii, *JRSAI* 13 (1903), p. 67. The O'Conors were thoroughly beaten down by 1316.

71 The following quote from the Annals of Loch Cé for the year 1307 testifies to the increased strength of the O'Kellys: 'The foreigners of Ros-Comain were all slain by Donnchadh Muimhneach O'Ceallaigh, a short time before his death, at Ath-escrah-Cuan to wit, where Philip Munter, and John Munter, and Matthew Drew fell along with seventy others who were either slain or taken prisoners; where the sheriff of Ros-Comain, and Diarmaid Gall Mac Diarmada, and Cormac Mac Ceithernaigh were taken prisoners; but their forces were still allowed to depart; and they themselves were let go after a while; and they afterwards made peace for the burning of the town by Edmond Butler.'

72 It states: 'A great victory over Toirdhelbhach O'Conchobhair king of Connacht, by Clann-Cellaigh; Toirdhelbhach himself was wounded there, and taken prisoner; and his horse and clothes were left there by him, together with a great slaughter of people.'

73 See Hall, *Women and the church*, chapter 6, where Hall explains some of the social aspects of convent life, including the matter of enclosure and enforcement, the interactions between nuns and the lay community around them, and the services, both spiritual and social, that the nuns provided. She meticulously scrutinises the range of activities that made up the spiritual life of women at this time. From the hagiography of women saints such as Bridget of Kildare, Ite of Killeedy (Co. Limerick), Moninne (Darerca) of Cell Shleibe Cuilinn (Killeevy, Co. Armagh) and Samthann of Cluain Bronaig (Clonbroney, Co. Longford) it is clear that professed nuns were involved in church-building, hosting clerics, fostering and educating children, pastoral care and caring for the sick. Hagiography also records nuns reading and writing, teaching psalms and lending manuscripts. In 'Priests' wives and brides of Christ', chapter 8 of *Land of women: tales of sex and gender from early Ireland* (Ithaca and London, 1996), Lisa Bitel provides several insights into the role of medieval nuns. In particular she mentions (p. 185) a boatload of wool which St Samthann's nuns received from Í, presumably for making wool, and states that the nun Ciar made clothes for St Cóemgen.

74 H.S. Sweetman, *Calendar of documents relating to Ireland, 1302–1307* (Longmans, 1886), p. 224.

75 P.W. Joyce, *The origin and history of Irish names of places*, i (Dublin, 1910), p. 150. Joyce (1827–1914) has stated that Liathán was the mother of St Kieran or was another woman of the same name. St Kieran was allegedly born near Fuerty in northern Hy-Many; hence St Mary Kyllin was seemingly rededicated to an Uí Maine woman.

76 Variations of the name, found in old documents, include 'Killithain', 'Killethean', 'Kyllheayn', 'Kyllcheayn', 'Kyllyhayn', 'Killehayn', 'Kyllihane', 'Killyane', 'Killiane', 'Killehan', 'Killihane', 'Cillian', 'Killyon' and 'Killian'.

77 Scanty information in papal letters of the fifteenth and early sixteenth centuries indicates that Killyan church functioned up to the Suppression, but on occasions had no vicar. In 1492 it was being served by a priest from the Cluniac monastery of the Apostles Peter and Paul de Innocentia near Athlone. In the same year it was united, but perhaps not permanently, with the neighbouring vicarage of Cill ar Ghualainn (now Ballygar parish); M.J. Haran (ed.), *Calendar of papal letters relating to Great Britain and Ireland, xv, 1484–1492* (Dublin, 1978), pp 434–5. For now, Killyan and Ballygar parishes are united.

78 The family broke into opposing branches: O'Conor Rua and O'Conor Donn.

79 Note the bizarre 'annexe' on the northern side; there is no entrance to the space enclosed and the walls seem to serve no purpose other than as a repository for fallen nunnery stones.

80 By deed dated 9 August of that year, for a certain sum of money and with the agreement of Edward Kinge, dean of Elphin (and next to be bishop in that diocese), and of his whole chapter; M.C. Griffith, *Irish patent rolls of James I*, patent roll 12, section CV1, p. 277.

81 James Hardiman, *The history of the town and county of Galway* (Dublin, 1820), p. 235, footnote f. It was said of John Lynch (allegedly by Sir James Ware) that 'he lived a concealed, and died a public papist'. He wasted and destroyed the diocese, 'leaving it not worth 200 marks'.

13
The Trinity College harp: the most exotic musical instrument in the world!

Brian Manners

Thought to date from AD 1400, the 'Brian Boru' or Trinity College harp is one of the oldest harps in the world. A fascinating number of stories and mythologies have attached themselves to this instrument over the past half-millennium. The most famous of all is that it once belonged to Brian Boru himself.

This essay is about the struggle for survival of an ancient tradition and an ancient instrument that has been long forgotten. The Trinity College harp is a very distinct type of harp. It is in fact a very different species from the typical harp that you see today in Ireland. We may for convenience call this type of harp the *cláirseach*, or simply the Gaelic harp, to distinguish it from the type current today.

Scientific research is being conducted into the *cláirseach* as we speak. Almost mythological in nature is the research already completed by Ann Heymann, one of the people spearheading the revival. A leading exponent, Heymann attests that these instruments only work at their optimum if strung in high-carat gold![1] Study of the exterior appearance of a typical Gaelic harp (like the Trinity College harp) is in its infancy, but early indications are that perhaps only the Book of Kells could outdo it for the arresting colourfulness of its design! Alas, however, its sweet, bell-like sound is almost never heard today, and we are only familiar with its worn and antiquated appearance.

Be that as it may, it is the Gaelic harp and not the modern version that has become the dominant symbol for Ireland. Henry VIII stamped its shape on the very first British coin in Ireland, and subsequent rulers have followed suit. It has quite an extraordinary visual presence in everyday Irish life, from commerce to sport and from education to politics (unionist and nationalist).[2] The newly formed Irish Free State adopted it as its emblem in 1922.

We are the only country in the world that has a musical instrument as its national emblem. We must also be the only country in the world whose national instrument is rarely ever heard. We are indifferent to it and to the world that it represents; most Irish people assume a knowledge of Gaelic Ireland, just as they assume that they've heard its harp, yet in reality they know little about either and appreciate them even less.

Firstly, what is important to realise is that the harp type seen today in Irish music sessions (or, indeed, in competition at Fleadh Cheoil na hÉireann) was invented in the nineteenth century by Dublin instrument-maker John Egan.[3] Its ancestor is not the Gaelic harp at all but rather the European orchestral harp. Gut-strung like a European harp, this 'portable Irish harp' no longer felt or sounded like the metal-wired instrument prevalent in the high Gaelic cultures of Ireland and Scotland. As Gaelic harp scholar Simon Chadwick states: 'The Gaelic revival demanded Romantic harps to accompany Gaelic singing in the parlours of Dublin and Edinburgh', and therefore it was designed so that 'classically trained polite aristocratic ladies could easily play it . . . Beyond the playing of certain melodies, there was no musical or technical connection between the two instruments.'[4]

The John Egan invention is often referred to as the 'neo-Irish' harp. In contrast to the neo-Irish and European traditions, the Gaelic harp was placed on the left shoulder rather than the right, utilising the right hand for the bass and the left for the treble. Strung in metal wire, the Brian Boru (Trinity College) harp, its contemporary in Scotland, the Queen Mary harp, and harps like them were plucked with the fingernails rather than the fingers, helping to create their distinctive sound. There are eighteen original Gaelic harps in existence; they are to be found in museums and in private ownership across Ireland and Scotland (with one in the Boston Museum of Fine Arts, USA).[5]

The history of the Gaelic harp stretches back at least 1,000 years in Ireland, although the oldest of the instruments dates only from the late medieval period, when harpers still enjoyed aristocratic status and the patronage of kings. Alongside the *file* (poet) and the *reacaire* (reciter), they were part of the high artistic culture of Gaelic society. They were not 'bards', as is often lazily stated by academics, but rather a distinct social class in themselves whose lives were solely dedicated to the excellence of harp-playing. It could take twelve years of intense study to reach the status of *ollam* (professor).[6] They enjoyed all the privileges of—and no doubt all the prejudices of—aristocratic life. Harpists were freed from manual labour of any kind under the highly sophisticated Gaelic law code (Brehon law), and it was illegal to cause them to break a nail or, indeed, to inflict any injury at all that would affect their playing.[7]

Today the harp is an internationally recognised symbol of Ireland. Many attribute this to a certain beer, but in reality this has been the case long before anyone drank a drop of Guinness.

Even the most prejudiced of outside observers of Ireland were in awe of the skill of the Irish harpist—most famously Gerald of Wales, who in the twelfth century wrote a work of propaganda justifying the Anglo-Norman invasion. A well-travelled man, he had spent time in the royal courts of Europe, no doubt coming into contact with the most celebrated musicians of that time.[8] Despite his desire to emphasise that all aspects of Ireland were repugnant, he couldn't help but be inspired by the music of the 'Irish savages':

> It is only in the case of musical instruments that I find any commendable diligence in these people—they are altogether more skilled than any other people I have seen.[9]

The Anglo-Norman invasion caused a major social and cultural upheaval, but the settlers were eventually almost swamped by the native culture. They were surrounded by a people that claimed a history almost as old as time itself.[10] The newcomers would very quickly have come into contact with this highly developed artistic culture, with its beautiful books and its harps strung with precious metal—all of which must have seemed extremely alluring. And just as they enjoyed the new, exotic women and the imaginative paganish love of life, so they would eventually come to appreciate the strict and elaborate legal code, representing a sophisticated and ancient society that it was dangerous to underestimate.

Ultimately, as medieval scholar Michael Richter states, '. . . the strength of Irish society meant that in the first part of the Middle Ages . . . it could absorb both the impact of the Vikings and that of the English'.[11] Becoming 'more Irish than the Irish themselves', the invaders Gaelicised their names, showed reverence for the Irish laws and surrounded themselves with poets and harpists like the natives. Real English power was limited to Dublin and some other urban centres, but, as historians are increasingly showing, trade with the Gael and the language of the Gael gradually became ever-present features of these 'English cities'.[12]

During the course of the twelfth century, and lasting until the seventeenth, new traditions in Irish poetry were invented. 'The new methods of composition were so strict and were observed so closely that experts find it nearly impossible to determine on the basis of language when or where a particular poem was written.'[13] This demonstrates remarkable cultural stability and unity, and a highly trained and organised scholarly culture (not to mention material wealth). It follows, therefore, that the *cruitire*, whose role was the virtuosic harp accompaniment of the reading of poetry in Gaelic courts, must also have been trained in this strict and sophisticated manner.

It is important to mention that the sustained patronage of these scholarly élites required not only an abundance of food and shelter but also all the other hallmarks of a functioning economy over many centuries. It must also be noted that the materials for the creation of books and musical instruments were expensive by European standards—particularly a musical instrument as technologically advanced as the Gaelic harp, with all its artistic adornments. Outside of the church organ, the Brian Boru harp, as attested by scholar Joan Rimmer, had a wider range of notes than any other musical instrument on the Continent at that time.[14]

Much as in the politically disunited Italy and Germany of the late Middle Ages,[15] the Irish kings and chieftains competed with one another not just materialistically and in the art of war but also, paradoxically, in artistic taste and hospitality. Their status was enhanced by how many poets and harpists they could patronise and by how many books they owned. How beautiful were those books! How beautiful were those harps and the music that sang of the kings' greatness! All this and more played its part in the elevation and power of a king in the minds of his subjects. The perfect metre of a poem, or the popularity of an accompanying tune, written in their honour was the perfect propaganda for these ambitious kings. Though this was rooted in political self-interest, it encouraged the considerable cultural and artistic achievement of the Gaelic world.

At the beginning of the seventeenth century the Tudor conquest took hold and the Irish earls took flight, and thus began the end of the Gaelic aristocratic society on which the harpist depended for his patronage. Despite the best attempts of British officialdom to repress all the Irish arts and language, the traditions were too strong, too established and too highly developed to be wiped out. Nevertheless, the glory days were over for the Irish harpist, who was now degraded to the status of a wandering minstrel. For a while, however, there was something of a false dawn, when Gaelic culture again showed its allure and resilience. Patronage was found in a seemingly unlikely place—amongst the Anglo-Irish aristocracy. The Gaelic harps became larger, so as to play the new hybrid Irish music that the new patrons demanded. Turlough O'Carolan's music is the great example of this style—Irish mixed with European baroque. He is the personification of these great wandering musicians.

It was inevitable that some harpists would leave for a new life on the Continent. During the seventeenth century their skill as musicians was famed throughout Europe and the Irish harper was found in many royal courts, from Spain to Poland. An oil painting from 1622 shows an Irish harpist amongst the Danish aristocracy.[16] Even some English writers praised the music of the Irish harp. Philosopher and scientist Francis Bacon—who was, amongst other things, lord chancellor and attorney general of England—stated that 'no instrument hath the sound so melting and prolonged as the Irish harp'.[17]

Patronage in Ireland reached its zenith in the important Belfast harp festival of 1792.[18] Realising 'how the mighty had fallen', the festival was supposed to help revive a tradition that was badly in need of reinvigoration. An invitation was sent out, to gather together as many harpists as possible from around Ireland. At this festival an eager young musician (but not a harpist) named Edward Bunting wrote down for posterity the music and the technical aspects of what he saw. Much of the Irish harp music that exists today is a direct result of this Protestant upper-class event and of Bunting's transcripts. Wolfe Tone (an attendee at the event) and Robert Emmet would later declare in their fight for Irish freedom that 'the harp is new strung and shall be heard'.[19]

One of Bunting's many interesting observations concerned the tuning of the harp. Two of the strings are tuned to the exact same 'G', breaking the diatonic run of the notes. The harpists at the time described these in English as the 'sister strings'. Bunting, other observers and even the harpists themselves had no musical explanation for this—it was merely tradition. Bunting noted that these strings 'nearly divided the instrument into bass and treble'. As Ann Heymann states, 'their recorded usage spanned at least 750 years, from twelfth-century glosses in Leabhar na hUidhre to an interview with harpist Patrick Byrne in 1849'.[20]

With no musical explanation in sight for this peculiarity, one must look beyond the musicality of the instrument and consider the harp through the eyes of an Irishman or woman over the course of these centuries. This was an aristocratic musical instrument that was a supreme example of Gaelic art and science, played by a people whose pagan roots were still strong. The Irish for 'sister strings' was the much less modest *comhluighe*, meaning 'lying together' (with sexual connotations), which therefore suggests that one string is male and the other female. Leading scholars Ann and Charlie Heymann give an explanation:

> Right and left in Gaelic Ireland were often equated with male and female. For example, the right side of the hearth was the man's and the left was the woman's. Men sat on the right side of the church and women on the left. If the cláirseach was thought to encompass both male and female voices, then the harper's left (female) and right (male) hands sounded the appropriate voices.[21]

The appropriate voices were the treble and the bass, the right (male) hand playing the bass and the left (female) hand the treble. This seemingly pagan Gaelic need for symmetry in nature has its modern-day equivalent in the Far Eastern philosophy of Yin and Yang.

Unfortunately, the Belfast festival did not have the desired effect and the tradition limped on into the nineteenth century.[22] John Egan invented his portable Irish harp, which, as mentioned above, became the Irish harp of modern times, leaving the Gaelic harp's bell-like sound to pass unheard into history—and the harp itself to be ultimately used as a national symbol and commercial logo. Historian Simon Chadwick states:

> Beyond the playing of certain melodies, there was no musical or technical connection between the two traditions . . . The most interesting thing is that the terms such as 'Irish harp' and 'clarsach', its national symbolism, its romantic and mythological associations, in fact all of the non-musical and non-technical baggage that the harp has always carried along with it, was transferred from the former to the latter with almost no interruption.[23]

In the twentieth century, however, the extinction of a lost art form was not acceptable to some. Major Irish composer Seán Ó Riada regarded the modern interpretation of this ancient art as weak and wholly inadequate.[24] In fact, he wouldn't allow modern Irish harpists in his famous ensemble Ceoltoirí Chualann. In *Our musical heritage* he shows his distaste: 'The present day harp technique with its soft, rather blurred sound has given rise to rather feminine drooping musical figures, while the older traditional sharp-toned technique gave rise to a vigorous masculine music'.[25]

Anyone familiar with Ó Riada's music will be aware of how much the harpsichord is played.[26] He felt that the plucking action of the harpsichord was closer to the sound and feel of the Gaelic harp. One of the many legacies of Ó Riada's short life was the revival of the harp music of O'Carolan.[27] Indeed, his fascination with the ancient tradition could lead in only one direction: an accurate reconstruction of the Brian Boru harp. In the mid-1960s he began this work with his friend Christopher Warren. Unfortunately, as he died some years later at the age of 40, he was never able to fully explore the ancient playing technique. His dream of restoring the Gaelic harp to its rightful place in the tradition was to be taken up by others.

One such advocate was a collaborator of Ó Riada's, Gráinne Yeats, who took up the mantle in the 1970s, along with others, such as American Jay Witcher, who began to make accurate reconstructions of the Trinity College harp.[28] Around this time Ann Heymann read a book by Edward Bunting and bought herself a Jay Witcher harp—the modern revival had begun!

Derek Bell of The Chieftains began to play the Gaelic harp in recordings.[29] Other individuals, such as David Kortier in the USA and Davy Patton in Ireland, began making accurate replicas. Gaelic harpist Paul Dooley built his own harps and did important work on the 'ap Huw' collection of music. Of Welsh and Irish origin, the 'ap Huw' manuscripts contain the oldest harp music in Europe. Siobhán Armstrong, an early music specialist and harpist who specialised in Baroque and opera, founded the Historical Harp Society of Ireland in 2002. Operating a summer school every year for young and old, it is one of the most important cultural and musical organisations operating in Ireland today.

Like research into the world it represents, at present only a handful of musicologists and musicians are doing important work on this very under-studied Gaelic art form, the most outstanding of which is the work of Ann Heymann. Her *Secrets of the Gaelic harp* was the first tutorial book on the harp, and she continues to lead the way in developing our understanding of the tradition. According to Heymann, one of the problems faced by the three oldest extant Gaelic harps that date from the period of Gaelic aristocratic patronage is tuning.[30] She explains:

> Over the past thirty years many imitations . . . have been built, but most differ significantly from the museum originals in ways that directly affect the stringing . . . [the] few copies that accurately follow the museum prototypes and are strung according to historical prototypes display dramatically decreased string tensions . . . in the bass octave, leading to progressively poorer tone and making tuning elusive for the longest strings.[31]

Reliable historical sources state that Gaelic harps were strung in silver,[32] although gold-stringed harps are mentioned in poetry and mythology. After extensive work and research, utilising a Brian Boru replica and stringing according to historical prototype, Heymann decided to use gold strings in the bass section. The harp now stayed in tune! The problem of 'elusive tuning' was solved. She further explains:

> Silver would have served the same purpose as gold only less effectively . . . and was more likely to serve as a complementary transition between the gold in the bass and brass in the high treble.[33]

Heymann's successful experiments, backed by a belief amongst scholars in the historical possibilities of gold and, indeed, the obvious enhanced sound quality of precious metals, has led others (including Siobhán Armstrong and Simon Chadwick) to follow her lead. Alas, no Gaelic kingships exist anymore to patronise this expensive stringing; though perhaps not ideal, modern brass strings suffice quite well musically for many. When the queen of England visited Trinity College in 2011, Siobhán Armstrong played her gold-stringed Brian Boru replica in the famous Long Room.

Unfortunately, and understandably, her replica harp lacked colour, as no proper study of the colour of the instrument has been carried out to date. Ironically, our national emblem, housed for the last 200 years in the esteemed seat of learning that is Trinity College, is very under-studied in its entirety. Only the Bunworth harp (housed in the Boston Museum of Fine Arts) and the Cloyne harp (owned by the National Museum of Ireland) have been reproduced in their true colourful splendour.

Ann Heymann holding the Mac Liag harp.

Researcher Karen Loomis has done some fascinating work on the Queen Mary harp in the University of Edinburgh—the sister instrument of the Brian Boru harp and dating from roughly the same period.[34] Employing the latest technology, she has made many fascinating discoveries, including traces of vermilion red on the body of the harp. Using vermilion red—the ultimate status symbol in medieval Europe—was almost like painting in gold leaf. It was used only in the most prestigious decoration of art in Renaissance Italy and in other periods of European history.[35] This provides clear evidence of the high standing of the harpist and of music in general in Gaelic society.

The true scientific replication in sound and in visual form of our national emblem must be an important objective for all those interested in our history and music. I believe that success in bringing this tradition back to life depends on this. What is of concern is that amongst the small troupe of true Gaelic harpists (the tiny minority that they are) playing today there is either a cost issue or a conservatism, or a desire to be fashion-conscious, because almost all of their harps remain colourless. Considering that most of the eighteen extant Gaelic harps show traces of very elaborate decoration, this is a bland and historically inaccurate representation of our harp, worryingly echoing the invention of the neo-Irish harp in the nineteenth century. Though we as yet lack scientific understanding of the historical colouring of most of these instruments, for the time being I see no reason for the modern replicas not to be designed in a style that seems appropriate to the player and tastefully nods to the Gaelic/Celtic design principals. The Mac Liag harp (a Brian Boru-inspired design) by Ann Heymann is a good example of this ideal.

Though not every Gaelic harp that has survived was coloured, this general disregard of colour is a problem: at a cursory glance all harps look the same to most people. Even the organisers of the Dublin St Patrick's Day festival use the straight-forepillared European Classical harp for branding. At a recent event for foreign dignitaries in Dublin Castle a Classical European harp was displayed—presumably all neo-Irish and Gaelic harp replicas were lost under the bed that day!

The vibrant, distinctive, colourful design of a Gaelic harp, with its large soundbox and greatly outcurved forepillar, could not be ignored and would light up any great room. Looking more closely, one would see precious-metal strings, and it would seem undeniable that this instrument represented a sophisticated artistic society.

Its visual beauty, colourful aesthetic and resonating bell-like sound will raise the harp from its position of obscure interest to a dedicated few to what it should be: not a symbol of commerce or of a disinterested Irish state but rather a symbol of Ireland's ancient high culture. Small and relatively light, the Brian Boru harp is ideally suited to the impromptu nature of an Irish music session (neo-Irish harps are often missing from pub sessions owing to their impractical size). Rarely heard now, it will be newly coloured and newly strung again and again, and heard wherever the Irish—or, indeed, the Scots—gather in the world!

Perhaps even the Irish state could be shown the potential cultural (and, indeed, economic) value of a renewed interest in our instrument. Foreign dignitaries or Irish citizens whom the state wishes to honour could be given a true replica of our national symbol in all its colour and precious-metal splendour. Indeed, its 'trophyesque' size would be ideal for this purpose; the image of an Irish Taoiseach presenting the Brian Boru/Trinity College harp to an American president would create some buzz of interest in our diaspora for this 'newly seen' instrument. No longer would it be just a two-dimensional symbol to be seen wherever Ireland is mentioned; it would be restored to its historic position as a real working musical instrument of national and international significance—still standing and still being heard in all its glamour after a thousand years!

Historian Donnchadh Ó Corráin alerts us to 'the woolly and foolish notions about wandering tribes and barbarous chiefs' which most Irish people possess when thinking about the history of their country (interestingly echoing the lasting effects of Cambrensis-style propaganda).[36] These notions would be given their marching orders by the sight and sound of this most exotic and beautiful of instruments. At the very least, the powers that be should realise that 'hanging the Gaelic harpists and breaking their instruments'[37]—or, indeed, just ignoring them—is not in their material interest . . . or rather not in the interest of what they call 'Brand Ireland'.

For another thousand years, let the *cláirseach* be newly coloured, newly strung and newly heard! *Cáid cach ceól co cruit*—'all music is sweet until compared to the harp'.[38]

Notes

1 A. Heymann and C. Heymann, 'Strings of gold', *Historical Harp Journal* 13 (3) (2003), pp 9–15.

2 S. Ó Brógáin, *The Wolfhound guide to the Irish harp emblem* (Dublin, 1998), p. 13.

3 M.L. O'Donnell, *Ireland's harp: the shaping of Irish identity,* c. *1770–1880* (Dublin, 2014), pp 87–105.

4 S. Chadwick, 'The early Irish harp', *Early Music* 36 (4) (2008), p. 521.

5 There are sixteen complete Gaelic harps in existence, and a further two that are in a fragmented state (see http://www.earlygaelicharp.info/instruments/; accessed April 2015).

6 See F. Kelly, *A guide to early Irish law* (Dublin, 1988; repr. 2001), pp 43–9, for a discussion of the legal position of the *file* within Gaelic society. Elsewhere in this book Kelly explains the divisions of rank. In the uppermost echelons of Gaelic society was a class of people described as *nemed* ('sacred'). The main members were kings (various grades), lords (those in possession of a certain number of client farmers), clerics (from low-ranking clergy to archbishops/abbots) and poets. An honour-price of seven *cumals* (units of currency, one *cumal* being normally equal to three milch cows) is allotted to the lowest grade of king, but also to a bishop and to a master-poet (a poet with the rank of *ollamh*). A provincial king, an archbishop and some abbots are awarded twice that, i.e. fourteen *cumals*, although not all sources are in agreement on the exact honour-price. It should be noted that the majority of these laws were written down in the seventh and eighth centuries but continued to be copied and edited by legal scribes up to the fall of Gaelic society.

7 Ibid., pp 129–57; http://www.brehonlawacademy.ie/#!Irish-Manuscripts-Uraicecht-Becc-–-The-Short-Primer/c19ap/0EF73336-9BED-4C04-B1C0-AD07BB4DDC29; *Urraicheacht Becht*: 'Nadbi cainfoltach nibi cainfuillmech' ('He who is not well qualified is not well remunerated').

8 See http://www.historyireland.com/medieval-history-pre-1500/giraldus-cambrensiss-view-of-europe/ (accessed April 2015).

9 John J. O'Meara (trans.), *The topography of Ireland by Giraldus Cambrensis* (Dundalk, 1951), p. 87.

10 'Goídel Glas', the grandson of Pharaoh, is claimed as the creator of 'Goídelc' (the Gaelic language) and hence as the ancestor of the Gaels; R.A.S. Macalister (ed. & trans.), *Lebor gabála Érenn: the book of the taking of Ireland* (5 vols, Dublin, 1932–42), ii, 107.

11 M. Richter, *Medieval Ireland: the enduring tradition* (Dublin, 2005), p. 188.

12 'Gaelic seeped into the Pale in spite of efforts to keep it out . . . by the sixteenth century children of

English descent were being coerced to learn their own language at their parent's expense'; P. Somerville-Large, *Dublin* (London, 1981), p. 85. At the start of the 1600s Fynes Moryson, an English administrator and chronicler with an overt anti-Irish bias, amongst numerous complaints about the Old English adopting Irish customs, had this to say about the Irish language: '. . . the English Irish and the very Cittizens . . . Commonly speake Irish among themselves . . . and my selfe and others often observed, the Cittizens of Watterford and Corcke having wyves that could speake English as well as wee, bitterly to chyde them when they speake English with us . . .'; C. Hughes (ed.), *Shakespeare's Europe: unpublished chapters of Fynes Moryson's Itinerary* (London, 1903), p. 213.

13 Richter, *Medieval Ireland*, p. 136.

14 J. Rimmer, 'The morphology of the Irish harp', *Galpin Society Journal* 17 (1964), pp 39–49.

15 Richter, *Medieval Ireland*, p. 9.

16 S. Chadwick, http://www.earlygaelicharp.info/history/17th.htm (accessed April 2015).

17 F. Bacon, *Sylvarum Sylva, or a natural history in ten centuries* (London, 1627), items 146, 223 and 278; J. Spedding *et al.* (eds), *The works of Francis Bacon* (15 vols, London, 1857–9), ii, 399–400, 420, 433; W. Bray (ed.), *The diary of John Evelyn* (London, n.d.), pp 273 and 418 (entries for 20 January 1654 and 14 November 1668).

18 G. Yeats, *The harp of Ireland: the Belfast harpers' festival, 1792, and the saving of Ireland's harp music by Edward Bunting* (Belfast, 1992).

19 Ó Brógáin, *The Wolfhound guide to the Irish harp emblem*, p. 22.

20 A. Heymann and C. Heymann, 'Cláirseach: the lore of the Irish harp', *Éire-Ireland* 26 (3) (1991), pp 84–7.

21 Ibid.

22 See O'Donnell, *Ireland's harp*, *passim*, for a general description of this period.

23 S. Chadwick, http://www.earlygaelicharp.info/history/19th.htm (accessed April 2015).

24 O'Donnell, *Ireland's harp*, pp 139–40.

25 T. Kinsella and T. Ó Cannain, *Our musical heritage* (Dublin, 1982), pp 78–9.

26 *Ó Riada's farewell*, his final album, is a solo harpsichord recording exploring Irish harp music (catalogue no. CC12CD, Claddagh Records).

27 G. Yeats, 'The rediscovery of Carolan', in B. Harris and G. Freyer (eds), *Integrating tradition: the achievement of Seán Ó Riada* (Irish Humanities Center & Keohanes, 1981), 78–94.

28 Derek Bell, *Carolan's receipt* (Claddagh catalogue no. CC18CD; barcode 7497730018208; released in 1975). The following is printed on the cover: 'It is the first record on which a real metal-strung Irish harp is used by an Irish Harper'.

29 Ibid.

30 The Lamont, the Brian Boru/Trinity College and the Queen Mary are the oldest Gaelic harps in existence. Somewhat distinguished by their small size, they are described as low-headed Gaelic harps. For more on the description of various Gaelic harps see S. Chadwick, http://www.earlygaelicharp.info/stringing/history.htm#osb (accessed April 2015).

31 Heymann and Heymann, 'Strings of gold', pp 9–15.

32 S. Chadwick, http://earlygaelicharp.info/stringing/history.htm (accessed April 2015).

33 Heymann and Heymann, 'Strings of gold', pp 9–15.

34 K. Loomis, https://www.academia.edu/11082480/The_Lamont_and_Queen_Mary_Harps (accessed April 2015); 'Vermilion pigment has so far only been detected on the forepillar, but the dark waxy substance found in the decorative work and surface crevices on the soundbox also appears in cracks and crevices on the forepillar'.

35 An expensive and desirable commodity during the Renaissance, it tended to be forged. 'Always buy vermilion unbroken, and not pounded or ground. The reason? Because it is generally adulterated, either with red lead or with pounded brick'; Cennino d'Andrea Cennini, *The craftsman's handbook: the Italian 'Il libro dell' arte'*, trans. D.V. Thompson Jr (New York, 1933), p. 40.

[36] D. Ó Corráin, 'Brian Boru, master of psychological warfare', *The Irish Times*, 8 March 2014.

[37] W.H. Grattan Flood, *The story of the harp* (London, 1905). On 28 January 1603 Queen Elizabeth herself ordered Lord Barrymore 'to hang the harpers wherever found, and destroy their instruments'. Whether Flood can be relied on as regards this quotation is debatable; we do know, however, that royal edicts were grandly pronounced, such as 'Execute by marshall law . . . harpers rymers barde', cited in A.J. Fletcher, *Drama and the performing arts in pre-Cromwellian Ireland: a repertory of sources and documents from the earliest times until* c. *1642* (Cambridge, 2001), p. 185, and taken from MS Harley 697 (f. 143v) in the British Library, with a date of 20 January 1603. Whether these orders were carried out could largely depend on the individuals on the ground, who may or may not have felt it politically desirable to obey. The above quotation is from an 'Edict of the Lord President and Council of Munster', with the following (summarised) text: 'We . . . haue thoughte it fitte to sette forthe and publishe this her Maiesties Proclamacion hereby in her Highnes name to declare . . . that the Marshall of this Province is . . . Commaunded to execute by Marshall lawe . . . Bardes, rymers, harpers . . . which he . . . shall fynde travaileinge or resydeinge within this Province . . . without the lycense or pasporte of his Master . . . being a knowne Subiecte . . .'

[38] Old Irish proverb; see Kelly, *A guide to early Irish law*, p. 64. There is some dispute amongst scholars as to the original meaning of *cruit*.

14

A woman's place: the functions of Queen Medb in Gaelic literature

Lora O'Brien

'Celtic' warrior queen of Connacht, sovereignty goddess, guardian and initiator, with fierce sexual prowess and an arrogance that led her men to downfall: this is the general popular perception of Medb today (according to the author's daily experience managing the Rathcroghan Visitor Centre), but on what is this perception based? This essay will examine references to the Queen Medb character in Irish literary sources, and explore the recorded themes. These are by no means comprehensive listings but merely an adequate sampling as space allows for the purposes of a foundational essay. Further research is needed on Medb, and particularly interesting will be work that looks at the social, political and cultural context in which her tales were recorded, and the influence that Gaelic culture exercised on the character development of the Connacht queen.

For now, though, where does Medb show up in the stories, and what themes are recorded? She is best known as a character in the *Táin Bó Cuailnge*,[1] but we see even in the pre-tale 'How the Bulls were Begotten' that 'the other [maggot] got into the well-spring Garad in Connacht, where a cow belonging to Medb and Ailill drank it'. And in 'The Adventures of Nera',[2] sometimes called *Táin Bó Aingen*, the stage is further set, as we see Medb speaking 'in the manner of an oath: I swear by the gods that my people swear by, that I shall not lie down, nor sleep on down or flockbed, nor shall I drink butter-milk nor nurse my side, nor drink red ale nor white, nor shall I taste food, until I see those two kine fighting before my face'.

What of Medb's history before the *Táin*? It is soon told. During the 'pillow talk' in *Táin Bó Cuailnge*[3] we hear how she became queen of Connacht: 'my father was in the high-kingship of Ireland, namely Eochu Feidlech ... He had six daughters ... I was the noblest and worthiest of them. I was the most generous of them in bounty and the bestowal of gifts. I was best of them in battle and fight and combat. I had fifteen hundred royal mercenaries of the sons of strangers exiled from their own land and as many of the sons of native freemen within the province ... I had these as my standing household', said Medb, 'and for that reason my father gave me one of the provinces of Ireland, namely, the province of Crúachu. Whence I am called Medb Chrúachna.' She hasn't mentioned, though, that Cruachan was previously ruled by her sister (as stated in *Aided Meidbe*):[4] 'Now Clothru was queen in Cruachu before Medb took the sovereignty; that [was] by force from Eochaid'.

And what of Medb's family? It is soon told. The aforementioned tale of Medb's death also records: 'The three daughters [of Eochaid Feidlig were] Eithni Uathach . . . (Eithni the terrible), namely, she used to eat the flesh of infants so that the children always disliked her to be mentioned, and Medb of Cruachu, and Clothru of Cruachu'.[5] From the *Ban-shenchus*, 'the Lore of Women',[6] we learn that 'Croind . . . was the wanton consort of Eochu Feidlech and mother of valiant Medb of Cruachan (glorious, perverse, extravagant and liberal) . . . There were six daughters . . . Mugain, Medb the hazel-kernel, and Lothra, Derbriu, Ethni and beauteous Clothru'. And her children are named: 'The seven Mane were Medb's great sons, the sons of Ailill who was not jealous. Three others (by whom good poetry was framed) were by Fergus, possessor of wealth. Their names were Ciar, Corc, and Conmac. They were three mighty chiefs in truth. There was Mane Mingor, Mane Morgor, Mane Mathremail who was not slow, Mane Athernail of the lies, Mane Mo Epert, Mane Mór who kept all and Mane Andoe lord of the district.' Her sons are named slightly differently in 'The Raid for the Cattle of Regamon':[7] 'Maine Morgor (Maine with great filial love), Maine Mingar (Maine with less filial love), Maine Aithremail (Maine like his father), Maine Mathremail (Maine like his mother), Maine Milbel (Maine with the mouth of honey), Maine Moepert (Maine too great to be described), Maine Condageb-uile (Maine who combined all qualities): now this one had the form both of father and mother, and had all the glory that belonged to both parents'.

What of Medb as royal host? It is soon told. In 'The Exile of the Sons of Uisliu', the Ulstermen 'went to Connacht, to Ailill and Medb—not that this was a home for Ulstermen, but that they knew these two would protect them'.[8] 'The Battle of Airtech'[9] tells that on the election of a new king the nobles of Ulster requested Fergus Mac Róich to come back to the fold, and he left Connacht—despite Medb's attempted bribery with female slaves—with his wife Flidais and stayed in Ulster until her death, 'after which he went back to Ailill and Medb, for his house-holding in the East was not good after Flidais'. In 'The Dream of Oengus',[10] Dagda brings his lovesick son 'to Ailill and Medb, for the girl is in their territory'. The party was welcomed with a week of feasting and drinking, and after an adventure with the Síd-dwellers . . . 'This is how the friendship between Ailill and Medb and the Macc Oc [Oengus] arose, and this is why Oengus took three hundred to the cattle raid of Cuailnge'. Another *Táin*, 'The Raid for Dartaid's Cattle',[11] shows Medb and Ailill summoning a king for a Samhain feast, and he receives aid from the Síd to fit his party out in splendour to impress them in Connacht. In 'The Cattle Raid of Fraech',[12] the hero does such a fine job of the same splendid fitting out of his party, with the help of the Síd, that sixteen are smothered to death in the crush to view them upon arrival at Cruachan. After feasting for three days and three nights, Fraech must face a monster in a lake to prove his worth to Medb and Ailill, but then they command that 'a bath of fresh bacon broth be prepared . . . and bid them with adze and with axe the flesh of a heifer full small to mince: Let the meat be all thrown in the bath, and there for healing let Fraech be laid', after which 'he passed from their sight out of Croghan; For that night from earth was he freed, and he dwelt with his kin, the Síd-dwellers, in the caverns of Croghan's deep Síd'.

What of Medb's judgement? It is soon told. In *Fled Bricrenn*,[13] Medb commands 'that women go out to meet the [arriving Ulster] warriors, and that beds be made ready and tubs of cold water prepared, so as to appease their frenzy'. She then feasts them for three days and three nights, after which she tests them (all of which is reminiscent of Fraech's visit), when 'three ferocious cats from the Cave of Cruachain were set loose against the three warriors'. When Aillil refuses to judge the warriors, she upbraids him for cowardice and does it herself, tricking each one into thinking himself the winner and packing them off home to Ulster. Medb is again seen as a decision-maker in the tale of 'The Battle of Magh Mucrama',[14] when she was counting the pigs that could not be counted: 'Medb was in her chariot. One of the pigs jumped across the chariot. "That pig is an extra one, Medb", said everyone. "It won't be this one", said Medb, seizing the pig's shank so that its skin split on its forehead and it left the skin in her hand along with the shank and it is not known where they went from that time onwards.' In 'The Colloquy of the Two Sages',[15] we see a brief reference to a poet's robe being conferred by Medb and Ailill. In 'The Driving of the Cattle of Flidais',[16] when Fergus comes to Ailill with a problem regarding another man's wife (Flidais) who loves him, Ailill says, 'we will consider this in counsel with Maev', who then proposes how they should proceed.

What of Medb's many lovers? It is soon told. 'The Battle of the Boyne'[17] is also called 'Medb's Men', and tells a long tale of the husbands of Medb, but her husbands end with Ailill, who 'assumed the kingship of Connacht thereafter, with the consent of Meadb'. In 'The Melodies of Buchet's House',[18] there is reference to 'Medb of the Red Side, the wife of Art, who took the Kingship [of Kells, the 'Royal Seat'] after Art's death, and did not suffer Cormac'. In the *Táin Bó Cuailnge*,[19] we see that the demands she makes of a husband are quite high, and why: '... a husband without meanness, without jealousy, without fear. If my husband should be mean, it would not be fitting for us to be together, for I am generous in largesse and the bestowal of gifts ... If my husband were timorous, neither would it be fitting for us to be together, for single-handed I am victorious in battles and contests and combats ... If the man with whom I should be were jealous, neither would it be fitting, for I was never without a man in the shadow of another.' In 'The Death of Fergus Mac Róich',[20] she seems to be having a rather agitated sexual encounter: 'As Fergus entered the lake, all there was of gravel and of stones at the bottom of the lake came to the surface. Then Medb went till she was on the breast of Fergus, with her legs entwined around him, and then he swam around the lake. And jealousy seized Ailill. Then Medb went up.'

So, what of Medb's womanhood? It is soon told. Her menstrual cycle is noted:

'Then her issue of blood came upon Medb and she said: "Fergus, cover the retreat of the men of Ireland that I may pass my water". "By my conscience", said Fergus, "It is ill-timed and it is not right to do so." "Yet I cannot but do so", said Medb, "for I shall not live unless I do" ... Medb passed her water and it made three great trenches in each of which a household can fit.' And at the end of it all, even Fergus seems to turn against her: '"This day was indeed a fitting one for those who were led by a woman", said Fergus. [Seven untranslated words] said Medb to Fergus ... "As when a mare goes before her band of foals into unknown territory, with none to lead or counsel them, so this host has perished today".'

And what of Medb's death? It is soon told. In *Aided Meidbe*, 'The Violent Death of Medb',[21] 'They say indeed that Medb killed her [sister Clothrú] and that through her side the swords brought forth Furbaide . . . Medb assumed the kingship of Connaught and took Ailill into sovereignty with her . . . Medb happened to be bathing herself early in the morning in the well ... "Who is that?" Furbaide asked. "The sister of your mother," all answered. He was eating a piece of cheese. He did not then tarry to seek a stone. He put the piece [of cheese] in the sling. When Medb's forehead was towards them, he let fly the piece [of cheese] and it struck her on the crown of the head so that he killed her by the one cast in vengeance of his mother. That is the death of Medb.'

Have we seen the Medb character here as a warrior, a sovereignty figure representative of the land, a guardian, an initiator, or a sexual and arrogant queen, as per the surviving popular view? Arguments could be made for Medb representing any of those functions, using the examples above, but this is not the full picture. Further research is certainly needed to explore whether the character of Medb was written throughout Gaelic culture as an educational tool or to preserve the details of older beliefs and mythology. Or perhaps Queen Medb fulfilled both functions?

Notes

1 T. Kinsella, *The Táin* (New York, 1970).
2 K. Meyer, 'Echtra Nerai (The adventures of Nera)', *Revue Celtique* 10 (1889), pp 212–28.
3 C. O'Rahilly, *Táin bó Cualnge from the Book of Leinster* (Dublin, 1970).
4 V. Hull, 'Aided Meidbe: the violent death of Medb', *Speculum* 13 (1) (1938), pp 52–61.
5 Ibid.
6 M.E. Dobbs, 'The Ban-shenchus', *Revue Celtique* 47 (1930), 283–339.
7 A.H. Leahy, *Heroic romances of Ireland*, ii (London, 1906).
8 Kinsella, *The Táin*.
9 R.I. Best, 'The battle of Airtech', *Ériu* 8 (1916), pp 170–90.
10 J. Gantz, *Early Irish sagas* (London, 1981).
11 Leahy, *Heroic romances of Ireland*, ii.
12 Ibid.
13 M. Dillon, *Early Irish literature* (Chicago, 1948).
14 W. Stokes, 'The battle of Mag Mucrime', *Revue Celtique* 13 (1892), pp 426–74.

[15] *Idem*, 'The colloquy of the two sages', *Revue Celtique* 26 (1905), pp 4–64.
[16] Leahy, *Heroic romances of Ireland*, ii.
[17] J. O'Neill, 'Cath Boinde', *Ériu* 2 (1905), pp 173–85.
[18] Dillon, *Early Irish literature.*
[19] O'Rahilly, *Táin bó Cualnge.*
[20] K. Meyer, *The death-tales of the Ulster heroes* (Dublin, 1906).
[21] Hull, 'Aided Meidbe'.

15

The Tallaght hills: a landscape of kingship and assembly

Colette Allen

The civil parish of Tallaght, with 49 townlands, is one of the largest in the country, and about a third of it lies in the mountain area known as the Tallaght hills. The Tallaght hills have been variously portrayed over the centuries as a place of escape or sanctuary (from the Gaelic point of view) or as the den of rebels (from the point of view of the English administration). Their proximity to the city of Dublin accentuated this perception.

The passage tombs crowning the hills of south-west Dublin and west Wicklow are a prominent feature of the landscape and are said to 'demarcate a sacred and political territory'.[1] There is also a demarcation between the groupings of passage tombs of south-west Dublin and the portal tombs to the east. This pattern continued in the Iron Age, with a concentration of hillforts and ring-barrows noted in south-west Dublin, and a major ceremonial landscape based along the western flanks of the Dublin mountains at Tallaght and Saggart.[2] The prehistoric evidence therefore points to the emergence of a strongly symbolic cultural landscape pattern from the time of its earliest inhabitants. In the Ordnance Survey letters for Dublin, Eugene O'Curry noted the significance of Tallaght Hill and its neighbours. He discussed and illustrated a range of mounds in the Tallaght area and cited some of the striking names among those cairns, such as Láthair na Ríogh.[3] This hilltop site had a great prospect over several counties and may have been an inauguration or *oireachtas* site. Assembly places were often sited on hilltop locations that featured prehistoric burial mounds.

The pair of stones at the western base of Tallaght Hill in Boherboy frame the view of Láthair na Ríogh. The place-name Boherboy is found at the foot of hills associated with assembly, such as Drung Hill and Mount Brandon in County Kerry, Church Mountain in County Wicklow and near Cullen in County Cork. The place-name element *buí* and landscapes of sovereignty have been discussed in the first volume of these essays.[4] According to Eoin Mac Neill, the pass between these hills was the suggested setting for the death of Laoghaire Mac Neill, a mythical king of Tara.[5]

There are place-names in the Tallaght hills that appear to parallel those in the early Irish saga called *Togail bruidne Da Derga*, which relates the accession, kingship and death of Conaire Mór, another legendary king of Tara. 'Togail bruidne Da Derga was an important tale which enjoyed widespread popularity and, as such, there were

Standing stone pair Adam and Eve in Boherboy, after the harvest. The hilltop summit in the distance was the site of Láthair na Ríogh. (Photo: Colette Allen)

probably many written and oral variants on the central theme of Conaire's tragic downfall.'[6] One of those oral variants may have been told in the hills of Tallaght, as the site of the mythical Da Derga's hostel is taken to be at the head of Glenasmole. T.M. Charles-Edwards points out that Conaire entered upon his reign via the Slighe Chualann and left it by returning to Leinster by the same route, travelling to his death at the hostel of 'Da Derga of the Leinstermen'.[7]

The manor of Bohercolyn has been traced by Liam Price from documents dating from 1171 to 1660,[8] demonstrating that this manor extended from east to west across the townlands of the parish of Tallaght, from Oldbawn to Boherboy in Saggart. The Slighe Chualann was assumed to follow the eastern coast 'chiefly on the account of the name Booterstown and its problematic etymology as Baile an Bhóthair'.[9] He gives the route of the Slighe Chualann as Dublin, Tallaght, Saggart, Rathcoole and so on, forming the main road to the south-east. Boherboy townland and the roadway or route that is inferred by the name is without doubt on the Slighe Chualann. Boherboy probably lay on an important nodal point, as the Slighe Chualann ran through it on an east–west axis, but Boherboy is also where the main route south that skirts the granite massif of the Dublin and Wicklow hills commences.

The sense of Conaire's impending doom would have been heightened if the listener, knowing the local landscape, imagined his journey along Bohercolyn and past Lysnacally[10] (the otherworld abode of the *cailleach* and the early name for Old Bawn). Nearby is Cairn na Dearg Laoich;[11] this place-name may commemorate the three red horsemen from the otherworld who preceded Conaire to the hostel. Conaire moves onwards through Bohernabreena, the road to the hostel and Glenasmole. Glenasmole was noted in the folklore record as meaning 'the glen of the black patch', from the embers of the burning hostel.[12] Dineen notes *smóil* as meaning 'ember'.[13]

Conaire Mór would have been perceived as being hemmed in by the mountains on either side of the glen and facing the great wall of Kippure mountain, thus increasing the impending sense of danger. He finally arrives at the putative location of the hostel near Mareen's Brook (mBruidne?), at the source of the Dodder, where Da Derga's hostel was said to have the river running through it.[14] The meeting with the three reds and allowing a single woman to enter the hostel are two of the *gessa* that Conaire breaks *en route*, and as he reaches the hostel he says, 'All of my *gessa* have overtaken me tonight'.[15]

Mac Neill traced other local place-names associated with this saga,[16] following the journey of Conaire's foster-brothers, the plunderers or *diberg*: Glencullen, Kilmasogue, Montpelier Hill, Tallaght Hill and Saggart Hill. From these place-names we form the impression of the *diberg* congregating on the hills above Glenasmole in pursuit of Conaire. Two names eluded Mac Neill: Crecca, which is probably Cruagh near Kilmasogue, and Sescenn Uarbeoil, which also fits this locale, as Mountseskin is one of the townlands on the summit of Tallaght Hill.

In her work on royal inauguration in Gaelic Ireland Elizabeth Fitzpatrick states that 'the rod of kingship which the comarba, ua Dubhtaig, gives to the king of Bréifne during his inauguration must be cut from the sacred hazel tree of St Máedóc at Díseart Máedóic in Sescenn Uairbeóil (Mount Seskin, Tallaght) in Leinster'.[17] Indeed, the parish of Tallaght still has two *bilí* in the form of St Maelruan's Tree at the Dominican priory and St Anne's Tree (a corruption of Sanctan) in Glenasmole.

Another legendary king of Tara, Cormac, has a *geas* associated with these hills. Given the association of Sescenn Uairbeoil with the rod of kingship and the inauguration rites of Bréifne, it is surprising to find that, according to the Fianna tales, 'it was forbidden for the king in Tara to hold the moss of Sescann Uairbeoil'.[18] The motifs of *gessa*, prophecies and omens that face the kings of Tara in these hills are significant and they lend an otherworldly aspect to these hills, which can be viewed from Tara on the southern horizon.

What was the Anglo-Norman/English administration's attitude to this area? In 1326 Archbishop Alen's register records the mountain land above Tallaght as 'laid waste and amongst the Irish'.[19] An Irish parliament in 1455 called for barriers to be erected on the bridges between Lucan and Kilmainham and all the fords between, to stop the Irish enemies.[20] The parliament had clearly lost control of the lands just a short distance from the capital. A report on the state of Ireland in 1515 said that only half of the county of Dublin was subject to the king's laws.[21]

This tension between the people of the hills and the new English settlers is reflected in Seán Ó Neachtain's poem 'Cath bearna Chroise Bhríde'. He outlines the story of a great faction fight between the people of the Tallaght hills and the people of the lowlands (*idir lucht luathfar láidir na bpátuidh agus drong ghreamach na pise*) at harvest time.[22] The people of the hills are described as the 'noble honourable kindred of the potatoes', while the lowlanders, the people of the grain, are represented as 'deceitful and treacherous'. Lughnasa was the time of the new potatoes and harvest time for crops. The people of the Tallaght hills were presumably the poet's audience and spoke Irish later than the main population of County Dublin.

This 'fight' was said to have taken place at 'the scalp'. In a translation of the poem, N.J.A. Williams questions Robin Flower's suggestion that the location of the poem is 'the scalp above Tallaght',[23] and wonders whether it lies at the Scalp near Enniskerry.[24] Although the place-name St Brigid's Cross is lost, it is almost certain to be the crossroads near the Gap of Ballinascorney (similar to a *scailp* in terrain), known as the festival site.[25] These roads would have led in a number of directions to churches dedicated to St Brigid.[26] The poem describes the assembly:

Do tóigeadh tinntidh arda
publibh bána is lachtna
do geaéagaidh gorma is uaidhne
cuireadh suas taibernacuil

High tents were erected,
pavilions white and grey;
tabernacles were set up of
blue and green branches.[27]

There follows a long list of personal names and place-names given to the ranks on either side of the fight as they join the assembly, and the poem degenerates into a long rendition of the fight. It could be read as having a local interest, playing upon the opposition between the Gaelic Irish of the hills and the New English of the plain, such as the Bulkeleys of Old Bawn. Sir Richard Bulkeley wrote of his great success on planting maize, which, he claimed, 'should render useless the cultivation of the field white pea'.[28]

Ó Neachtain was probably financially rewarded by those whose views he represented, the Irish-speaking hillsmen, and so the poem illustrates the local social customs, local topography, personal names and place-names. Owing to concentration on its satirical content, the poem has not heretofore been interpreted as having a

Detail of Old Bawn House by Robert Newcomen, 1654. (RCB Library D6/132/1: The Lordship of Tallagh Latlie Belonginge to the Bishope of Dublin)[29]

Lughnasa assembly theme. The poem's theme of the great assembly, taking place on a hill with a wide prospect, at harvest time, the inclusion of a place-name associated with St Brigid and the subject-matter of faction fighting between two groups are motifs that Máire MacNeill has indicated as being part of the Lughnasa tradition.[30]

Although it lies outside the parameters of this essay, the Tallaght Hill area continued into the modern era as a landscape of political assembly. It was a muster point for the 1798 rebellion. In 1803 Robert Emmet and his men were on the run in Tallaght following the failure of his rebellion, moving from house to house on the hill at Lughnasa. On 24 July 1803, General Archer wrote to Secretary Marsden in Dublin Castle: 'notice of a Pattern to be held at the Brakes of Ballinascorney this day has been widely diffused in New Street and a Large assembly is expected there'.[31] This was the entire communication, which must indicate that the administration in Dublin was familiar with both the place and the threat associated with such gatherings. In 1867 there was another great assembly, as up to 7,000 men gathered on Tallaght Hill as part of the Fenian rising.[32]

Although it lies just a few miles south of Dublin city, the place-names and history of Tallaght Hill retain references to landscapes associated with mythological kingship, old Gaelic sagas, medieval kingship rituals and the assembly sites of the Gaelic tradition.

Notes

1 G. Stout, 'Wicklow's prehistoric landscape', in K. Hannigan and W. Nolan (eds), *Wicklow: history and society: interdisciplinary essays on the history of an Irish county* (Dublin, 1994), p. 9.
2 G. Stout, 'Patterns in the past', in M. Stout and G. Stout (eds), *Dublin city and county from prehistory to present: studies in honour of J.H. Andrews* (Dublin, 1992), p. 8.
3 Ordnance Survey letters, Dublin (1928), p. 25.
4 C. Allen, 'A shadowy figure behind the chiefs: the Cailleach Bhéarra as a symbol of sovereignty', in K. Simms (ed.), *Gaelic Ireland (c. 600-c. 1700): politics, culture and landscapes* (Dublin, 2013), pp 105–10.
5 E. Mac Neill, 'Sescenn Uarbeoil of the sagas and other ancient place-names to the south of Dublin', *Journal of the Royal Society of Antiquaries of Ireland* (hereafter *JRSAI*) 5 (1935), pp 12–22, at p. 20.
6 M. West, 'The genesis of *Togail bruidne Da Derga*: a reappraisal of the "two-source" theory', *Celtica* 23 (1999), pp 413–35.
7 T.M. Charles-Edwards, '*Geis*, prophecy, omen, and oath', *Celtica* 23 (1999), pp 38–59, at p. 43.
8 L. Price, 'The manor of Bothercolyn', *JRSAI* 14 (1944), pp 107–18.
9 C. Ó Lochlainn, 'Roadways in ancient Ireland', in J. Ryan (ed.), *Féil-sgríbhinn Eóin Mhic Néill: essays and studies presented to Professor Eóin Mac Néill* (Dublin, 1940), pp 465–74, at p. 473.
10 See https://www.logainm.ie/1166671.aspx.
11 See https://www.logainm.ie/1414132.aspx.
12 National Folklore Collection, University College Dublin, Schools' Manuscript Collection; S MS 0795:027.
13 P.S. Dinneen, *Foclóir Gaedhlige agus Béarla: an Irish–English dictionary* (Dublin, 1927), p. 1068.
14 P. Healy, *Glenasmole roads* (Dublin, 2006), p. 54.
15 J. Gantz, *Early Irish myths and sagas* (Harmondsworth, 1981), p. 73.
16 Mac Neill, 'Sescenn Uarbeoil', p. 22; and see Dinneen, *Foclóir Gaedhlige agus Béarla*, 'S. Uairbeoil near Tallaght', p. 1019.
17 E. Fitzpatrick, *Royal inauguration in Gaelic Ireland, c. 1100–1600: a cultural landscape study* (Woodbridge, 2004), p. 58.
18 J.F. Nagy, *The wisdom of the outlaw: the boyhood deeds of Finn in Gaelic narrative tradition* (Berkeley, 1985), p. 144.
19 C. McNeill, *Calendar of Archbishop Alen's register of early church documents, c. 1172–1534* (Dublin, 1950), p. 180.
20 Ibid.
21 Ibid., p. 181.
22 N.J.A. Williams, 'Cath bearna Chroise Brighde', *Zeitschrift für Celtische Philologie* 38 (1981), pp 269–338, at p. 275.
23 Ibid., p. 313.
24 Ibid., p. 314.
25 G. Little, *Malachi Horan remembers* (Dublin, 1945), p. xiv.
26 P. Healy, *All roads lead to Tallaght* (Dublin, 2004), p. 84.
27 Ibid., p. 301.
28 T. Hoppen, *Papers of the Dublin Philosophical Society, 1683–1709* (Dublin, 2008), p. 161.
29 RCB Library D6/Catalogue of the maps of the archbishops of Dublin, 1654–1850/1: The Lordship of Tallagh Latlie Belonginge to the Bishope of Dublin; R. Refaussé and M. Clark, *A catalogue of the maps of the estates of the archbishops of Dublin: 1654–1850* (Dublin, 2000), p. 80.
30 M. Mac Neill, *The festival of Lughnasa: a study of the survival of the Celtic festival of the beginning of the harvest* (Oxford, 1962), p. 424.
31 The National Archives of Ireland, MS 620/64/24, 'Rebellion Papers'.
32 S.I. Takagami, 'The Dublin rebellion', *Irish Historical Studies* 29 (1985), p. 358.

16
In the footsteps of the noble Gael

Con Connor

In 1956 A.T. Lucas produced his comprehensive and impressive report on known Irish footwear.[1] This short article looks at his 'Type 1' or LT1s, the medieval Irish high-status single-piece shoes that Lucas called 'astonishingly sophisticated'.[2] I first became interested in these LT1s about ten years ago, but modern copies of them could not be found and the only information available consisted of on-line snippets from the journal essay by Lucas. When I first saw the Lucas sketches of these shoes, I was amazed at their unnecessary complexity. I made my first pair in 2007, using the sketch from the Lucas essay to mark out a pattern on 3mm leather. These shoes were sown inside out and then soaked in water until they became soft enough to be turned outside in. Dried slowly on my feet (which were wrapped in cling-film) by the heat of an open fire, they moulded themselves to my feet, but in so doing they shrank. This shrinkage exposed thread in the toe and heel areas, and this style of one-piece leather shoe must have invisible stitching. Because they were too tight and now permanently hardened despite regular applications of vegetable oil, they could not be worn for very long, nor could I walk very far without discomfort. I realised that more medieval leathercraft skills remained to be discovered and learned.

Lucas Type 1 Gaelic slipper.

I had the pattern and the goosefoot awl-hole spacings and stitching technique right. This showed me that the Lucas pattern was true, because I'd achieved a 'remarkable cut' and 'the shapeliness of the shoes' as

Lucas Type I pattern shown whip-stitched, with goosefoot awl in place for display purposes.

well. My versions were unwearable, however, because I had believed that they must be full turn-shoes. I therefore tried another method, used in the shoes pictured here, which gives flexibility in the middle of the shoe while also completely hiding the thread because no gap is created from 'turning outside in'.

Using 2.5–3mm oak-bark-tanned shoulder leather from an adult cow, I overlay the Lucas LT1 pattern and trace the outline of the LT1 with a ballpoint pen. Then, using an extremely sharp knife, I cut away and trim until I've got a pure shape. I mark out the stitch holes using dividers and make multiple curved stitching holes using a goosefoot awl, taking care not to go through the outer skin; I loosely whip-stitch these holes to keep them open, because otherwise they would disappear when wet. No further trimming of the leather is possible from this stage onwards. I now soak the area that makes the heel in warm water until it is fully soft and pliable. This is then whip-stitched with new thread from the inner corner out, removing the first loose thread as I go.

It takes about twenty minutes plus to whip-stitch a heel tight. The wet leather is very pliable and, because it dries progressively, it has its own time-limit for sewing; once a heel or toe is started, you need to finish quickly to ensure that it dries evenly. Linen thread today has a breaking point of approximately 25lb., and when it snaps

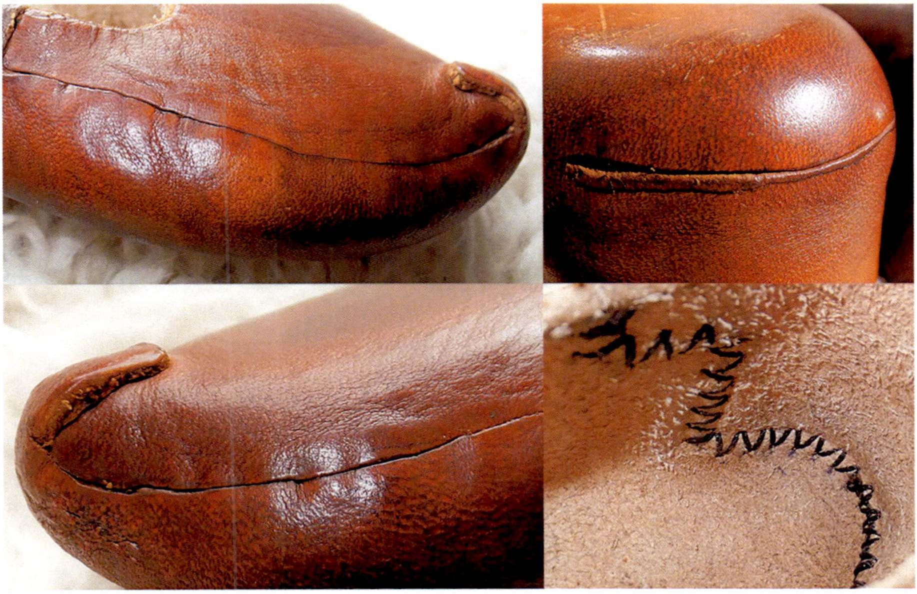

Clockwise, from top left: outside right foot, outside right heel, inside right heel, inside right foot.

you have to strip it back and start again. Because this has happened more than once, I now use waxed nylon thread with a breaking point of 35lb., and I cannot snap nylon thread by simple pulling as I tighten each stitch. I whip-stitch each pair of holes twice and twist around the first loop, creating a lock stitch on the second pass. While this may seem to be 'overdoing it a bit', it works well, resulting in a shoe that does not show any thread from the outside. When the heel is fully sewn, I carefully shape it by hand as I dry it near an open fire. If my hand gets too hot, then the shoe is too hot as well. I've lifted the heel seam off the ground by modifying the basic template provided by Lucas. This may help to slow water ingress but also looks better and suggests that I may have 'mastered' the making of LT1s, in that I can make my own modifications without departure from the core design concept. This 'non-turn-shoe technique' leaves the middle section soft with its normal flexibility, so that the shoe bends easily as you walk and no sewing thread is visible from the outside.

Once the heel area has dried enough and begins to hold its desired shape, I soak the under-toe area in warm water but only wet the upper toe or vamp area. The double whip-stitch method means that about 1.2m of thread and 30 minutes plus is needed for sewing the toe area of a 17cm-long finished shoe. The upper toe has all stitch holes spaced at approximately 4mm apart, and the under-toe has six holes spaced at about 4mm at the end of the sew line but at 6.5mm for most of the large curved area. As I begin to sew a left shoe, the thumb and first two fingers of my left hand begin shaping the under-toe area to meet the upper toe. I call this 'working the leather' and it requires renewed use of long-forgotten muscles. The needle is in my right hand when shaping and sewing the right shoe. Just like the heel sewing, the toe must be done in one go from start of sewing to finish.

Drying properly is crucial to the longevity of the shoe: too much heat and it will shrink too much in one spot and maybe crack; too little and it begins to lose its shape and appear lumpy. So I have to sit and dry it and shape it by hand, to dry the toe and then the heel and repeat the process, ensuring that the leather is evenly warm but not too hot. Three days later, a shoe made this way will have dried fully and its damp smell will have gone away completely. The wetted areas will show a gloss on the surface and there will be visible water-stain lines where it meets the middle dry area. The dye can now be applied. Applying several coats of oil dye a few hours apart is the best way to get that deep dark colour. After each dye coat has dried, I hand-polish with a cotton rag. Leather is a natural material with variations throughout, and if a beginner has chosen a piece from a shoulder for one shoe and a piece from a butt for the other shoe it will begin to show at this stage, causing confusion. I use natural vegetable oil to seal the shoe, although it may be that butter oil was used in times past. After oiling each shoe, I again polish or buff, always checking the stitch-lines, the smell and the evenness of everything, seeking the highest standard.

Making a pair of child-size LT1s usually takes place over a week, but once started there is a process to follow, so it takes experience and time to produce a high-quality finish. Approximately 24 hours of effort are needed for the labour aspect per pair of dyed and polished LT1 child-size shoes using vege-tanned cowhide. Getting the right raw materials, the tools and tool-sharpening and the skill/experience that is required are difficult to measure, as for me it has all been a self-teaching/learning process over many years. Lacing styles may vary and I'm unaware of any historically correct style of lacing. Having said that, the cross-over style that climbs up the leg is still current in Irish dancing and ballet shoes. It was also common in the Roman era, so it may have been one of the common lacing methods, and it also works well today. Shoes used only at home may have had a very simple or basic lacing style, so that the shoe could be easily pulled on or slipped off very quickly for convenience. Perhaps a woollen felt inner shoe or triangular woollen foot-wrap was used with these shoes to give greater comfort, as otherwise the skin of the foot quickly becomes chafed and sore. For outdoor use, I would guess that full cross-over wrap-around lacing up the leg may have been preferred. This would secure the felt inner shoe or woollen foot-wrap to the foot and to the woollen leg/shin-wrap. A wooden patten or clog may have also been added for the muddy season.

Back in the day, as they say, it would probably have been a long time before any apprentice was allowed to make these Lucas Type 1 shoes. He would have to show skill with materials and processes before being shown the technique of making high-status shoes from a single piece of leather. I can make a functional pair of bag-shoes

Lucas Type I Gaelic slippers, child size 6.

or pampooties in less than two hours, but it takes almost 24 hours to finish a pair of child-size LT1 shoes, making them up to twelve times more expensive in labour. This level of quality was part of an ostentatious display of wealth by the upper classes in the early medieval period in Ireland.

For the medieval shoemaker, the ability to make these shoes must have been highly prized. It may have meant that, as a craftsman, he would be attached to a noble family for life, and his food, shelter and creature comforts assured. He might have been excused 'battle duty' or menial work, simply because these shoes wear out and the owners would always want to be seen wearing new shoes. My own experience of wearing a pair at home, walking on wooden floors and cement floors covered in a rubberised paint, shows that they can last for six months or more. In times past, however, the normal life expectancy for a pair of shoes that still looked good may have been only three months, so perhaps the shoemaker was always busy making shoes for the nobility and their extended families.

Complex geometric carving or ornamentation on top of design complexity and craft skill declare these shoes to be part of the ultimate 'bling' for the nobility of the early historic period in Ireland. Wearing these Lucas Type 1 shoes would have brought instant recognition of status. The Gaelic nobles wore colourful costumes with contrasting braiding trim as unnecessary embellishment, and this was further supported by gold and silver jewellery. The noble Gael of the early medieval era proudly displayed his or her high status from head to toe, with a style that was astonishingly sophisticated and indigenous to Ireland.

Fifteen of these uniquely Irish single-piece, high-status leather shoes were known to exist in 1956, two in Northern Ireland and thirteen in the Republic. In his detailed report, A.T. Lucas calls these shoes Type 1 and says: 'In addition to these features [ornamentation or carvings] the whole group shows great uniformity in the remarkable cut of the shoes; the consistent presence of such details as the sewn-down tag at the tip of the toe, and the particular scoring on the vamp and heel; the shapeliness of the shoes themselves and the unvarying nature of the craftsmanship all of which combine to create the impression of a very homogeneous class confined to a fairly limited period [Early Christian]'.[3] Lucas also says that 'despite their complex pattern they remain single-piece shoes, although the writer, for one, is at a loss to understand why their makers should, apparently, have made things more difficult for themselves by keeping to the single-piece tradition by, as it were, a technical *tour de force*, when they might have achieved the same result by building up the shoe from separate pieces, a procedure which should have presented no difficulties to tradesmen of their accomplishments'.[4]

Notes

1 The 1956 A.T. Lucas essay 'Footwear in Ireland' can be found in the *Journal of the County Louth Archaeological Society* 13 (4) (1956), pp 309–94. The author extends his thanks to the National Museum of Ireland staff for providing a paper copy of the Lucas essay many years ago.

2 Ibid., p. 384.

3 Ibid., p. 381.

4 Ibid., p. 366.

Bibliography

Manuscript sources

Bodleian Library, Oxford

MS Rawlinson B 488, fol. 21v

British Library, London

Cotton MSS, Caligula E I

Lambeth Palace Library

Carew MSS, vol. 611

National Archives of Ireland

RC 7: Calendar of plea rolls

MS 620/64/24: Rebellion papers

Representative Church Body Library

RCB Library D6/Catalogue of the maps of the archbishops of Dublin, 1654–1850/1: The Lordship of Tallagh Latlie Belonginge to the Bishope of Dublin

The National Archives of the United Kingdom

MS C 47/10/29

MS E 101/315/23

SP 60, State papers, Ireland, Henry VIII

SP 61, State papers, Ireland, Edward VI

SP 62, State papers, Ireland, Philip and Mary I

SP 63, State papers, Ireland, Elizabeth I

Trinity College Dublin

MS 1288 (H 1 14): Catalogue of the battles of Hugh O'Byrne by Ferganainm McKeogh; tales and poems, transcribed by Hugh O'Daly in the year 1750

MS 813, fols 001r–400v [1641.tcd.ie] 1641 Depositions for Kildare

University College Dublin

National Folklore Commission: S MS 0795:027

Printed primary sources

Account of the facsimiles of national manuscripts of Ireland, edited by J.T. Gilbert (Dublin, 1882).

Accounts of the lord high treasurer of Scotland, edited by T. Dickson and J.B. Paul (4 vols; Edinburgh, 1877–1902).

Acts of the lords of the Isles, 1336–1493, edited by J. Munro and R.W. Munro (Edinburgh, 1986).

'Acts of the privy council in Ireland, 1556–1571', edited by J.T. Gilbert, in HMC, *Fifteenth report*, appendix iii (London, 1897).

Annála ríoghachta Éireann: Annals of the kingdom of Ireland by the Four Masters, from the earliest period to the year 1616, edited by J. O'Donovan (7 vols; Dublin, 1856; repr. 1990).

Annála Uladh, annals of Ulster; otherwise annála Senait, annals of Senat: a chronicle of Irish affairs, 431–1131, 1155–1541, edited by W.M. Hennessy and B. MacCarthy (4 vols; Dublin, 1887–1901; repr. 1998).

BACON, F., *Sylvarum Sylva, or a natural history in ten centuries* (London, 1627).

Books of survey and distribution: being abstracts of various surveys and instruments of title, 1636–1703, iii: County of Galway, prepared for publication ... by B. Mac Giolla Choille, introduction by R.C. Simington (Dublin, 1962).

BOWER, W., *Scotichronicon*, edited by N. Shead, W. Stevenson, D.E.R. Watt, A. Borthwick, R.E. Latham, J.R.S. Phillips and M. Smith (Aberdeen, 1991).

Calendar of documents relating to Ireland, 1302–1307, edited by H.S. Sweetman (London, 1886).

Calendar of entries in the papal registers relating to Great Britain and Ireland: papal letters, vol. v, 1398–1404, edited by W.H. Bliss and J.A. Twemlow (London, 1904).

Calendar of entries in the papal registers relating to Great Britain and Ireland: petitions to the pope, vol. i, 1342–1419, edited by W.H. Bliss (London, 1896).

Calendar of the Carew manuscripts preserved in the archiepiscopal library at Lambeth, 1515–1624 (6 vols; London, 1867–73).

Calendar of the justiciary rolls or proceedings in the court of the justiciar of Ireland, edited by J. Mills (2 vols; Dublin, 1905–14).

Calendar of the patent and close rolls of chancery in Ireland: Elizabeth I, 19th year to the end of her reign, edited by J. Morrin (3 vols; Dublin, 1861–2).

Calendar of the patent rolls preserved in the Public Record Office: Elizabeth I, vol. ii, 1562–1563 (London, 1948).

Calendar of the patent rolls preserved in the Public Record Office: Henry IV, vol. iii, 1405–1408, edited by R.C. Fowler (London, 1907).

Calendar of the state papers relating to Ireland, of the reigns of Henry VIII, Edward VI, Mary and Elizabeth, 1509–1573, edited by H.C. Hamilton (London, 1860).

Calendar of the state papers relating to Ireland, of the reign of Elizabeth, 1574–1585, edited by H.C. Hamilton (London, 1867).

Calendar of the state papers relating to Ireland, of the reign of Elizabeth, 1588, August–1592, September, edited by A.S.M. Hume (London, 1885).

Calendar of the state papers relating to Ireland, of the reign of Elizabeth, 1592–1596, edited by H.C. Hamilton (London, 1885).

Calendar of the state papers relating to Ireland, of the reign of Elizabeth, 1596, July–1597, December, edited by E.G. Atkinson (London, 1912).

Campaign journals of the Elizabethan Irish wars, edited by D. Edwards (Dublin, 2014).

A census of Ireland, circa *1659*, edited by S. Pender (Dublin, 1939).

Cogadh Gaedhal re Gallaibh, edited by J.H. Todd (London, 1867).

DAVIES, Sir J., *A discovery of the true cause why Ireland was never entirely subdued nor brought under obedience of the crown of England until the beginning of his majesty's reign* (London, 1612).

Foedera, conventiones, litterae et cuiuscunque generis actapublica, edited by T. Rymer (20 vols; London, 1727–35).

HOLINSHED, R., *The . . . chronicles of England, Scotlande and Irelande . . .* (London, 1577), edited by J. Hooker *et al.* (3 vols; 1587) and by H. Ellis (6 vols; 1807–8).

Inquisitions and extents of medieval Ireland, edited by P. Dryburgh and B. Smith (Kew, 2007).

Irish patent rolls of James I: facsimile of the Irish record commissioners' calendar prepared prior to 1830, with foreword by M.C. Griffith (Dublin, 1966).

Leabhar Branach: The book of the O'Byrnes, edited by S. MacAirt (Dublin, 1944).

Leabhar mór na ngenealach: The great book of Irish genealogies, edited and translated by N. Ó Muraíle (5 vols; Dublin, 2003).

Letters and memorials of state in the reigns of Queen Mary, Queen Elizabeth, King James, King Charles the first, part of the reign of King Charles the second, and Oliver's usurpation, edited by A. Collins (2 vols; London, 1746).

Letters and papers, foreign and domestic, Henry VIII, edited by J.S. Brewer and R.H. Brodie (21 vols; London, 1862–1932).

Literary remains of King Edward the sixth: edited from his autograph manuscripts, with historical notes and a biographical memoir, edited by J.G. Nichols (2 vols; London, 1857).

LODGE, J., *The peerage of Ireland, or a genealogical history of the present nobility of the kingdom*, edited by M. Archdall (7 vols; 1789).

'Lord Chancellor Gerrard's notes of his report on Ireland: with extracts from original Irish records exhibited by him before the privy council in England, 1577–8', edited by C. McNeill, *Analecta Hibernica* 2 (1931), 92–291.

LYNCH, J., *De praesulibus Hiberniae* [1672], edited by J.F. O'Doherty (2 vols; Dublin, 1944).

Miscellaneous Irish annals, edited by S. Ó hInnse (Dublin, 1947).

Report on the manuscripts of Lord de l'Isle & Dudley preserved at Penshurst Place (6 vols;

London, 1925–66).
Rotuli Scotiae, 1292–1516, edited by D. MacPherson (2 vols; London, 1819).
'Sir Henry Sidney's memoir of his government of Ireland', edited by H. Hore, *Ulster Journal of Archaeology* 7 (1860), 179–95.
SPENSER, E., *View of the state of Ireland written dialogue wise between Eudoxus and Irenus by Edmund Spencer Esq. In the yeare 1596* (repr. Dublin, 1809).
STANYHURST, R., 'History of Ireland under Henry VIII', in Raphael Holinshed's *Chronicles* (London, 1577).
TAYLOR, G. and SKINNER, A., *Maps of the roads of Ireland surveyed 1777* (London and Dublin, 1778).
The annals of Clonmacnoise: being annals of Ireland from the earliest period to AD 1408, edited by D. Murphy (2 vols; Dublin, 1896).
The annals of Loch Cé: a chronicle of Irish affairs, 1014–1590, edited by W.M. Hennessy (2 vols; London, 1871; Dublin, 1939).
The Black Book of Limerick, edited by J. MacCaffrey (Dublin, 1907).
The calendar of Ormond deeds, edited by E. Curtis (6 vols; Dublin, 1932).
The complete peerage of England, Scotland, Ireland, Great Britain, and the United Kingdom, edited by G.E. Cokayne (6 vols; Gloucester, 1987).
The diary of John Evelyn, edited by W. Bray (2 vols; London, *c.* 1901).
The Irish cartularies of Llanthony Prima & Secunda, edited by E. St John Brooks (Dublin, 1953).
The Irish fiants of the Tudor sovereigns during the reigns of Henry VIII, Edward VI, Philip & Mary, and Elizabeth I (4 vols; Dublin, 1994).
The pipe rolls of Cloyne: Rotulus pipae Clonensis, edited by K. Nicholls and P. MacCotter (Cloyne, 1996).
The topography of Ireland by Giraldus Cambrensis, translated by J.J. O'Meara (Dundalk, 1951).
'A viceregal progress through the south and west of Ireland in 1567', edited by J. Buckley, *Journal of the Waterford and South-East of Ireland Archaeological Society* 12 (1909), 61–76, 132–46, 179–84.
The works of Francis Bacon, edited by J. Spedding *et al.* (15 vols; London, 1857–9).

Secondary sources

ARCHDALL, M., *Monasticon Hibernicum: or, a history of the abbeys, priories, and other religious houses in Ireland, pt 12, vol. ii. Counties of Galway and Kerry* (Dublin, no date).
BARDON, J., *A history of Ulster* (Belfast, 1992).
BARRY, T.B., FRAME, R. and SIMMS, K. (eds), *Colony and frontier in medieval Ireland: essays presented to J.F. Lydon* (London, 1995).
BARTLETT, R., *The making of Europe: conquest, colonisation and cultural change, 950–*

1350 (London, 1993).

BARTLETT, T., '"What ish my nation?": themes in Irish history 1550–1850', in T. Bartlett, C. Curtin, R. O'Dwyer and G. Ó Tuathaigh (eds), *Irish studies: a general introduction* (Dublin, 1988), 44–59.

BAYNE, G.C., *Select cases in the council of Henry VII* (London, 1958).

BECKETT, J.C., 'The Confederation of Kilkenny reviewed', in M. Roberts (ed.), *Historical Studies II* (London, 1959), 29–41.

BEGGAN, G., 'Ballygar: the Hy-Many royal seat', in K. Simms (ed.), *Gaelic Ireland (c. 600–c. 1700): politics, culture and landscapes: studies for the Irish Chiefs' prize* (Dublin, 2013), 87–95.

BEGGAN, G., 'The Carmelite house of Holy Cross, Slewshancogh, diocese of Elphin', *Journal of the County Roscommon Historical and Archaeological Society* 13 (2016), 111–15.

BEIRNE, F.M. (ed.), *The diocese of Elphin: people, places and pilgrimage* (Dublin, 2000).

BERLETH, R.J., *The twilight lords: Elizabeth I and the plunder of Ireland* (Lanham, Maryland, 1978; repr. 2002).

BEST, R.I. (ed. & trans.), 'The battle of Airtech', *Ériu* 8 (1916), 170–90.

BITEL, L.M., *Land of women: tales of sex and gender from early Ireland* (Ithaca and London, 1996).

BRADSHAW, B., *The Irish constitutional revolution of the sixteenth century* (Cambridge, 1979).

BRADY, W.M., *The Irish reformation, or, the alleged conversion of the Irish bishops at the accession of Queen Elizabeth* (London, 1867).

BRAND, P., 'The early history of the legal profession of the lordship of Ireland, 1250–1350', in D. Hogan and W.N. Osborough (eds), *Brehons, serjeants and attorneys: studies in the history of the Irish legal profession* (Dublin, 1990), 15–50.

BRAND, P., *The origins of the English legal profession* (London, 1992).

BREATHNACH, L. (ed.), *Uraicecht na Ríar: the poetic grades in early Irish law* (Dublin, 1987).

BROWN, J., 'Dartrey: the rise and fall of an Irish estate', *The Clogher Record*, 18 (2) (2004), 269–78.

BYRNE-ROTHWELL, D., *The Byrnes and the O'Byrnes, i. A new insight upon Irish history* (Isle of Colonsay, 2010).

CANNY, N., 'The 1641 depositions as a source for the writing of social history: County Cork as a case study', in P. O'Flanagan and C. Buttimer (eds), *Cork: history and society: interdisciplinary essays on the history of an Irish county* (Dublin, 1993), 249–308.

CANNY, N., 'What really happened in Ireland in 1641?', in J. Ohlmeyer (ed.), *Ireland from independence to occupation, 1641–1660* (Cambridge, 1995), 24–42.

CANNY, N., 'Religion, politics and the Irish rising of 1641', in J. Devlin and R. Fanning (eds), *Religion and rebellion* (Dublin, 1997), 40–70.

CANNY, N., *Making Ireland British, 1580–1650* (Oxford, 2001).

CAREY, V., '"Neither good English nor good Irish": bi-lingualism and identity formation in sixteenth-century Ireland', in H. Morgan (ed.), *Political ideology in Ireland, 1541–1641* (Dublin, 1999), 45–61.

CARLISLE, N., *A topographical dictionary of Ireland* (London, 1810).

CARRIGAN, W., *The history and antiquities of the diocese of Ossory* (Dublin, 1905).

CENNINI, C.d'A., *The craftsman's handbook: the Italian 'Il libro dell' arte'* (trans. Daniel V. Thompson Jr) (New York, 1933).

CHADWICK, S., 'The early Irish harp', *Early Music* 36 (4) (2008), 521–32.

CHARLES-EDWARDS, T.M., '*Geis*, prophesy, omen, and oath', *Celtica* 23 (1999), 38–59.

CHAVASSE, C., *The story of Baltinglass* (Kilkenny, 1970).

CLAFFEY, J.A., *Irish Historic Towns Atlas No. 20: Tuam* (Dublin, 2009).

CLARKE, A., 'The policies of the "Old English" in parliament, 1640–41', in J.L. McCracken (ed.), *Historical Studies V: papers read before the Sixth Irish Conference of Historians* (London, 1965), 85–102.

CLARKE, A., 'The Irish economy, 1600–60', in T.W. Moody, F.X. Martin and F.J. Byrne (eds), *A new history of Ireland, iii. Early modern Ireland, 1534–1691* (Oxford, 1976), 168–86.

CLARKE, A., 'The genesis of the Ulster rising of 1641', in P. Roebuck (ed.), *Plantation to partition: essays in Ulster history in honour of J.L. McCracken* (Belfast, 1981), 29–45.

CLARKE, A., 'The 1641 rebellion and anti-popery in Ireland', in B. Mac Cuarta (ed.), *Ulster 1641: aspects of the rising* (Belfast, 1993), 139–57.

CLARKE, A., *The Old English in Ireland, 1625–42* (Dublin, 2000).

CLARKE, H.B., PRUNTY, J. and HENNESSY, M., *Surveying Ireland's past: multidisciplinary essays in honour of Anngret Simms* (Dublin, 2004).

COKAYNE, G.E., *The complete peerage of England, Scotland, Ireland, Great Britain, and the United Kingdom*, vol. 6 (2nd edn, Gloucester, 1987).

CONNEELY, D., *The letters of Saint Patrick* (Maynooth, 1993).

CORISH, P., 'The rising of 1641 and the Catholic confederacy, 1641–5', in T.W. Moody, F.X. Martin and F.J. Byrne (eds), *A new history of Ireland, iii. Early modern Ireland, 1534–1691* (Oxford, 1976), 289–316.

COSGRAVE, A., *Late medieval Ireland, 1370–1541* (Dublin, 1981).

COUNTY WICKLOW HERITAGE PROJECT, *The last county: the emergence of Wicklow as a county, 1606–1845* (Wicklow, 1993; repr. 2006).

CRAMPTON, C., 'Wicklow biographies, no. 8: Feagh Mac Hugh O'Byrne', *Journal of the West Wicklow Historical Society* 3 (1989), 15–16.

CRAWFORD, J.G., *Anglicizing the government of Ireland* (Dublin, 1993).

CUNNINGHAM, B., 'The composition of Connacht in the lordships of Clanricard and Thomond, 1577–1642', *Irish Historical Studies* 24 (1984), 1–14.

DAVIS, T., *The Patriot Parliament of 1689* (London, 1893).

DE PAOR, L., *Saint Patrick's world: the Christian culture of Ireland's apostolic age* (Dublin, 1996).

DE PAOR, M. and DE PAOR, L., *Early Christian Ireland* (London, 1958; repr. 1978).

DILLON, M., *Early Irish literature* (Chicago, 1948).

DINNEEN, P.S., *Foclóir Gaedhlige agus Béarla: an Irish–English dictionary* (Dublin, 1927).

DOBBS, M., 'The Ban-shenchus', *Revue Celtique* 47 (1930), 283–339.

DUFFY, P.J., 'Social and spatial order in the MacMahon lordship of Airghialla in the late sixteenth century', in P.J. Duffy, D. Edwards and E. FitzPatrick (eds), *Gaelic Ireland c. 1250–c. 1650: land, lordship and settlement* (Dublin, 2004), 115–37.

EDWARDS, D., 'The MacGiollaPhádraigs of Upper Ossory, 1532–1641', in P.G. Lane and W. Nolan (eds), *Laois: history and society: interdisciplinary essays on the history of an Irish county* (Dublin, 1999), 327–75.

EDWARDS, D., 'Collaboration without anglicization', in P.J. Duffy, D. Edwards and E. FitzPatrick (eds), *Gaelic Ireland c. 1250–c. 1650: land, lordship and settlement* (Dublin, 2004), 77–97.

EDWARDS, D., LENIHAN, P. and TAIT, C. (eds), *Age of atrocity: violence and political conflict in early modern Ireland* (Dublin, 2007).

EDWARDS, D., LENIHAN, P. and TAIT, C., 'Early modern Ireland: a history of violence', in D. Edwards, P. Lenihan and C. Tait (eds), *Age of atrocity: violence and political conflict in early modern Ireland* (Dublin, 2007), 9–33.

EGAN, P.K., 'The Carmelite cell of Bealaneny', *Journal of the Galway Archaeological and Historical Society* 26 (1954–6), 19–25.

EGAN, P.K., *The parish of Ballinasloe: its history from the earliest times to the present century* (Dublin, 1960; facsimile reproduction, 1994).

EISENBICHLER, K. (ed.), *The premodern teenager: youth in society, 1150–1650* (Toronto, 2002).

EMPEY, C.A., 'The cantreds of the medieval county of Kilkenny', *Journal of the Royal Society of Antiquaries of Ireland* 101 (2) (1971), 128–34.

ETCHINGHAM, C., 'Episcopal hierarchy in Connacht and Tairdelbach Ua Conchobair', *Journal of the Galway Archaeological and Historical Society* 52 (2000), 13–29.

FITZPATRICK, B., *Seventeenth-century Ireland: the war of religions* (Dublin, 1988).

FITZPATRICK, E., *Royal inauguration in Gaelic Ireland c. 1100–1600: a cultural landscape study* (Woodbridge, 2004).

FLETCHER, A.J., *Drama and the performing arts in pre-Cromwellian Ireland: a repertory of sources and documents from the earliest times until c. 1642* (Cambridge, 2001).

FLOOD, W.H.G., *The story of the harp* (London, 1905).

FLYNN, L.J., 'Hugh MacMahon, bishop of Clogher 1707–15 and archbishop of Armagh 1715–37', *Seanchas Ardmhacha: Journal of the Armagh Diocesan Historical*

Society 7 (1) (1973), 108–75.

FOSTER, R.F., *Modern Ireland, 1600–1972* (London, 1989).

FRAME, R., 'Ireland after 1169: barriers to acculturation on an "English" edge', in K. Stringer and A. Jotischky (eds), *Norman expansion: connections, continuities and contrasts* (Farnham, 2013), 115–41.

FROST, J., *The history and topography of the county of Clare, from earliest times to the beginning of the 18th century* (Dublin, 1893).

GANTZ, J., *Early Irish myths and sagas* (Penguin Classics, 1981).

GIBLIN, C., 'Catalogue of Irish material in the "Nunziatura di Fiandra", Vatican archives: part i, vols 1–50', *Collectanea Hibernica* 1 (1958), 7–136.

GILLESPIE, R., 'The end of an era: Ulster and the outbreak of the 1641 rising', in C. Brady and R. Gillespie (eds), *Natives and newcomers: essays on the making of Irish colonial society, 1534–1641* (Dublin, 1986), 191–213.

GWYNN, A., *The twelfth-century reform: a history of Irish Catholicism*, ii, pt 1 (Dublin, 1968).

GWYNN, A. and HADCOCK, R.N., *Medieval religious houses: Ireland: with an appendix to early sites* (Harlow, 1970).

HALL, D., *Women and the church in medieval Ireland,* c.*1140–1540* (Dublin, 2002).

HAND, G.J., *English law in Ireland, 1290–1324* (Cambridge, 1967).

HANDCOCK, W.D., *The history and antiquities of Tallaght in the county of Dublin* (Dublin, 1991).

HANNIGAN, K. and NOLAN, W. (eds), *Wicklow: history and society: interdisciplinary essays on the history of an Irish county* (Dublin, 1994).

HARDIMAN, J., *The history of the town and county of Galway from the earliest period to the present time* (Dublin, 1820).

HAYES, R., 'Biographical dictionary of Irishmen in France', *Studies: An Irish Quarterly Review* 21 (124) (1942), 477–92.

HAYES-MCCOY, G.A., *Scots mercenary forces in Ireland, 1565–1603* (Dublin, 1937).

HAYES-MCCOY, G.A., 'The royal supremacy and ecclesiastical revolution, 1534–47', in T.W. Moody, F.X. Martin and F.J. Byrne (eds), *A new history of Ireland, iii. Early modern Ireland, 1534–1691* (Oxford, 1976), 39–68.

HAYES-MCCOY, G.A., 'Conciliation, coercion, and the Protestant reformation, 1547–71', in T.W. Moody, F.X. Martin and F.J. Byrne (eds), *A new history of Ireland, iii. Early modern Ireland, 1534–1691* (Oxford, 1976), 69–93.

HEALY, P., *All roads lead to Tallaght* (Dublin, 2004).

HEALY, P., *Glenasmole roads* (Dublin, 2006).

HERITY, M. (ed.), *Ordnance Survey letters, Mayo* (Dublin, 2009).

HERITY, M. (ed.), *Ordnance Survey letters, Galway* (Dublin, 2009).

HEYMANN, A. and HEYMANN, C., 'Cláirseach: the lore of the Irish harp', *Éire-Ireland* 26 (3) (1991), 84–7.

HEYMANN, A. and HEYMANN, C., 'Strings of gold', *Historical Harp Journal* 13

(3) (2003), 9–15.

HICKEY, S., KENNY, L. and BEHAN, P. (eds), *Nás na Ríogh: from Poorhouse Road to the Fairy Flax ... an illustrated history of Naas* (Naas, 1990).

HOLLAND, P., 'The Anglo-Norman landscape in County Galway: land-holdings, castles and settlements', *Journal of the Galway Archaeological and Historical Society* 69 (1997), 159–93.

HOPPEN, T. (ed.), *Papers of the Dublin Philosophical Society, 1683–1709* (Dublin, 2008).

HORE, H.F. and GRAVES, J., *The social state of the southern and eastern counties of Ireland* (Dublin, 1870).

HOROWITZ, D., *The deadly ethnic riot* (Berkeley, 2001).

HUGHES, C. (ed.), *Shakespeare's Europe: unpublished chapters of Fynes Moryson's Itinerary* (London, 1903).

HULL, V., 'Aided Meidbe: the violent death of Medb', *Speculum* 13 (1) (1938), 52–61.

JACKMAN, N., 'Kilbegly Mill: the excavation of an early medieval mill in south Roscommon', *Journal of the County Roscommon Historical and Archaeological Society* (2012), 23–6.

JEFFRIES, H.A., 'The Kildare revolt: accident or design?', *Journal of the County Kildare Archaeological Society* 19 (3) (2004–5), 447–59.

JENNINGS, B. (ed.), *Wild geese in Spanish Flanders 1582–1700* (Dublin, 1963).

JORDAN, W.K., *Edward VI: the young king: the protectorship of the duke of Somerset* (Cambridge, Mass., 1968).

JOYCE, P.W., *The origin and history of Irish names of places*, i (Dublin, 1910).

KALYVAS, S., *The logic of violence in civil war* (Cambridge, 2006).

KEENAN, D., 'A case study of tower houses in County Mayo' (unpublished MA thesis, University College Dublin, 2012).

KEHNEL, A., *Clonmacnois: the church and lands of St Ciarán: change and continuity in an Irish monastic foundation (6th to 16th century)* (Münster, 1997).

KENYON, J. and OHLMEYER, J., 'The background to the civil wars in the Stewart kingdoms', in J. Kenyon, J. Ohlmeyer and J. Morrill (eds), *The civil wars: a military history of England, Scotland, and Ireland, 1638–1660* (Oxford, 1998), 3–40.

KENYON, J., OHLMEYER, J. and MORRILL, J. (eds), *The civil wars: a military history of England, Scotland, and Ireland, 1638–1660* (Oxford, 1998).

KINSELLA, T. (trans.), *The Táin* (New York, 1970).

KINSELLA, T. and Ó CANNAIN, T., *Our musical heritage* (Dublin, 1982).

KNOX, H.T., 'The early tribes of Connacht', *Journal of the Royal Society of Antiquaries of Ireland* (5th ser.) 10 (4) (1900), 343–56.

KNOX, H.T., 'The de Burgo clans of Galway', *Journal of the Galway Archaeological and Historical Society* 1 (1900–1), 124–31.

KNOX, H.T., 'Occupation of Connaught by Anglo Normans after AD 1237', *Journal of the Royal Society of Antiquaries of Ireland* (5th ser.) 12 (1902), 132–8, 393–406; 13 (1903), 58–74, 179–89, 284–94.

KNOX, H.T., 'The expansion of two royal tribes of Connacht', *Journal of the Galway Archaeological and Historical Society* 4 (1905–6), 99–101.

KNOX, H.T., *The history of the county of Mayo to the close of the sixteenth century* (Dublin, 1908).

LAWLOR, C., '1597–1997—the Firebrand and the Wicklow legend that's still burning', *Dunlavin–Donard–Davidstown Parish Link* 3 (6) (1997), 7.

LAWLOR, C., 'Some Wicklow history—originally recorded', *Dunlavin Festival of Arts Brochure* 21 (Naas, 2003), 49–52.

LEAHY, A.H., *Heroic romances of Ireland*, ii (London, 1906).

LENNON, C. and GILLESPIE, R., 'Reformation to Restoration', in S. Duffy (ed.), *Atlas of Irish history* (Dublin, 1997), 50–3.

LENNON, C., *Sixteenth-century Ireland: the incomplete conquest* (Dublin, 2005).

LEWIS, S., *A topographical dictionary of Ireland: comprising the several counties; cities; boroughs; corporate, market and post towns; parishes; and villages, with historical and statistical descriptions embellished with engravings of the arms of the cities, bishopricks, corporate towns, and boroughs* (2 vols, London, 1837).

LITTLE, G.A., *Malachi Horan remembers* (Dublin, 1945).

LIVINGSTONE, P., *The Monaghan story: a documented history of the County Monaghan from the earliest times to 1976* (Clogher Historical Society, 1980).

LONG, H., 'Three settlements in Gaelic Wicklow, 1169–1600: Rathgall, Ballincor, and Glendalough', in K. Hannigan and W. Nolan (eds), *Wicklow: history and society: interdisciplinary essays on the history of an Irish county* (Dublin, 1994), 248–56.

LUCAS, A.T., 'Footwear in Ireland', *Journal of the County Louth Archaeological Society* 13 (4) (1956), 309–94.

LYNOTT, J., 'The parish of Tober', *Dunlavin Festival of Arts Brochure* 12 (1994).

MACALISTER, R.A.S. (ed. & trans.), *Lebor gabála Érenn: The book of the taking of Ireland* (5 vols, Dublin, 1932–42).

MACCOTTER, P., *Medieval Ireland: territorial, political and economic divisions* (Dublin, 2008).

MAC CUARTA, B., 'Religious violence against settlers in south Ulster, 1641–2', in D. Edwards, P. Lenihan and C. Tait (eds), *Age of atrocity: violence and political conflict in early modern Ireland* (Dublin, 2007), 154–75.

MACCURTAIN, M., *Tudor and Stuart Ireland* (Dublin, 1972).

MACCURTAIN, M. and O'DOWD, M. (eds), *Women in early modern Ireland* (Dublin, 1991).

MAC DUINNSHLÉIBHE, P., 'The legal murder of Aodh Rua McMahon, 1590', *Clogher Record* 1 (3) (1955), 33–52.

MAC GABHANN, F., 'The place-names of Mayo', in G. Moran and N. Ó Muraíle (eds), *Mayo: history and society: interdisciplinary essays on the history of an Irish county* (Dublin, 2014), 101–32.

MACLEOD, N., '"Rogues, villaines and base trulls": constructing the "other" in the 1641 depositions', in E. Darcy, A. Margey and E. Murphy (eds), *The 1641 depositions and the Irish rebellion* (London, 2012), 113-27.

MAC NEILL, C. (ed.), *Calendar of Archbishop Alen's Register of early church documents, c. 1172–1534* (Dublin, 1950).

MAC NEILL, E., 'Sescenn Uarbeoil of the sagas and other ancient place-names to the south of Dublin', *Journal of the Royal Society of Antiquaries of Ireland* (7th ser.) 5 (1935), 12–22.

MAC NEILL, M., *The festival of Lughnasa: a study of the survival of the Celtic festival of the beginning of the harvest* (Oxford, 1962).

MAC NIOCAILL, G., *Ireland before the Vikings* (Dublin, 1972).

MAGINN, C., 'The Baltinglass rebellion, 1580: English dissent or a Gaelic uprising?', *Historical Journal* 47 (2) (2004), 205–32.

MAGINN, C., *'Civilizing' Gaelic Leinster: the extension of Tudor rule in the O'Byrne and O'Toole lordships* (Dublin, 2005).

MANNION, J., 'The Senchineoil and the Sogain: differentiating between the pre-Celtic and early Celtic tribes of central east Galway', *Journal of the Galway Archaeological and Historical Society* 58 (2006), 165–70.

MARSDEN, J., *Galloglas: Hebridean and West Highland mercenary warrior kindreds in medieval Ireland* (East Linton, 2003).

MEYER, K., 'Echtra Nerai (The adventures of Nera)', *Revue Celtique* 10 (1889), 212–28.

MEYER, K., *The death-tales of the Ulster heroes* (Dublin, 1906).

MOODY, T.W., 'The treatment of the native population under the scheme for the plantation of Ulster', *Irish Historical Studies* 1 (1938), 59–63.

MOODY, T.W., MARTIN, F.X. and BYRNE, F.J. (eds), *A new history of Ireland, iii. Early modern Ireland, 1534–1691* (Oxford, 1976).

MORGAN, H., 'Gaelic lordship and Tudor conquest: Tír Eoghain, 1541–1603', *History Ireland* 13 (5) (2005), 38–43.

MURPHY, B., 'The status of the native Irish after 1331', *Irish Jurist* 2 (1967), 116–28.

MURRAY, G., *The Cross of Cong: a masterpiece of medieval Irish art* (Dublin, 2014).

MURRAY, G., 'The establishment of Tuam as an archdiocesan capital in the twelfth century', in A. Tierney (ed.), *Glimpses of Tuam through the centuries* (Tuam, 2014), 15–17.

NAGY, J.F., *The wisdom of the outlaw: the boyhood deeds of Finn in Gaelic narrative tradition* (Berkeley, 1985).

NICHOLLS, K., 'Anglo-French Ireland and after', *Peritia* 1 (1982), 370–402.

NICHOLLS, K., 'The other massacre: English killings of Irish, 1641–2', in D.

Edwards, P. Lenihan and C. Tait (eds), *Age of atrocity: violence and political conflict in early modern Ireland* (Dublin, 2007), 176–91.

NICHOLLS, K. and QUINN, D.B., 'Ireland in 1534', in T.W. Moody, F.X. Martin and F.J. Byrne (eds), *A new history of Ireland, iii. Early modern Ireland, 1534–1691* (Oxford, 1976), 1–38.

NOONAN, K., '"The cruell pressure of an enraged, barbarous people": Irish and English identity in seventeenth-century policy and propaganda', *Historical Journal* 41 (1998), 151–77.

O'BRIEN, A., 'Phelim MacFeagh's revolt', *Journal of the Wicklow Historical Society* 2 (4) (1998), 78–86.

O'BRIEN, C., 'The Byrnes of Ballymanus', in K. Hannigan and W. Nolan (eds), *Wicklow: history and society: interdisciplinary essays on the history of an Irish county* (Dublin, 1994), 305–40.

O'BRIEN, C. (ed.), *Feagh McHugh O'Byrne: the Wicklow firebrand* (Rathdrum, 1998).

Ó BRÓGÁIN, S., *The Wolfhound guide to the Irish harp emblem* (Dublin, 1998).

O'BYRNE, E., 'The battle of Glenmalure, 25 August 1580: cause and course', in C. O'Brien (ed.), *Feagh McHugh O'Byrne: the Wicklow firebrand* (Rathdrum, 1998), 150–81.

O'BYRNE, E., *War, politics and the Irish of Leinster, 1156–1606* (Dublin, 2000).

Ó CORRÁIN, D., 'Brian Boru, master of psychological warfare', *The Irish Times* (8 March 2014).

Ó CORRÁIN, D. and MAGUIRE, F., *Irish names* (2nd edn, Dublin, 1990).

O'DONNELL, M.L., *Ireland's harp: the shaping of Irish identity,* c. *1770–1880* (Dublin, 2014).

O'DONOVAN, J. , 'Castlekelly', Ordnance Survey Letters, Roscommon.

O'DONOVAN, J., Ordnance Survey Field Name Books (1838).

O'DONOVAN, J., Ordnance Survey Letters, Galway, vol. 1.

O'DONOVAN, J. (ed.), 'The registry of Clonmacnoise, with notes and introductory remarks', *Journal of the Kilkenny and South-East of Ireland Archaeological Society* 1 (2) (1857), 444–60.

O'DOWD, M., 'Women and war in Ireland in the 1640s', in M. MacCurtain and M. O'Dowd (eds), *Women in early modern Ireland* (Dublin, 1991), 91–111.

O'FLAHERTY, R., *A chorographical description of West or h-Iar Connaught: written AD 1684* (Dublin, 1846).

O'HANLON, J. and O'LEARY, E., *History of the Queen's County*, pt ii (Dublin, 1907).

O'HART, J., *Irish pedigrees; or, the origin and stem of the Irish nation* (2 vols, Dublin, 1876).

OHLMEYER, J., 'The civil wars in Ireland', in J. Kenyon, J. Ohlmeyer and J. Morrill (eds), *The civil wars: a military history of England, Scotland, and Ireland, 1638–1660* (Oxford, 1998), 73–102.

O'LOUGHLIN, M.C., *The families of County Clare, Ireland: over one thousand entries from the archives of the Irish Genealogical Foundation* (Kansas, 2000).

Ó LOCHLAINN, C., 'Roadways in ancient Ireland', in J. Ryan (ed.), *Feil-sgribhinn Eoin Mhic Neill: essays and studies presented to Professor Eoin Mac Neill* (Dublin, 1940), 465–74.

Ó MÓRDHA, P., 'The MacMahons of Monaghan', *Clogher Record* 2 (1) (1957), 148–69.

Ó MÓRDHA, P.B., 'Colla Dubh MacMahon: his ancestors and descendants', *Clogher Record* 8 (2) (1974), 194–206.

O'NEILL, J. (ed. & trans.), 'Cath Boinde', *Ériu* 2 (1905), 173–85.

O'RAHILLY, C. (ed.), *Táin Bó Cualnge from the Book of Leinster* (Dublin, 1970).

ORDNANCE SURVEY IRELAND, *Map of monastic Ireland* (Dublin, 1979).

ORPEN, G.H., 'Richard de Burgh and the conquest of Connacht', *Journal of the Galway Archaeological and Historical Society* 7 (1911–12), 129–47.

OTWAY-RUTHVEN, A.J., 'The native Irish and English law in medieval Ireland', *Irish Historical Studies* 7 (25) (1950), 1–16.

OTWAY-RUTHVEN, A.J., *A history of medieval Ireland* (London, 1968).

PARKER, C., 'The internal frontier: the Irish in County Waterford in the later Middle Ages', in T.B. Barry, R. Frame and K. Simms (eds), *Colony and frontier in medieval Ireland: essays presented to J.F. Lydon* (London, 1995), 139–54.

PERCEVAL-MAXWELL, M., 'The Ulster rising of 1641, and the depositions', *Irish Historical Studies* 21 (1978), 144–67.

PERCEVAL-MAXWELL, M., *The outbreak of the Irish rebellion of 1641* (Montreal, 1994).

PHILLIPS, J.R.S., 'The Irish remonstrance of 1317: an international perspective', *Irish Historical Studies* 27 (106) (1990), 112–29.

PRICE, L., 'The armed forces of the Irish chiefs in the sixteenth century', *Journal of the Royal Society of Antiquaries of Ireland* (7th ser.) 2 (2) (1932), 201–7.

PRICE, L., 'The manor of Bothercolyn (Co. Dublin)', *Journal of the Royal Society of Antiquaries of Ireland* (7th ser.) 14 (1944), 107–18.

REFAUSSÉ, R. and CLARK, M., *A catalogue of the maps of the estates of the archbishops of Dublin, 1654–1850* (Dublin, 2000).

RICHES, D. (ed.), *The anthropology of violence* (Oxford, 1986).

RICHES, D., 'The phenomenon of violence', in *idem* (ed.), *The anthropology of violence* (Oxford, 1986), 1–27.

RICHTER, M., *Medieval Ireland: the enduring tradition* (Dublin, 2005).

RIMMER, J., 'The morphology of the Irish harp', *Galpin Society Journal* 17 (1964), 39–49.

ROBINSON, D.M., *Tintern Abbey* (Cadw Welsh Historic Monuments, 1986).

RUSHE, D.C., *Historical sketches of Monaghan: from the earliest times to the Fenian movement* (Dublin, 1895).

RUSHE, D.C., *History of Monaghan for two hundred years, 1660–1860* (Dublin, 1921),

291–338.

RYAN, J., *Toirdelbach O Conchubair (1088–1156): king of Connacht, king of Ireland co fresabra* (Dublin, 1966).

SCHLEGEL, D.M., 'Sir Brian and Lady Mary MacMahon', *Clogher Record* 15 (3) (1996), 133–44.

SIMMS, K., 'References to landscape and economy in Irish bardic poetry', in H.B. Clarke, J. Prunty and M. Hennessy, *Surveying Ireland's past: multidisciplinary essays in honour of Anngret Simms* (Dublin, 2004), 145–68.

SIMMS, K., *Medieval Gaelic sources* (Dublin, 2009).

SMYTH, W., *Map-making, landscapes and memory: a geography of early modern Ireland,* c. *1530–1750* (Cork, 2006).

SOMERS, D., *Endurance: heroic journeys in Ireland* (Dublin, 2005).

STEPHENS, J. and MOLL, H., *Monasticon Hibernicum, or, the monastical history of Ireland* (London, 1722).

STOKES, W., 'The battle of Mag Mucrime', *Revue Celtique* 13 (1892), 426–74.

STOKES, W., 'The colloquy of the two sages', *Revue Celtique* 26 (1905), 4–64.

STOUT, G., 'Wicklow's prehistoric landscape', in K. Hannigan and W. Nolan (eds), *Wicklow: history and society: interdisciplinary essays on the history of an Irish county* (Dublin, 1994), 1–40.

STOUT, G. and STOUT, M., 'Patterns in the past: County Dublin 5000 BC–1000 AD', in F.H.A. Aalen and K. Whelan (eds), *Dublin city and county from prehistory to present: studies in honour of J.H. Andrews* (Dublin, 1992), 5–41.

TAKAGAMI, S.I., 'The Fenian rising in Dublin, March 1867', *Irish Historical Studies* 29 (1995), 340–62.

UNDERDOWN, D., *Revel, riot, and rebellion: popular politics and culture in England, 1603–1660* (Oxford, 1985).

VOLKAN, V., 'The need to have enemies and allies: a developmental approach', *Political Psychology* 6 (1985), 219–47.

WALSH, P. (ed.), *The will and family of Hugh O'Neill, earl of Tyrone, with an appendix of genealogies* (Dublin, 1930).

WATT, J., *The church in medieval Ireland* (Dublin, 1972).

WEST, M., 'The genesis of Togail bruidne Da Derga: a reappraisal of the "two-source" theory', *Celtica* 23 (1999), 413–35.

WHITE, P., *History of Clare and the Dalcassian clans of Tipperary, Limerick and Galway* (Dublin, 1893).

WILLIAMS, N.J.A., 'Cath Bearna Chroise Brigde', *Zeitschrift für Celtische Philologie* 38 (1981), 269–338.

WOULFE, P., *Sloinnte Gaedheal is Gall: Irish names and surnames* (Dublin, 1922).

YEATS, G., 'The rediscovery of Carolan', in B. Harris and G. Freyer (eds), *Integrating tradition: the achievement of Seán Ó Riada* (Ballina and Chester Springs, 1981), 78–94.

YEATS, G., *The harp of Ireland: the Belfast harpers' festival, 1792, and the saving of Ireland's harp music by Edward Bunting* (Belfast, 1992).

Electronic sources

Albert O'Mallon: https://histfam.familysearch.org//getperson.php?personID=I158177&tree=Nixon.

Annals of Loch Cé: http://www.ucc.ie/celt/published/T100010A/index.html.

Annals of the Four Masters: http://www.ucc.ie/celt/online/T100005E/text008.html.

ARCHDALL, M., *Monasticon Hibernicum: or, a history of the abbeys, priories, and other religious houses in Ireland; interspersed with memoirs of their several founders and benefactors, and of their abbots and other superiors, to the time of their final suppression. Edited with extensive notes by the Right Rev. Patrick Moran, D.D., vol. ii* (W. B. Kelly, Dublin, 1876): https://archive.org/stream/monasticonhiber01archgoog/monasticonhiber01archgoog_djvu.txt.

Ballygaddy Bridge, Mapviewer, Ordnance Survey Ireland: http://maps.osi.ie/publicviewer/#V2,542019,753809,10,7.

Basilica Bruxellensis sive monumenta antiqua inscriptiones, et Coenotaphia . . . (1743), p. 119: https://lib.ugent.be/en/catalog/bkt01:000316995.

Bodleian Library, Oxford, MS Rawlinson B 488, fol. 21v: http://image.ox.ac.uk/images/bodleian/msrawlb488/f21v.jpg.

Bourke, Sir John: http://en.wikipedia.org/wiki/Sir_John_Bourke_of_Brittas.

BRADY, W.M., *The Irish Reformation or the alleged conversion of the Irish bishops at the accession of Queen Elizabeth* . . . (5th edn, London, 1857), 144–5: https://archive.org/stream/irishreformation00braduoft/irishreformation00braduoft_djvu.txt.

Buslé de Montpleinchamp, Jean-Chrysostome, *L'Histoire de l'archiduc Albert, gouverneur général et puis prince souverain de la Belgique* (1693): https://archive.org/details/bub_gb_6CtCAAAAcAAJ.

CHADWICK, S.: http://www.earlygaelicharp.info/history/17th.htm.

CHADWICK, S.: http://www.earlygaelicharp.info/history/19th.htm.

CHADWICK, S.: http://www.earlygaelicharp.info/stringing/history.htm#osb.

CHADWICK, S.: http://earlygaelicharp.info/stringing/history.htm.

CHADWICK, S.: http://www.earlygaelicharp.info/instruments/.

DONOVAN, B.C., 'The rise of Feagh McHugh O'Byrne in Gaelic Leinster': http://homepage.eircom.net/~nobyrne/The_rise_of_Feagh_macHugh_OByrne_in_Tudor_Leinster.htm.

Down Survey map of County Galway: http://downsurvey.tcd.ie/down-survey-maps.php#c=Galway.

EDWARDS, D., 'Feagh McHugh O'Byrne: forgotten leader of the Nine Years War': http://homepage.eircom.net/~nobyrne/Feagh_McHugh_%20Forgotten_Leader.htm.

FitzGerald, James FitzThomas: http://en.wikipedia.org/wiki/James_FitzThomas_FitzGerald.

FROST, J., *The history and topography of the county of Clare, from the earliest times to the beginning of the 18th century* (Dublin, 1893): http://www.clarelibrary.ie/eolas/coclare/history/frost/chap10_st_flannan.htm.

JENNINGS, B. (ed.), *Wild geese in Spanish Flanders, 1582–1700* (Dublin, 1964): http://www.irishmanuscripts.ie/digital/Wild%20Geese%20in%20Spanish%20Flanders%201582-1700/data/search.xml.

JOYCE, P.W., *The origin and history of Irish names of places,* vol. i (Dublin 1910): http://www.archive.org/details/originhistoryofi02injoyce.

KELLY, F., *A guide to early Irish law* (Dublin, 1988; repr. 2001): http://www.brehonlawacademy.ie/#!Irish-Manuscripts-Uraicecht-Becc-—-The-Short-Primer/c19ap/0EF73336-9BED-4C04-B1C0-AD07BB4DDC29.

KEMPE, A.J. (ed.), *The Loseley Manuscripts . . .* (London, 1836): https://archive.org/stream/loseleymanuscrip00kempuoft/loseleymanuscrip00kempuoft_djvu.txt.

Kiltonanlea: https://en.wikipedia.org/wiki/Kiltenanlea.

Knappogue Castle: http://en.wikipedia.org/wiki/Knappogue_Castle.

KNOX, H.T., *Notes on the early history of the dioceses of Tuam, Killala and Achonry* (Dublin, 1904): http://www.archive.org/details/notesonearlyhist00knoxiala.

Letter from Isabel to Conde de Gondomar (De Brusselas 12-II-1622) (Record no. 145178), https://realbiblioteca.patrimonionacional.es/cgi-bin/koha/opac-MARCdetail.pl?biblionumber=145178.

LOOMIS, K.: https://www.academia.edu/11082480/The_Lamont_and_Queen_Mary_Harps.

MacCarthaigh's book: http://celtucc.ie/published/T100013/index/html.

MAC EITEAGÁIN, D., *Feagh McHugh O'Byrne and the Ulster princes: his role in their castle escapes*: http://homepage.eircom.net/~nobyrne/Dublin_Castle_escape.htm.

Monastic Matrix: http://www.monasticmatrix.org.

MCINERNEY, L., 'Documents from the Thomond papers at Petworth House archive', *Archivium Hibernicum* 63 (2011), 7–55: http://www.clarelibrary.ie/eolas/coclare/history/images/Thomond_Papers_from_Petworth_House_Archive.pdf.

O'BRIEN, C., 'Feagh McHugh O'Byrne' (2000): http://www.historyireland.com/early-modern-history-1500-1700/feagh-mchugh-obyrne/.

O'BYRNE, E., 'FitzDermot (Mac Gilla Mo Cholmóc), Sir Ralph', in J. McGuire and J. Quinn (eds), *Dictionary of Irish biography* (Cambridge, 2009): http://dib.cambridge.org/.

O'BYRNE, E., 'Mac Gilla Mo Cholmóc, Diarmait', in J. McGuire and J. Quinn (eds), *Dictionary of Irish biography* (Cambridge, 2009): http://dib.cambridge.org/.

O'BYRNE, E., 'The rise of the Gabhal Raghnaill': http://homepage.tinet.ie/

~nobyrne/Rise_of_Gabhal_Raghnall.htm.

O'BYRNE, E., 'The battle of Glenmalure, 25 August 1580: cause and course': http://homepage.tinet.ie/~nobyrne/Battle_of_Glenmalure.htm.

Ó CLÉIRIGH, L., *Beatha Aodha Ruaidh Uí Dhomhnaill*: http://www.ucc.ie/celt/published/T100080.html.

O'CONOR-NASH, P., 'O'Conors: kings of Connacht, high kings of Ireland' (2001): http//clonalis.com/oconors-kings-of-connacht-high-kings-of-ireland/.

O'DONOVAN, J., Ordnance Survey Field Name Books (1838): http://places.galwaylibrary.ie/field-books.

O'DONOVAN, J. (ed.), *The tribes and customs of Hy-Many, commonly called O'Kelly country*: https://www.ucc.ie/research/celt/published/G105007.html.

Ó DUINNÍN, P., *Foclóir Gaedhilge agus Béarla* (Dublin, 1927): http://www.ucc.ie/celt/Dinneen1.pdf.

O'GRADY, D. (trans.), 'A lament for the rebel leader Fiach McHugh O'Byrne', by Aonghas Ó Dalaigh (sixteenth century): http://www.munsterlit.ie/Southword/Issues/17A/Poetry/ogrady_desmond.html.

O'LOUGHLIN, T., 'Giraldus Cambrensis's view of Europe': http://www.historyireland.com/medieval-history-pre-1500/giraldus-cambrensiss-view-of-europe/.

Ordnance Survey Ireland map of County Galway (1840): www.galway.ie/en/services/Library/1842OSmaps/.

Place-names database of Ireland: http://www.logainm.ie.

'Plantations of Ireland' on Wikipedia: https://en.wikipedia.org/wiki/Plantations_of_Ireland.

PARRE, V.S. (Ph.D thesis, University of Murcia School of Law): http://gw.geneanet.org/gerardlpdupon?lang=en;pz=capucine+agnes+rolande;nz=perrier;ocz=0;p=dom+emilio;n=o+mallun.

RUSHE, D.C., *History of Monaghan for two hundred years, 1660–1860* (Dublin, 1921), appendix i, pp 291–338: http://www.failteromhat.com/monaghanhearth.php.

Spanish Wild Geese: http://indigo.ie/~wildgees/s-wgeese.htm.

STANLEY, W., 'A calendar of manuscript material relating to Ireland, 1580–1602; Letter of Sir William Stanley, 31 August 1580': http://www.ucc.ie/celt/published/E580000-002/text002.html.

TAYLOR, G. and SKINNER, A., *Maps of the roads of Ireland surveyed 1777*: https://archive.org/details/TaylorSkinnerMapsOfTheRoadsOfIrelandSurveyed1777.

TCD, 1641 Depositions project (on-line transcript January 1970): http://1641.tcd.ie/deposition.php?depID<?php echo 809250r141?>.

Terms of Count Gondomar to Archduchess of Austria (London, 9-IV-1622) (Record no. 122054): http://realbiblioteca.patrimonionacional.es/cgi-bin/koha/opac-MARCdetail.pl?biblionumber=122054.

'The Dominican friary of Roscommon town, Co. Roscommon': http://www.culturalheritageireland.ie/index.php/heritage-sites-and-centres/98-the-dominican-friary-of-roscommon-town-co-roscommon.

'Tírechán's text in English' (trans. Ludwig Bieler) in Ego Patricius: http://www.confessio.ie/more/tirechan_english#.

WHITE, P., *History of Clare and the Dalcassian clans of Tipperary, Limerick, and Galway* (Dublin, 1893): https://archive.org/details/historyofclareda00whit.

Contributors

COLETTE ALLEN worked for many years in the Local Studies section of the County Library, Tallaght. She recently completed an MLitt. in NUI Galway entitled 'The landscapes of Buí: the Cailleach Bhéarra'.

GERARD BEGGAN was born in Limerick City in 1934. Educated at Patrickswell NS and Mungret College SJ, in 1952 he entered St Patrick's Training College, Drumcondra, where he qualified as a National Teacher in the First Division, obtaining therefrom a *Teastas Dhá-Theangach* or bilingual certificate. He taught as assistant teacher and principal teacher in a number of national schools in Wexford and Dublin before returning to university to study Mathematical Science at UCD full-time. Having graduated in second place in BSc. (Hons) in 1964, he specialised further in Mathematics and was awarded the MSc. (Hons). He was appointed in 1965 to the Inspectorate for Secondary Schools and served in Munster as an Inspector of Mathematics and Applied Mathematics. Following his appointment in 1971 to a Statutory Lectureship in Education in NUI Galway, he obtained an MA (Hons) in History and a Ph.D. He retired in 2000.

GORDON BOND completed a BA in History in 2013. Having since completed an MSc. in International Politics, he now works in the civil service but hopes to return to the study of History at some stage in the future.

CON CONNOR lives in north County Roscommon and is a leather craft designer, worker and teacher, registered with the Design and Craft Council of Ireland. He has displayed his craftwork in the National Museum of Ireland, the Museum of Country Living and at Interpretative Centres and festivals throughout Ireland. He has also studied Archaeology at NUI Galway. Roscommon town museum and the Clonalis O'Connor family museum have examples of Con's replica shoes on display. Con is also a Celtic druid with an on-line presence. You can see Con's craftwork at celticshoes.ie.

SIMON EGAN is a native of County Kerry. He graduated in 2011 from University College Cork with a First Class Honours BA in History and Modern Irish, before beginning his doctoral studies in History there under the supervision of Dr David Edwards. Simon's doctoral research was funded by the Irish Research Council and he graduated with a Ph.D in History in June 2016. He currently holds a Society for Renaissance Studies Postdoctoral Fellowship and is in the process of preparing his thesis for publication as a monograph.

STEPHEN HEWER is a Postgraduate Research Fellow in the Trinity Medieval History Research Centre, Trinity College, Dublin. He was an Irish Research Council Postgraduate Scholar at Trinity College. His Ph.D thesis was on the legal status of ethnic groups in the English royal courts in Ireland (1252–1318). His research examines the interactions of law and society, the wider implications of court records, and modern constructions of historical group identities.

DECLAN KEENAN is a Chartered Engineer from County Mayo. He also holds an MA in Early Modern History from UCD. Declan has a keen interest in and researches the history and cartography of early modern Ireland.

STEPHEN KESTELL served in the Irish Defence Forces for six years before attending University College Cork as a mature student in 2013. In 2016 he achieved a BA joint honours degree in Sociology and History. He has recently completed a Master of Research under the supervision of Dr Hiram Morgan, with his research topic focused on the demise of Feagh McHugh O'Byrne during the Tudor conquest of Ireland.

CHRIS LAWLOR is a retired secondary school teacher living in Dunlavin, Co. Wicklow. He is married to Margaret and they have three sons, Declan, Jason and Michael. He is the author of nine historical books and of numerous chapters and essays in historical and other journals. He won the Dunlavin Arts Festival short-story award in 2001, the Lord Walter Fitzgerald prize for original historical research in 2003 and the Irish Chiefs' prize for history in 2013. He holds an MA from NUI Maynooth and a Ph.D from DCU, and has lectured in Ireland, the UK and Australia.

BRIAN McCABE is a retired civil servant with an interest in history and archaeology. He is a founder member and Honorary Secretary of Clann Chába, the Clan Mc Cabe Society, and editor of their newsletter, *The Gallowglass*. He is a former Director of Clans of Ireland. He is also a Council member of the Kildare Archaeological Society and a regular contributor to their annual journal, as well as to those of the Royal Society of Antiquaries of Ireland, the Meath Archaeological and Historical Society, the *Dublin Historical Record* and Cumann Seanchais Bhreifne. He has also contributed articles to both *History Ireland* and *Archaeology Ireland*, and to many other publications.

EUGENE McMAHON is a retired history teacher and union president. Eugene and his wife Anne married in Dublin and have lived variously in Ireland, East Africa and Canada. Other writings of Eugene's include some short stories and contributory chapters to both the 2005 and 2006 editions of *Vanished Hamilton* by Margaret Houghton. He has also co-authored a genealogical study of *The McMahons of*

Trohanny with Patrick McMahon in 2008. More recently, Eugene has had a companion volume, *The McMahons of Kilbeg—a genetic and historic odyssey*, published in 2017.

BRIAN MANNERS and his brother John came upon an Irish harp summer school in County Kilkenny, quite by chance, on an August holiday weekend five years ago. They had played Classical and Irish traditional music their whole lives and assumed that they knew something about the harping tradition of Ireland. After attending a short performance by harpist Ann Heymann, they were both taken aback! This did not sound like the Irish harp they knew but rather more like bells that echoed and commanded the attention of the room. It suddenly became crystal clear why this harp was Ireland's national instrument. Thus began a journey of fascination with this lost instrument, this lost sound and the associated lost culture of the Gaelic world. Brian Manners plays the trombone and low whistle; once mastery has been achieved in these, the Gaelic harp will be his next conquest—he holds out hope! His recently published book entitled *The Trinity College Harp—Ireland and the most exotic music instrument in the world* can be viewed at www.trinityharp.ie.

GERRY MOLONEY is a lecturer in computing in the Institute of Technology, Carlow, with a particular interest in and concentration on new and emerging technologies. Outside of the education and computing industries, he has a wide range of active interests, including music, sport, astronomy, medicine and ancient history. He is an active member of a number of clubs, societies and organising committees in these areas.

LORA O'BRIEN is an Irish journalist, author and guide living in County Waterford, with a background in Irish heritage tourism and a focus on native Irish mythology. She spent over a decade living and working at Rathcroghan, Co. Roscommon, the home of Queen Medb, managing the heritage centre and liaising with officials, scholars and visitors on a daily basis. Her latest book, *Tales of old Ireland—retold* (2018), is published by Eel & Otter Press.

RUAIRÍ Ó hAODHA is a County Galway-based librarian and historian. He is a member of the editorial committee of the *Journal of the Old Tuam Society.*

DIARMUID WHEELER completed a BA in History and English at the National University of Ireland, Maynooth, in 2010, and an MA in Military History and Strategic Studies at the same institution in 2011. He was recently awarded a Ph.D in History at NUI Galway for his dissertation on the Tudor transition of Leix and Offaly from Gaelic lordships to English shires from *c.* 1547 to 1622.

The editors

DR JOSEPH MANNION is vice-chair of Clans of Ireland, and chairperson and historian of the Mannion Clan Association. He has written a biography of County Galway's earliest known ecclesiastic entitled *The life, legends and legacy of Saint Kerrill*, and a short but detailed family history called *The Mannion Clan historical trail*. He has also authored a wide range of journal articles and book chapters dealing with the medieval and early modern history of the South Connacht region.

DR KATHARINE SIMMS is a Fellow Emerita of Trinity College Dublin, where she was a Senior Lecturer in Medieval History to 2010. She is the author of *From kings to warlords: the changing political structure of Gaelic Ireland in the later Middle Ages* and *Medieval Gaelic sources*, together with numerous articles on the kings, clerics and learned classes in Gaelic Ireland from the thirteenth to the fifteenth century.